From The Shepherd To His Flock

By

Sheila Boyd Cook

Copyright 2017
By
Sheila Boyd Cook

ISBN 978-1-940609-90-4
All rights reserved
No part of this book may be reproduced or transmitted in any form or by any means, electronic or mechanical, including photocopying, recording, or by any information storage and retrieval system, without permission in writing from the copyright owner.

All scripture verses are from the
King James Version
This book was printed in the United States of America.

To order additional copies of this book contact:

Sheila Boyd Cook
4006 Sweethome Road
Ashland City, TN 37015
615-519-5518

FWB
FWB Publications
Columbus, Ohio

Dr. L.C. Johnson and Terry Boyd at Terry's Ordination Service

Bro. Terry Boyd

Table of Contents

Authors Preface 1
Dedication 3
Chapter 1 Behold the Lamb of God 5
Chapter 2 Silence before God 11
Chapter 3 Salvation Is Knowing God 23
Chapter 4 Spiritual Peace... 33
Chapter 5 The Father without a Name 43
Chapter 6 A Friend like Jesus 53
Chapter 7 We Would See Jesus 65
Chapter 8 What is Sin?.. 75
Chapter 9 A Good Man 85
Chapter 10 Degrees from God 97
Chapter 11 In the Book 107
Chapter 12 What will it Take?... 117
Chapter 13 Is It Finished?... 127
Chapter 14 What is a Christian? 137
Chapter 15 Look at Him! 149
Chapter 16 Fatherhood... 159
Chapter 17 Why Did Jesus Die? 171
Chapter 18 Casting Bread 185
Chapter 19 Jesus Spoke 195
Chapter 20 Four Aspects of God's Glory......................... 205
Chapter 21 Message continued from Chapter 20 219
Chapter 22 God's Plan for Your Life 231
Chapter 23 Marring God's Plan....................................... 245
Chapter 24 Waiting for Your Ship to Come In 255
Chapter 25 The Second Coming....................................... 263

Chapter 26 What Is Your Faith? 273
Chapter 27 Have You Kept Your Promise? 283
Chapter 28 Jesus Never Fails 289
Chapter 29 A Great Sermon by a Great Christian........... 301
Chapter 30 The Love and Justice of God 311
Chapter 31 Four Sides of the Gospel 323
Chapter 32 Perfecting the Saints 333
Chapter 33 The Voice of Jesus 341
Chapter 34 I Know.. 351

Author's Preface

This is book two of the sermons of my dad that I transcribed from the cassette tapes preserved by the Ashland City Free Will Baptist Church. Since my father's death, it has been a joy to listen to him once again through these tapes. It has been my way of dealing with his death and remembering he is in a much better place. Heaven seems a little sweeter to me now and as I listen and transcribe these tapes, I see why Dad loved the Lord so much and spent his life preaching the gospel. Life as a preacher's kid was not always easy, but the one thing I learned all those years growing up was that Jesus loved me and died to save me from a lifetime in hell. I am thankful for Christian parents that instilled the love of God in my heart and were an example to me of what Christian parents were every day of their life. As a daughter of the pastor, there are times when you don't feel like you really have a pastor to go to when things happen in your life. But I was always able to go to him and he would pray with me and lead me in the right direction. Dad was in the ministry for twenty years and pastored the Ashland City Free Will Baptist Church for twenty-four years. His sermons are from his heart and I believed he preached what the Lord laid on his heart to preach every Sunday morning, Sunday night and Wednesday night. In twenty-five years, he preached a lot of sermons, preached hundreds of funerals and performed many weddings. He enjoyed sharing God's word whenever he could.

From The Shepherd To His Flock

The title "From the Shepherd to the Flock" comes from what I heard my father say numerous times. By definition, in the early morning a shepherd would lead forth the flock from the fold, marching at its head to the spot where they were to be pastured. Here he watched them all day, taking care that none of the sheep strayed, and if any for a time eluded his watch and wandered away from the rest, seeking diligently till he found and brought it back. In those lands, sheep require to be supplied regularly with water, and the shepherd for this purpose has to guide them either to some running stream or to wells dug in the wilderness and furnished with troughs. At night, he brought the flock home to the fold, counting them as they passed under the rod at the door to assure himself that none were missing. Nor did his labors always end with sunset. Often, he had to guard the fold through the dark hours from the attack of wild beasts, or the wild attempts of the prowling thief. As a pastor, that was what my father did every Sunday morning, Sunday night and Wednesday night. **When a member of our church would pass away, Dad would always lay a red rose on the pillow in the casket with a note saying, 'love from the Shepherd to one of the flock'. Dad was a shepherd to many people who entrusted their lives and families to him. He guided them and protected them as the Lord led him. The definition of a shepherd is one who guides and directs his flock in a particular direction. To dad, that direction was always on God.**

Dedication

This book is lovingly dedicated to
my sister, Christi. For all those days
we played church in the hallway of our home and
for putting up with the fact that we were "Preacher's
Kids". I cannot imagine sharing
my life with anyone else. I love you!

From The Shepherd To His Flock

Chapter 1
Behold the Lamb of God
John 1:29-37

We have in John 1:29-37 John the Baptist's introduction to Jesus. *"The next day John seeth Jesus coming unto him, and said, behold the Lamb of God, which taketh away the sin of the world. This is he of whom I said, after me cometh a man which is preferred before me: for he was before me. And I knew him not: but that he should be made manifest to Israel, therefore am I come baptizing with water. And John bare record, saying, I saw the Spirit descending from heaven like a dove, and it abode upon him. And I knew him not: but he that sent me to baptize with water, the same is he which baptizeth with the Holy Ghost. And I saw, and bare record that this is the Son of God. Again, the next day after John stood, and two of his disciples; and looking upon Jesus as he walked, he saith, Behold the Lamb of God! And the two disciples heard him speak, and they followed Jesus"*.

Some people say that John the Baptist was born to say one sentence; that he was born to make one exclamation. The ministry of John the Baptist was like Peter's ministry. He rose suddenly in the barren desert, he delivered his message and just as quickly, he disappeared from the scene. His ministry was very quick and sudden and it seemed he was born for one purpose. God chose John the Baptist as the one who would introduce his son the Lord Jesus Christ to the world. With the introduction by John the

Baptist, Jesus began his public ministry. Had you been chosen of God to introduce the Lord Jesus Christ how would you have introduced him? Had God said to you I want you to go out and when you see the Lord coming, I want you to introduce the Lord Jesus Christ to the world in words they will not forget, what would you say?

I am sure some people would say, Behold the man who can feed the poor. Behold a man who can feel all of those who are hungry. What a hay day the reporters would have with a front page caption like that. Behold a man that can take loaves and fishes and can feed the poor. I have come to believe that our government has a complex about those who do not work or those who do not care; those who will not support themselves through honest work. I think it is a wonderful thing for all of those in the world, through sickness or some other thing out of their control to be supported and helped. We have a guilt complex in America, I think that sends the rest of us to work for those who will not. We have seen in the past few years tens of thousands different welfare programs that absolutely grow more insane as they are being implemented by our local governments. Had we had the opportunity to introduce a man who could feed the poor what a great enthusiastic way we could have introduced our Lord.

Perhaps we could introduce him like this, Behold the man that can call down legions of angels. Jesus said on one occasion, I have but to say the word and I can call down 72,000 angels to do my bidding. Can you imagine the devastation 72,000 could cause at the word of God? So perhaps we could have introduced the Lord as a man with power to call down legions of angels from heaven. We could have said, behold a man who can heal the sick. Certainly any man who has a reputation of being able to heal the sick would have a great multitude of followers. Behold the man who can open the eyes of the blind, ears of the deaf, and can cause those who are crippled to walk again. Behold a man that controls nature. Behold a man who can go out to the sea when it is raging and say, peace be still and the waves suddenly obey his voice and the sea becomes calm. Can you imagine how exciting it would be to introduce the Lord in so many ways? A man that can feed the poor, heal the sick, call legions of angels and a man who has the power over nature. John the Baptist was chosen of God to introduce his son. John the Baptist said these words, "Behold the Lamb of God which taketh away the sin of the world".

Let's think for a moment about the sin of the world. Here is a man from God, John, who said, Jesus was the Lamb of God and came for one purpose and that was to take away the sin of the world. God says that is what is wrong with the world. God says it's not inflation, it's not suffering and diseases, it's not crime or corruption in high places, but sin is what is wrong with the world. That is at the root of all crime, inflation, violence, bloodshed, and sickness – sin. I am amazed at how, for so many years, ministers who preach the gospel or supposed to preach the gospel have totally ignored or buried and forgotten the old doctrines that our forefathers preached. Now that the world is in such terrible shape with crime rate, inflation rate, and with all the other things happening in the world, more and more ministers are becoming aware again of that old doctrine our forefathers preached and that today's psychologist laugh at. Ministers are becoming aware that sin is exactly what is wrong with the world today. The things that our forefathers preached: total depravity, sin nature, that's what they preached and that is what God said was wrong with us and people are becoming aware of the monster we are facing in the world is exactly what is described in the Bible as sin. Our preachers in the past called it total depravity. They preached that people are born sinners. They are not entering in some kind of sin as they live, but sin has entered our whole personality and emotion. Man is totally depraved. They preached sin, heaven and hell. Do you know when hell became so great in our streets? When the hell left the pulpits, it went into the streets. If there was hell preached from the pulpit, you didn't find it in homes and in the streets. Now that it is not in the pulpit, we find our homes and streets filled with it. Those who hold on to the fundamental truths of the word of God still preach it. Our problem is exactly what the Bible says – SIN!

I read something the other day from the Minnesota crime commission report. I want to read you what the crime report said, "What we call delinquency or delinquent behavior is not anything new. What we call delinquent behavior is as old as man itself. It is not something that just moronic segment of our society is liable for but no infant is born a finished product. Every baby starts life like a savage. Every child is born with urges, aggressiveness, anger, fear, love, no control, completely self-centered and he wants what he wants when he wants it. He wants his bottle, he wants his mother's attention, he wants his uncle's watch and if you deny them that they see with rage and aggression and would commit murder were they not helpless". It goes on to say, "the child is dirty, has no morals, no knowledge, so skill, they are born delinquent and if permitted to continue to grow up like that, every one of them will be criminals, thieves, killers and rapists. Every child as he grows up, it is normal for him to fight, grab, tear things apart, and talk back and disobey. Every child must grow out of delinquent behavior". The report finished by saying these words, "what we need then is discipline. Discipline in the homes, discipline in the school because every child is a delinquent and must grow out of delinquency". What are they saying? They are saying what the Bible says, men are born sinners. Men are born totally depraved. Unless something happens to that individual, they will become increasingly evil as they get older. Therefore, they conclude what we need is discipline. And John the Baptist came to say, "Behold the Lamb of God, which taketh away the sin of the world".

I am reminded of what Paul said in Romans 14:14, *"I know and am persuaded by the Lord Jesus, that there is nothing unclean of itself..."* I got to thinking about that. You mean to tell me that whiskey is alright; that gambling is alright; that adultery is alright? Then I read it again. Paul said, I am persuaded that nothing within itself is unclean. I began to say how can I make that all work out in my thinking. So let's take alcohol for example. There is nothing wrong with alcohol. There could be no practice of medicine without it. It is the solvent that carries almost all of our medicines. There is nothing wrong with alcohol until you add sin to it. You add sin to it and you have a disaster. Playing cards, dominoes and checkers are not wrong until you add sin to them. The gun was one of the finest instruments invented until you add sin to it. You add sin to the gun and you have murder, bloodshed, blackmail and all the other things. To take sin out of those things; to take sin out of our heart, God's remedy for man is to Behold the Lamb.

How does it work? God took away our penalty, our judgment when he took upon himself our sin. More than that, he took upon himself the very wrath of God for our sins. He bore our iniquities on the tree of Calvary. It is in our accepting that grace and accepting what Jesus Christ did for us that the stain of sin is washed away. Our souls are cleansed and he forgives us our iniquity. He creates in us a new heart and a new life; not only in this life but in the life to come. Did you ever think about the fact that when Jesus went to heaven he didn't go alone? When Jesus went to heaven he put his arm around the thief he saved on the cross. The man who, died beside the Lamb of God, went to heaven with Jesus. He died beside the Lamb of God who takes away the sin of the world. Tremendous thought.

John the Baptist had the rare privilege of pointing to the whole world and saying, that's the Lamb of God; that's the son of God. There is no greater privilege in the whole world than to point to the Lamb of God. That to me is the greatest joy, that though the word of God, I point you and others to the Lamb of God and say to you, Behold the Lamb of God which takes away the sin of the world. That was what John the Baptist was called to do. Will you trust him? Will you receive him? Will you accept him as your personal savior? Behold the Lamb of God today.

Chapter 2
Silence before God
Romans 3:19

I want us to recognize that the word is the sword of the spirit. The Apostle Paul, in the first three chapters of Romans, takes the sword of the Spirit of God and he turns it into an instrument of death killing every pretense, every excuse, all of man's righteousness and turns us to the only one that can save us and that person is Christ Jesus. Paul uses the sword of the spirit very skillfully, especially in the first three chapters of Romans.

Now in the 19th verse of our message, Silence before God, it reads, *"Now we know that what things soever the law saith, it saith to them who are under the law: that every mouth may be stopped, and all the world may become guilty before God"*. I have been watching the news lately about all the folks on trial for murder. We are getting more and more of these multiple murders. Where one man is maybe tried for two out of twenty-eight suspected murders. Sometimes, I wonder what goes on in the mind of a criminal when he is awaiting trial. Have you ever wondered what a criminal thought about after his case has been presented, after he sat in the witness chair and gave his testimony and the witnesses were called by the prosecution and they established a motive, the place, the instrument used and then the defense presented character witnesses. After all that was over and the criminal is led away to await sentencing, have you ever wondered in the quietness of that moment, while he is awaiting to hear the verdict, what goes through his mind?

Probably he thinks about the maximum sentence and the minimum sentence that could be his and perhaps he's praying that through the skill of his defense attorney or maybe through some fault of the prosecution and maybe through the mercy of the judge and jury, he would receive the minimum sentence. I suppose even then they might even pray that some kind of miracle would come between them and the circumstances. Notice again what Paul says in Romans 3:19, *"Now we know that what things soever the law saith, it saith to them who are under the law: that every mouth may be stopped, and all the world may become guilty before God"*. I have noticed in our earthly courts there is sometimes a postponement between the time of trial and the date of sentencing. A man who stands guilty, condemned in an earthly court might feel a sense of false security because the Day of Judgment has been postponed and he has not yet appeared before the judge. He might feel a little secure that it is being put off till later, but not every man. Paul says that every man be warned and be rightly instructed and have no false sense of security that they shall ever escape standing before God in the divine court. God's patience will one day run out. The day of God's mercy will come to an end and he will become the angry judge. No man will give an excuse, no man will have any reason for being absent, no man shall escape because the sentence is sure and God will enter in one day into the Holy temple and the bailiff will say, "Order in the court". That is the same thing as the scripture says the Lord is in his holy temple let all the earth keep silent. The Lord is in his holy temple today and he says let all the world worship and praise. Let everything that hath breathe please God. Let the voices sing, and let the birds sing and let all of nature give praises unto God. But the day will come when he will say, the Lord is in his holy temple, not to be worshipped, but to pass sentence, therefore let all the earth shut up, let all the world keep silent. He is not there to be worshipped anymore, he is there as the judge to pass sentence.

Now when Paul says, whatsoever things the law saith to them who are under the law, the primary application is to Israel. But is has a secondary application. Whatsoever the law says it says to everyone, to anyone who has any code of standard of right or wrong by which to live. If any man lives by a standard, a law, he will be judged. All of us have some things we will not do. We have a code of ethics, a code of standards. There is some conduct we have decided that we will live our lives. We will do this, but we will never do that. This is alright, this is questionable and this will never be done. And we live our lives by some kind of standard. Paul goes on to say that the whole world, not just our little corner of it, but the whole world lives in sin. The whole world lives in wickedness. All of us have our standards, code of ethics. All of us have ideas of what should be and should not be done. If you want to see what Paul is talking about here in reality and have your own experience of it, go to what we call heathen lands. If you were to go to the heathen lands, you would be shocked. When you saw the way people live, the standard of living, their conduct, it would absolutely shock you. If you were to go to parts of the world today, you would see, as you walked through the marketplace, maybe half of a roasted dog hanging in the store window waiting to be sold. You would see blood sacrifices being made in heathen temples, you would see dead bodies lying beside the street and people passing by without paying any attention to it. It would shock your western culture. It would shock you to death.

The only difference between that and the way people live in America, is the difference between sin in rags and sin in silk. Free Will Baptist people have always seemed to be poor people. We thought that was the only way to get to heaven, so we stayed poor. That's right, rich folks can't go to heaven so Lord help us not to get rich. And if you get a dollar or two, don't let anyone know about it, they may vote you out of the church. But a few years ago, Free Will Baptists, along with everybody else, began to experience what we call the affluent society. We began to raise our standard of living. Folks began to have money. A lot of our good Free Will Baptist folks that used to live out in the country began to move uptown. Because they had money now to involve themselves in better entertainment and better housing and automobiles. They found themselves in a whole new circle of friends. They found themselves in high society. We have lost a lot of good Free Will Baptists to high society. A lot of them still go to church, but we lost them. They meet wherever the high society folks meet and they live wherever the high society folks live. They entertain wherever high society folks entertain. They drink red wine, they wear low neck dresses and they gamble, commit adultery – that's high society. There is another place in our town, if the truth be known, a red light should be hanging in the window. They too drink, wear low cut dresses, gamble and commit adultery. So what is the difference – just the street address brother, that's the only difference? The difference between sin in rags and sin in silk, Paul says all are guilty before God. There is no difference.

The Bible says that the whole world lies in sin and when Jesus comes to earth the second time, there is going to be more than one judgment, by the way. There is going to be a judgment of the nations. All nations will be turned into hell with those that forget God. God is going to judge the nations when he comes again. Paul says when he comes he will find the whole world lying in sin and in wickedness. You know, this whole world is corrupt. This whole society is wicked and the whole world is lying in sin. Why are the nations of the world experiencing such crisis today? We do nothing because we have to play Paul against Peter. This man has oil, this person's got gold. And we all want our part of it so we have to be careful not to upset the apple cart. Folks don't know what to do about nothing.

Our president is not going to solve our problems. He is not going to get us out of this mess, folks. He doesn't know the answers. Our congressmen and senators don't know how to deal with problems in our own cities and counties, much less the whole world. It seems the answers have eluded everyone. Why is the world in such a condition? The Psalmist said it in the 9th chapter of Psalms and the 15th verse. *"The heathen are sunk down in the pit that they made: in the net which they hid is their own foot taken"*. He said the heathen would have sunk down in the pit of their own digging and in the net that they hid their own foot was caught. If we said it in America, we'd say we did it to ourselves. We are to blame. Paul says it a little bit differently. The heathen lands today – who are the heathen lands? Africa, China, Great Britain, the United States and so on are the heathen nations of this world. The whole world lies in sin and wickedness and Paul tells us that we are in that condition because we departed from God. That may seem to you an over simplification but look in Romans chapter 1 with me to verse 21. Paul not only tells us why the world is lying in wickedness, but he tells us the very steps we took in order to get in that shape. Notice what he says in verses 21-23: *"Because that, when they (that is the nations of the world) knew God, they glorified him not as God, neither were they thankful; but became vain in their imaginations, and their foolish heart was darkened. Professing themselves to be wise, they became fools. And changed the glory of the incorruptible God into an image made like to corruptible man, and to birds, and four footed beasts, and creeping things"*. The first thing I want you to notice in verse 21 is that Paul says there was a time when everybody knew God. There was a time on earth when all men knew God and when they knew God, they were not thankful and then he gives us the steps of our going away from God. It was our vain reasoning, our ungratefulness, our profession to be wise, our hearts were darkened and we became fools. Not only did we become fools, but we turned away from God and began to worship every imaginable thing under heaven, even creeping things. I believe its verses 24, 26, 28 where it says and God gave them over and God gave them up. That's what happened. That's why the world is in the shape it is today. God has given up. Not that he has given up because he doesn't know what to do. He has given up because that's the judgment of the nations. He has given them over to a reprobate mind. They don't know what to do. That's the reason they can't come to any conclusions. They don't know what to do because God has given them over to a reprobate mind. The whole world, when we began to experience affluence, began to get so greedy that it was pitiful. The oil companies – listen brother, don't tell me about the oil shortages and all this kind of poor stuff and about reinvestment of billions of dollars to find more fuel. They stuck a gun in your back and robbed you. When you go to the grocery store to buy groceries, there are manufacturers of food products that are sticking a gun in your back and robbing you, just as if they had caught you on the street. I know because I worked for a grocery company and I know what it is to gouge and get every dime you can while you can get it.

God gave them over to a reprobate mind. And all over this world individuals are hearing the gospel of Jesus Christ and individuals are responding by receiving Christ as their Savior, but the nations are doomed to hell and will never become righteous. Our blessed nation of America will never be a righteous nation again until Jesus returns. The nations are getting set for the judgment of God. While you may be saved our nation can't. While the Chinese might be saved, China can't. God gave them up.

Why do we have so much trouble in Iran? Folks think that it was all political. Brother that was the hand of God. You see God took a little bitty stick and he whipped us. He humiliated us before the whole world. Why? Because we are turning away from God. He humiliated us in the courts of this nation with a little bitty insignificant country. He had a little stick and brother we didn't learn anything from that and God's got a big stick. If we don't respond to the little stick God uses the big stick.

Romans 1 gives us the reason for being in the shape we are in. Chapter 2 gives us the principle by which God will bring nations and individuals into judgment. It says there will be no respecter of persons. Each man will be judged as he is, all excuses swept away. Romans 3 tells us there will be a complete examination of every individual. It says from the crown of his head to the soul of his feet, tells us every avenue of our bodies which we turn away from God. We will be brought before the judgment of God. He tells us that every mouth will be stopped.

If you and I stepped outside the church this morning and a car swerved and came upon the steps and pinned me and you between the car and the steps and we became what they call dead men. And you are ushered into the presence of God. By the way, all those jokes about meeting St. Peter at the gate are just Irishmen jokes. You are not going to meet any St. Peter at any gate. God gave St. Peter the keys to the kingdom, that's right and Peter turned the first key on the Day of Pentecost, when he opened up the Gospel to the Jewish nations. He used the second key when he preached the first non-Jewish sermon in the house of Cornelius and opened up the gospel to the gentile world and from that day to this the gate has been wide open. You are not going to meet St. Peter at the gate, but you will meet God. When you stand before God and God should ask you by what right, and notice the word right, by what right do you have to enter my heaven, what would you say? All of you expect to go to heaven, none of you are planning on going to hell. But if God were to ask you, by what right do you enter into my heaven, what would you say? Many of you already know the answer to that.

First, we meet the man, Paul says, is trusting in his own righteousness and in his own works and his own deeds, by his own standard of conduct. He is trusting in that and he is going to let God scrutinize his life and he is depending on that to get him to heaven. Not by works of the flesh, Paul says. The deeds of the law shall no flesh be justified but we still believe we can live our lives and do it right and get before God and say, God here is my record. So one fellow would say, well preacher, when I get to heaven and he asks me by what right I enter into his heaven, I would say here is my record. Scrutinize my life, you will find no serious crimes, you will find I was a good neighbor. Every time Bro. Boyd asked to borrow something I let him and every time I caught him on the side of the road out of gas, I stopped and helped him. I paid my debts, I was good to my wife and children. Here is the record of my life. Paul says that is what some folks are going to say. If you are planning on that, let me give you an illustration. Suppose you were to get in your car after church and you were to fly out of our parking lot and through town and run all the red lights, break the speed limit and ignore the sirens as they began to chase you. When you were finally pinned and caught you jumped out of your car and slapped the policeman. You were brought into court and when they added up all the laws you had broken it added up to a thousand dollars and you didn't have any money to pay it and you stood before the judge guilty. The policeman was there that you slapped and you can't pay the thousand dollar fines and you are in a real mess. Then your brother walks in and he pays your fine and you turn around to start to walk out of the courtroom. The policeman, who you slapped, grabs you by the arm and says by what right do you walk out of this courtroom? Are you going to say, here's my record, sir? I'm the man that was speeding. I am the man that ran the red lights. I am the man that slapped you. Here is my record, examine it. By my record, I leave this courtroom. Would you say that? You know what you would say? Sir, my fine has been paid. That is the only excuse you have – your fine has been paid.

People think they are going to stand before God and say, here's my record. Brother, it won't be your record that will get you through. It is your record that got you there. I am always arguing with my family and folks I grew up with. Why? I ask why the thief went to heaven if he wasn't baptized. Everybody knows that, he died under the law. He was saved before Jesus died, he died and was saved under the law. Brother, it was the law that nailed him to the cross. It wasn't the law that saved him. It was the law that got him there. No, you say my fine has been paid. My elder brother, the Lord Jesus Christ, paid my fine when he died on the cross.

I was talking to a man not long ago who said almost these exact words, "I don't go to church, I don't go to Sunday school, but I'm a member of the lodge and if I live up to the obligations of my lodge, I'll be alright". When I first went to Nashville to preach, I was invited to attend a lodge meeting. I'm not preaching against lodges. Never been to one before but one of the members of the church was in it over his head. He wanted me to take part in one of the opening meetings and I went and I never got up and down so many times in my life. When we walked out of the building he said, Brother, wasn't that beautiful? If a man just lived that, there would not be a need to go to church". I'm going to tell ya'll something. I don't know how many of you belong to a lodge. None of my business, really. If you want to belong to a lodge and you want to share a common benevolence, if you want to have a secret handshake and go through drills and have passwords and all that, go right ahead. But if you ever tell me that you are going to heaven because you kept any of society's obligations, I'll take the word of God and fight you all the way to hell and watch you go through the gate. Not by the deeds of the flesh shall any be justified by the law. Here is my record. No serious faults. Here's my record.

If you were to ask someone else, if you were to stand before God and he asked you by what right do you have to enter into my heaven, they would say, brother, I wouldn't have a thing to say and that is exactly right. The whole world, every mouth, will be stopped and the whole world guilty before God. The scripture says that there is coming a time when you who have trampled underfoot the Lord Jesus Christ shall stand and look him square in the face, not as your Savior, but as your judge. And you will never, the scripture says, open your lips. There will be no defense, no excuses, no place to hide, but you will see the truth, you will understand the truth and you will offer no defense.

If the sinner could speak you know what the sinner would say? He would say I hate salvation by the blood of Jesus Christ. I want to do it my way. I hate you God for not letting me do it my way. I hate Christians, I hate Christ, and I hate God. I hate, I hate I hate and your voice will trail off into nothing. That's about all the sinner would say.

I know what I would say. What would you say? If you were to use any of the two I talked about – here's my record or I have nothing to say – you have reason to wonder if you are saved or not. I want you to ponder that question, every one of you. I don't care how long you've been in the church, I don't care what office you hold, I want you to answer that question in your soul – what would you say? I would say Jesus is my right, because Jesus has become my righteousness and because Jesus is in my heart, I can't be kept out of his heaven.

Those who will be able to answer God through the righteousness of Jesus Christ will see that they are forever accepted in the beloved.

When from the dust of death, I rise
To claim my mansion in the skies
Even then this shall be my plea
Jesus lived yes Jesus died for me.

Chapter 3
Salvation Is Knowing God
Hebrews 11: 1-2

"Now faith is the substance of things hoped for, the evidence of things not seen. For by it the elders obtained a good report."

We tell folks an awful lot about God. We preachers are always preaching about God and giving folk's information, quoting scripture, but as you begin to deal with folks on a one to one basis and when you have conversation and fellowship together you begin to wonder really how much do we really know God. Not how much we know about Him but how much do we know God. Salvation is knowing God. There has been a rise the past few years of the camp of the Atheist. Those people who would take from our society any resemblance of Christianity or any worship of God. By the way, they will never succeed at that. They make us mad. They're like a hornet in our bonnet, but God's people will see to it they won't succeed. Because of some changes in our society, they have been loud and they have been very much in the media, championing the cause of the atheist and they are led by folks like Madelyn O'Hare and others who are nothing but reprobates. The movement they are in is nothing new, it is old as the hills. It just never was paid too much attention to until folks began to want to live without God. Folks wanted to live as though there was no God, so they began to pick up a great deal of converts.

If you go all the way back in history and read about the great atheist (I say great because they were well known). There was a man by the name of John Stewart Mill who said that, "my father taught me that I could never answer the question who made me. Because to ask the question who made me brings up a question far greater than that and that is who made God. Therefore, I will never answer the question where did I come from". You see the atheist is a person who does not know where they came from. He is the person who does not know who made them. An atheist is someone who doesn't know where he is going. He doesn't know where he came from and by their own admission, they don't know where they are going.

All of you know that story about the atheist in town who died and he was at the funeral home and a lot of people went to the service out of curiosity to find out what the preacher was going to say. There was a great number of people who came to view the body and one little lady was heard to say, "my, my, what a shame, he is all dressed up and nowhere to go". An atheist is someone who doesn't understand the source and he doesn't understand his destiny. But more than that, he doesn't understand life. You see the atheist says to fight against the Christian faith, they say things like this: God is a good God and if God is a God of love, why did He make such things as a lie, snakes, and why did he create a man like Adolf Hitler? Why did He make men who are murderers? If God is God why do we have floods, why do we have storms and fires that destroy people and why is there diseases? They don't understand life. They don't know where they came from and where they are going and they don't know what to do with the life they have in the meantime.

The man of faith has some answers. I am glad that we know who made us, where we are going when we leave this earth and I am glad we have some answers to the life in which we are now living. The Psalmist said, "The fool hath said in his heart there is no God". The Bible says call no man a fool. Anyone who calls someone a fool is in danger of hell fire, but God says there is a man that is a fool. He is a fool because he does not know where he came from or where he is going. He does not understand his source nor his destiny and he can't deal with life. He is a fool.

Some people have the idea that theologians discovered God. That we preachers discovered God, sort of like Columbus discovered America. That someone stumbled across this idea of God and he began to develop it and theology is simply the brainchild of theologians. Man could not have discovered God, had not God chosen to reveal Himself to mankind. I want us to think briefly three ways in which God has revealed Himself to mankind.

In the first place, God has revealed himself to mankind in nature. The scripture says that all the heavens above us and the earth beneath us declare God. When we look into a sunset or look into the sky or even look in the face of a tornado it is God saying, "Here I am". It is God declaring there is a great God. There is the great creator and God revealed himself. When God created this earth, He expressed himself in creation. He expressed his mind in creation. Some of the most fascinating things exist in nature. They say a salmon will lay its eggs in the St. James River and no matter where he goes, he will return to that same spot every four years unless he dies on the way. He will go back to the place where he was spawned. When you see the geese flying south, you wonder who set their time table. Who told them there was a winter to avoid and a warm place to go? I told you the story about my dog who moved all the puppies back several miles during the night. Who put all that in order into nature? God expressed himself in nature. Every time you see a sunrise or a sunset, when you think about the planets and how they revolve in perfect order and in timing, you have to see that it is God saying, "Here I am". That must have been what the Psalmist said when he said, "The heavens declare the glory of God and the firmament showeth his handiwork". I love that word "handiwork". Handiwork is something you do while you are waiting to do something else. When you go down into the basement and you do woodworking, you have a handiwork. When I read where the Psalmist said, "the firmament showeth His handiwork and I look into the heavens and see all that, I say, "God that's what you did when you were waiting to do something else". What else you did must be awfully spectacular. God declared himself in nature. Job was much smarter than our scientist and astrologers back when Columbus discovered America. We thought the world was flat. Job said, "God made the circle of the earth and hung it in nothing". Up until 250 years ago, we believed that the world was flat. Just before that, folks believed that the world sat on a giant elephant. One Buddhist student said to his Buddhist teacher, "What does the earth rest on?" The teacher said, "it rests on the back of a large elephant". The student said, "What does the elephant stand on?" The teacher replied "on the back of a giant turtle". And the student said, "What does the turtle stand on?" The teacher replied, "Let's change the subject". Job said God hangeth the earth on nothing. Isaiah said, "Lift up your eyes and behold He who created these things". I can't help but laugh when fellows tell us that all that we enjoy and see among us happened by chance. They say there was an explosion somewhere and all of this came into being. There have been many theories about creation and evolution and I told you that when I was going to George Peabody College, our teachers taught us that spaceships came close to earth from outer space and they had to empty their garbage, so they opened the portals and the garbage settled down and that's where we came from. People taught that. Someone said, I don't remember who it was, said to say that the world got here by chance is like saying the unabridged dictionary is a result of an explosion in a printing factory. We have to believe there is order because God expressed order when he created the world.

He revealed Himself, secondly, in history. History is, of course, the story of man and God has the story of man in the Bible. God created history when he created man. Someday, God will end history just as He started it. Remember in the Old Testament, when God called a man named Abraham. He asked him to leave his family and his homeland and go to a land that he would show him. This man Abraham was living among his people, who were idol worshippers. He began to hear the whisper of God in his ear and in his heart. God began to reveal himself to this man. Abraham had not seen God in the stars, but rather he had no doubt been exposed to idol worship. God began to speak to this man in his heart and told him to leave and he did. And Abraham told his son Isaac about God and Isaac told his son Jacob about God and so on and so on. God began to reveal himself in a personal way to the men he created – Moses, Elijah, David, Isaiah, and all the other men of the word of God. There came a time when this God spoke to the King of Egypt. He said to the king, let my people go. In the events of what happened from that day, until the Roman Era came in, Jehovah God was the undisputed God of history. He was the Lord of Glory. He had revealed himself to mankind in spectacular ways that could not be denied. By the time the Romans took over, he was undisputed. Jehovah was God.

Finally, God revealed himself, not only in nature, not only in history, but he revealed himself in the person of man. God says, here I am in nature, here I am in history. But most clearly, he said, here I am in man. I think how wonderful it was when God sent forth his Son. And when, in the fullness of time, God sent forth his Son, Galatians says, "born of a woman, born unto the law". Then later it says, being made a curse by the law that he might redeem us from the law, the curse. John said the word became flesh and dwelt among us and we beheld his glory, as the only begotten of the Father, full of grace and truth.

When Tiberius Caesar was the Roman emperor, there was a strange looking fellow who was preaching in the wilderness, who ate a strange diet of locust and wild honey. By the way, locust was not a bug, it was a fruit, we believe. In fact, they gather the locust fruit in Israel today. He dressed in camel's hair and he ate strange food and he came to the river Jordan. He was preaching and baptizing and when he gave the invitation a young Jewish man came forward and ask John to baptize him in the river Jorden. When John baptized him and brought him up out of the water, the heavens opened and God said, "This is my beloved Son". Here I am. God revealing himself to us in the person of Jesus Christ. God found a direct and personal way to say, here I am. For years, the prophets has said, "listen to me for I have the word of God". But when Jesus came, he said, listen to me, I am the word of God". He became very real. Not only did he become known to us but he got involved. There had been other gods, but they never got involved. They stayed where it was safe. They never fooled around with crosses and tombs. They survived not because they got involved, but because they withdrew. They have a great following today because of survival, but Jesus Christ came and got involved. He got in the front line trenches. He came where we live. He took on the form of man, and became the servant of man. He knew every pain we know, He knew every happiness we know, every joy. He knew what it was like to go to a wedding and rejoice. When we have a wedding, in our country, we turn the lights out, light the candles and everybody comes in real slow and nobody says anything. It is the most sober most sorrowful thing in all the world. There ought to be bells ringing, folks ought to be beating on the bottoms of pots and pans and folks ought to be happy when folks get married. But we don't dare say a word. Those folks knew how to throw a wedding and Jesus knew the happiness of seeing a man and woman become one. He also knew what it was like to stand beside the grave of a friend and weep. He knew everything that we know. He even knew death. He became obedient even unto the death of the cross. Back there at Bethlehem, God wrapped himself in a few pounds of human flesh. The Virgin Mary, when she picked that baby up from delivering him and wrapped him in swaddling clothes and laid him in the straw, she whispered Immanuel, I'm sure, which means God is with us. Here I am. You know Jesus talked the day he was born. Jesus had a conversation, a beautiful conversation with God the Father. We find it in the scriptures, it is a marvelous conversation going on inside the Godhead. Someday I'll preach on it.

Jesus got involved with our problems and our temptations. He got involved with our death. He came to live among men and he could say there has no temptation taken you but such as is common to man. What he is saying is that no temptation taken you but what I have already experienced. I know God will give you the grace to bear it. You have to know about something before you can tell about it.

During the Vietnam War, I didn't go to Vietnam or Korea, but all I know was what Huntley and Brinkley told me on the evening news. But if you want to know what it is like to be in the jungles of Vietnam or on the slopes of Korea ask somebody who was there. Jesus didn't come to give us pretty statements, he came to get involved in life and we know he knows what life is all about. That's why it is so wonderful to go to him because he understands.

Men want to have faith in a God who said, here I am. How do we have faith? Romans 10:17 says, *"So faith cometh by hearing, and hearing by the word of God"*. That is a marvelous statement, because seeing the things in nature may not allow you to see God. You may not see God in the sunset. You may experience nature and not see God. You might believe in God, and not believe in Jesus Christ. You do not believe him because you have not seen him. But faith cometh by hearing and hearing cometh by the word of God. You do not come to church on Sunday morning, Sunday night and Wednesday night to see God. But you come to hear him. When you hear God, you believe God.

There were many people in the scriptures who looked at Jesus, who heard the witnesses, who saw his teaching, who saw all the miracles that he performed, but they rejected him as Lord. They rejected him as the Messiah. Faith doesn't come by seeing. Faith cometh by hearing. A beautiful example of that is Thomas, one of the disciples, who was absent when they found that Jesus was resurrected from the dead. Thomas was that kind of fellow. I'm glad that the story of Thomas is in the Bible. He was a man who wanted to believe, but he had some honest doubts. And God met him right where he was. Thomas said I don't believe it and you'll never make me believe until I see with my own eyes where the nails went. Jesus said to Thomas, reach hither thy fingers and touch the scars and reach your hand into my side. Thomas said when he saw the scars and saw the side, he fell on his face and said, oh my Lord my God. Then Jesus said something to him that's very important to us. "Thomas, because you have seen you have believed. Blessed are those who have not seen yet believed. Faith cometh by hearing not by seeing, and hearing from the word of God. The greatest sin in all the world is not knowing Jesus. Do you know that Jesus today? Have you accepted Him as your personal Savior? If not, I ask you come to Him today.

From The Shepherd To His Flock

Chapter 4
Spiritual Peace
Romans 4:1-8

I want to talk to you about the next best thing to being in heaven and that is having spiritual peace. Our scripture is Romans 4:1-8, but first I want to read a few words of the Psalmist. Because in Romans chapter 4, the apostle Paul quotes the words of the Psalmist in Psalm 32. I want to talk about a man who is blessed, a man that is happy, and a man who has spiritual peace. The Psalmist said, *"Blessed is he whose transgression is forgiven, whose sin is covered. Blessed is the man unto whom the Lord imputeth not iniquity, and in whose spirit there is no guile"*.

In Romans chapter 4, Paul says, *"What shall we say then that Abraham our father, as pertaining to the flesh, hath found? For if Abraham were justified by works, he hath whereof to glory; but not before God. For what saith the scripture? Abraham believed God, and it was counted unto him for righteousness"*. What was counted as righteousness, not works but his belief in God was counted to him for righteousness. Let's continue with verse 4, *"Now to him that worketh is the reward not reckoned of grace, but of debt. But to him that worketh not, but believeth on him that justified the ungodly, his faith is counted for righteousness. Even as David also describeth the blessedness of the man, unto whom God imputeth righteousness without works, Saying, Blessed are they whose iniquities are forgiven, and whose sins are covered. Blessed is the man to whom the Lord will not impute sin".*

David and Paul are talking about a man, a certain man, a particular man who is at peace with God, a man who has spiritual peace. The word blessed in our text means spiritual peace. The man whose sins are forgiven is at spiritual peace. The man to whom God imputeth not iniquities has a spiritual peace. A man who is counted righteous without works has a spiritual peace. This peace or this blessedness is because, as Paul and David both say, that God's wrath has been appeased. Do you realize that the sinner builds up the wrath of God? It just keeps building up like a mighty stream being held back by a dam. And the wrath of God keeps building up, getting higher, filling every inlet and indention until finally the force is so great that the dam breaks and the wrath of God comes down on the unbeliever. David said, and Paul quoted him, "Blessed is the man that does not have that wrath of God. Blessed is the man who has found forgiveness of sin and has appeased the wrath of God.

If I felt like I was under the wrath of God, if I felt like my sins were not forgiven, I would not leave here today, without any unforgiven sin in my heart. I do not want to go around with the burden of knowing God's wrath is not appeased, as far as my life is concerned. But I've got some wonderful news for you today. The Psalmist said it like this, he said, *"mercy and truth are met together, righteousness and peace have kissed each other"* (Psalm 85:10). Now Paul quoting from Psalm 32 is speaking not of mankind in general. Blessed is the man whose sin is forgiven. Blessed is the man whom God imputeth righteousness without works. It is a certain man, not mankind in general, bur a particular man. Paul and David both use the term, 'the man'. Blessed is THE man, a particular man. A man who has met certain criteria to be called a blessed man. And then he says, blessed is the man. What man is he speaking of? Is he talking about a good man? Blessed is the man who is a good neighbor. Blessed is the good man who pays his bills. No, he is not talking about a good man because Romans 3:12 says *"there is none that doeth good, no not one"*. He is not talking about a good man being at peace with God here. Now there are some things men do today that are good. In fact, our world has a lot of good men and women. There are a lot of good folks living in this country of ours. And if being good could be used some way as a means of obtaining spiritual peace, then all of mankind could receive the peace of God on their own merit. So he is not talking about a good man. Is he talking about a heritage, or a culture, or a particular family? No, Paul says in Romans 2:11 *"there is no respect of persons with God"*. Doesn't make any difference where you live, what kind of house you live in, what color your skin is, the size of your bank account. God doesn't look at you any different than he looks at any other mankind on the face of this earth. There is no respect of persons with God. He looks at all men alike. He is certainly not talking about the wealthy man. We read in the book of Luke, chapter 16 of a man who had plenty who faired sumptuously every day, who was wrapped in royal robes. He had everything money could provide for him and the scripture says he died and in hell he lifted up his eyes.

What man is this particular man that is blessed? I want to give you a few aspects of this man and why he is blessed. Romans 4 verse 6, *"the man whom God imputeth righteousness without works"*. That simply means the man who has received the best that God has to offer without working for it. Our sin, the scripture says, will not be imputed against us. This blessed man is blessed of God. If you are here today and you are a child of God, you have been to the cross, you have bowed, somewhere, your heart before God and it need not have been in the church or in the presence of any other living soul. It need not have been at an altar someplace. But someplace you had your own private altar and you confessed the fact that you were a sinner by birth. If you confessed the fact that Jesus died for your sin and you believed on him and received him as your Savior, you are a blessed man and your sin will not be imputed unto you. You have a righteousness today that is very precious. It is not yours, you didn't earn it. You didn't deserve it, but nevertheless, you have a perfect righteousness.

Paul said, "Blessed is the man who has been counted righteous without works". Your righteousness today before God is because God has imputed righteousness unto us. We did not earn it or deserve it. God clothed us with righteousness because, why? Abraham believed and it was counted unto him as righteousness. I don't care what you are doing in life today. You may be a preacher, a missionary, whatever you are, don't ever try to stand before God in your own righteousness. Because it won't stand up.

11 Corinthians 5:21 tells how we are imputed this righteousness. The scripture says, *"For He (that is God) hath made Him (that is Jesus) to be sin who knew no sin; that we might be made the righteousness of God in Him"*. Isn't that a marvelous thing? All of us were filled with sinfulness. God found someone who had no sin and God took all of our sinfulness and placed it on the sinless one and we became righteous. That is a wonderful thing. Our faith is today what Jesus did. Our faith is in what Jesus did at Calvary, not what we have done, but what he did. We rest in his finished work.

Romans chapter 10 verse 10, says *"For with the heart man believeth unto righteousness"*. Not with works, not with giving, not with being good, but with the heart of man believeth unto righteousness. Matthew chapter 25 verse 46, says, speaking of those who are not clothed in righteousness, *"And these shall go away into eternal punishment, but the righteous into life eternal"*.

Why is this man blessed? Because he has been imputed righteous before God. And this righteousness is apart from works. Titus chapter 3 verse 5 tells us, *"Not by works of righteousness which we have done, but by his mercy he saved us, by the washing of regeneration, and renewing of the Holy Ghost"*. That simply means that man has received something. Man got something that he had no part in getting. That is what grace is. And blessed is that man who has obtained righteousness through his belief in Christ. It is all from God. If it required work on our part, as Paul said in Romans, then to receive it would be payment for what we had done. And in heaven, Paul said, we would have whereof to boast. But it came from God without works. Verse 3 says, *"For what saith the scripture? Abraham believed God, and it was counted unto him for righteousness"*. Today religion adds almost everything you can imagine to salvation. In almost every branch of religion today, man has felt that God needed a little help and so they have added a little something to this thing of being saved. To some, it is a baptismal experience. Baptismal regeneration –you are born again, regenerated again by the works of baptism – that's adding works. Some say if you quit certain things, give up certain things – that is adding works. Some say it is through church membership or a particular church membership – that is adding works. Abraham simply believed God. He believed what God's word said. That belief made Abraham righteous in the sight of God. You and I today believe God's word. We believe what he said about Jesus. We believe what he said about us and we have accepted what God said about us and that is counted unto us righteousness. God took the belief of Abraham and put it on account of righteousness. Blessed is the man that has been imputed righteous without works. We need to get a hold of that truth and when you do, bless your heart, you will have spiritual peace.

Then he says, "Blessed is the man whose sins are forgiven". Our sin is not imputed unto us. Impute means to put on one's account. It is also translated as counted. The scripture says he put our sins on Christ's account and put Christ's righteousness on our account. I don't know why. I am not even sure I know how, but praise God it's true. He took what I had, which was bad, and put it on Christ and took what Christ had which was righteous and put it on me. If you ever see me laying in a casket somewhere and someone is preaching my funeral, don't you ever believe that Terry Boyd ever accounted for one second on his own righteousness, nor his own goodness. If it weren't for Jesus Christ, I'd die and go to hell. I deserve to die and go to hell. Praise his holy name, I'm not. I'm not worthy of that, but bless God it makes it exciting.

He came to his own and his own received him not but to them that did receive Him to them gave he the power to become the sons of God. That is what makes the Christian life exciting. Of course, you are not worthy, but he made you worthy. God will not impute our sins or count our sins against us. Now once we are justified, we have peace with God. Paul says, once we are justified and have peace with God our record contains not our sins, but Christ's perfect righteousness. It also tells us that our record can never contain sin. We do sin and this sin breaks our fellowship with God, but our sin has been covered. It has been paid for. Our record will never contain sin. He'll keep a record of your works and one day you will be rewarded for your works, but your sin is remembered no more. Once you are justified, your record never again contains sin. It has been forgiven. It has been taken away. How blessed can you get? I want to make sure you get it. God does not record the sins of a justified man or woman. They have been forgiven. The word in the Old Testament was 'covered'. It was used to describe the priest who went in once a year and took the blood of the sacrifice into the Holy of Holies and there he covered the altar. As the blood covered the altar, the sin of the one making the sacrifice was covered. It wasn't taken away, but covered. The scripture says when Christ came, he was the Lamb of God, slain from the foundation of the world. He went in himself with his own precious blood and he covered the altar once and for all. Our sins were not covered, but taken away. You get that. God will not impute sin to man who is justified. Our sin has been taken away not just covered. The scripture says that when Jesus offered his sacrifice, it was of such quality that it didn't just cover our sins, it paid the penalty of sin once and for all. We ought to rejoice greatly because our sin has been done away with and remembered against us no more. And the scripture says they are removed as far as the east is from the west. I'm glad the scripture didn't say as far as the north is from the south. The Holy Spirit used east and west. You know why? If you are in the south and you head north, you'll get there. If you are in the west and head east, you'll never get there. The Bible didn't say he took your sin as far as the north is from the south because there is a limit there. You can go to the North Pole and South Pole. But He said as far as the east is from the west. In other words, never will they be remembered again. Oh, the blessedness of the man whose sin is not imputed against him. God is not keeping a record of your sin if you have been imputed righteous in his sight through his Son, the Lord Jesus Christ.

Do you know how David sinned? A horrible sin before God. He lost his fellowship with God and he even lost four children and yet Nathan, the prophet of God, speaking to David said these words, "the Lord hath also put away thy sin. Thou shalt die". David expected to die. But his sin had not been charged to his account. He did not die. If God had put his sin and your sin against your record, you would die immediately. But your sin has been taken away. Blessed is the man whose sins are forgiven. Forgiveness is more than you think it is. Because we cannot think of forgiveness the way God thinks about it. If someone asked us to forgive them, we say yes we forgive you, but we never forget it. If I get the opportunity, I'll remind you of it. Isn't that the way we handle it? Forgiveness is more than we think it is. It's more than paying the penalty. It's more than going back and doing something over again or doing something right. Forgiveness is more than saying, I forgive you. Forgiveness involves the heart of the forgiver. I want you to get this. If you want to know forgiveness from God's point of view, look at the story of the prodigal son. The father in that story projected real forgiveness. He is the picture of God. You see, the father in that story, had been sinned against. But the father who has been sinned against instituted forgiveness. It came from his heart. The prodigal son didn't have anything to do with it, the father instituted forgiveness. He didn't have to, but he wanted to. It came from his heart. The son, you remember, planned to offer some work in order to be forgiven. But the father said, no you are forgiven. I forgive you. It involved the heart of the forgiver. The father forgave that son without any output on his part.

When Jesus hung upon the cross, he had you on his mind. And he said, "Father, forgive them". It's a matter of his heart. He instituted forgiveness. And just as that prodigal son was folded in the arms of forgiveness of that father, so are you and I enfolded in the arms of God's forgiveness. Such a man is blessed indeed.

Psychiatrist tell us today that most of the sickness that's in the world is because a man or woman cannot forgive themselves of certain things. Listen to me and get it straight – God has already forgiven you for everything you have every done. God has forgiven you. Your past is clean, your present is clean, and your future has been presented clean by the Son. Will you accept that truth today? Your sins have been forgiven and blessed is the man whose sin is forgiven. What man? The man whom the Lord will not impute sin. This is the best part. The first man, righteousness without works. The second man, sins are forgiven. The third man, sin is not imputed unto Him. Your sin and my sin has not been put on our account. If it had we'd already be dead. But it was put on Christ's account, and we have been imputed righteous in God's sight. On how blessed it is because God will not impute our sin against us. Romans 8:1 says, *"There is therefore now no condemnation to them which are in Christ Jesus who walk not after the flesh, but after the Spirit"*. There is no condemnation. There is no condemnation today, tomorrow and there will be no condemnation in the future. Hebrews chapter 10 verses 10-14 says the same thing. *"By the which will we are sanctified through the offering of the body of Jesus Christ once for all"* (verse 10). *"But this man, after he had offered one sacrifice for sins forever, sat down at the right hand of God;"* (verse 12) *"and by one offering he hath perfected forever them that are sanctified"* (verse 14). That is how you can have spiritual peace. There is no sin on your account today. God wiped it away. Now God sees you righteous, because Christ finished the work on Calvary. That's why you are blessed. There is a sadness to all of this. A sadness that we have to take into account. There are some perhaps, even in this congregation, and the world is filled with people, who have not yet been imputed righteous. That is simply because they will not believe. If you really believe, that by a simple act of faith, Christ could take away your sin of the past, present and future and forever have a clean record. If you really believed that, you would accept it. And yet there are some who have not been imputed righteous because they simply will not believe. And that man is not blessed. Sometime turn to Acts 13:39 and read these words, *"And by him (Christ) all that believe are justified from all things"*. Blessed is that man.

What is holding you back? If you are here today and you have not been imputed righteous, want you come and accept this righteousness of God? It is not in you, it is not in me, it is not in anybody in this room, but it is in Christ. Come and take it and let God wipe your record clean, past, present, and future.

And never again can a sin be recorded on that record. If you will, you will become that man, the Bible talks about, as being a blessed man and brother that is spiritual peace.

Chapter 5
The Father without a Name
Luke 15:11-24

I want to speak from this particular passage in a way perhaps it has not been used by me in a long time, if ever. I want to preach to you on the subject of the unknown father. Scripture says there was a certain man, no name, no address. We don't know who he was except we do know the parable is about God the Father. It certainly applies to every man, especially unto every father. The younger son in this family, I identify with, I also had an elder brother, like this younger boy had. The younger son was displeased with things at home, with family life. That is not uncommon. All of us, at one time or another, as sons have been fed up with the father and the things that go on around the house, so we decide we will show them and we leave home. I left home at least a hundred times. One time I got 20 miles from home before I turned around and went back. Every man goes through that. But the time came when this young boy left his father's house and is also common, he went into a life of sin. After a while, he recognized his condition and he realized his position as a son. So he made a decision to go back to the father's house. He was a smart kid after all. And the father received him with open arms. He does not have a name, this father. We don't know him, but we can attach some credibility to him. There are four attributes I want to speak on today.

First of all, he was a godly father. I'm not going to take the time to explain what I mean by a godly father. I don't mean he sat around with a Bible in his hand all day, I mean he was a man of principle. He was a man that believed in being a good man. He lived right. He was also a very giving father. There is nothing any more wonderful than a giving father. This father was also a loving father and a forgiving father. I want us to talk about those four attributes. He was godly, giving, loving and forgiving. I want you men, as we talk about this unknown father, to evaluate your own manner of being a father. I want to tell you fellows, the two most important jobs you have is that of being a husband and a father, if you are married and have children. If you fail at that, you are a failure no matter what else you accomplish. You fail in life.

He was a godly father. How do we know? Simply, because he was in the Bible. Let's look at verse 18. What did the son say when he got into trouble and realized that he had sinned? He said, "I will arise and go to my father and I will say to him, I have sinned against heaven and before thee". How do he know he had sinned against heaven? How did he know he had sinned against his father? Because his father was a man of God with principles. You see, he taught his children and lived his life before his children in such a way that every child in that family knew their father was a godly man. When he messed up, as all of us do, he realized he had sinned. Not only against God, but he had sinned against his own father's godly principles. He had broken his father's heart. His father's dreams had perished, his father's hopes for this young boy had perished. No doubt he was still praying, but he was a godly man because when the boy sinned, he knew he had sinned. Not many people today may know what sin is or maybe we call it by another name. It doesn't seem to me today that there are an awful lot of families who are turning out children who know anything about godly principles. Children, today, young children ten, eleven, twelve years old, roam God knows where. All over this country, moms and dads don't know where their children are and some of them don't care as long as they don't bother them. We are raising a generation who have no godly principles. Mom and dad didn't teach them godly principles.

But this young man knew and he made a confession. Notice how the father dealt or deals with the son when he returns. Praise God, this father dealt with that young boy, who came back from a life of sin, just like God deals with every one of us. Now listen, there is not a one of us that hasn't been a prodigal sometime in our life. Some of us are prodigals today. But we know where the Father's house is. And this father dealt with this young son, just like God deals with us – in grace, undeserving, but grace. By the way, there is another biblical principle here and you wives can say, Amen, when I say something that sounds good to you. But the father, under God, is supposed to be the spiritual leader of the home. The God given responsibility for the spiritual leadership in the home, God gave it to the man. Let me tell you this, the success of the home will depend largely upon the father's relationship to God. Listen, you wives, you ought to urge your husband to seek God's will, not only for his life, but for his family. A man that walks with God is a better father. A man who walks with God and seeks God's will have less problems that he cannot deal with. Problems are not insurmountable to a man who walks with God. A man who walks with God does not seek his own will, but he seeks the will of his heavenly Father.

Secondly, he was a giving father. Notice in verse 12 it says he divided unto them his living. The word 'living' here, of course, is talking about a monetary or financial gift. He gave this young boy his inheritance early. He gave him money. And when it says he gathered all, he may have even given him so many cows and so many sheep. He divided unto them his living. He gave himself to his family. His family was the most important institution on the face of God's earth in his heart and in his eyes. That is a picture of Christ giving Himself for all of us, his family.

Now I may duck behind the pulpit a time or two in the next minute or two. But we have too many selfish fathers. Let me tell you something. A man who comes home from work on Friday night and spends every minute of his time, until he goes back to work on Monday morning, for himself is a selfish man. A man who comes home from work at 3 o'clock in the afternoon, spends all his time on himself from then to bedtime, is a selfish man. I know a man needs time to himself, but I know some fathers who don't spend any time with their family. If you can go play golf with your buddies, you can take your boys to the park. You can take your boys fishing. And if you can spend time, fishing with your buddies, you can go shopping with your wife. Now I have to say like Paul, I have no word from the Lord but that's my opinion. Most of the time, and I guess this was the way it was in my family, the only time a father spends with his children anymore, is when he has to discipline them. After all, the mother has been saying all day, "Wait till her daddy gets home".

The father gave them a good home. There is no evidence anywhere except this was a good home. The boy had been reared to realize that the kind of life he was living was wrong. Something else he knew – he knew if he went home, his father would forgive him. Now I don't care what your son or daughter does, and I don't care how you discipline them and you have to sometimes. Don't let a son or daughter bankrupt you. Spend all your money keeping a boy out of jail, let him go to jail. Let him pay for his own sins, but don't you every close the door on him. Don't ever day, 'Don't ever step back in my house again'. Don't ever close that door. That son or daughter out there has got to know that they can go home. And they have got to know that if they are sincere, they will be forgiven when they get there. What kind of home have you provided for your family? I'm not talking about size. I'm not talking about beauty, but does love exist in your home? It's not chandeliers and cathedral ceilings, but have you taught your children that you love them? Have you taught your children bib ical standards? Do they know Dad's home is a godly home? We see in this scripture a young man that knew things were right at home.

The father also gave them a good name. The scripture says a good name is rather to be chosen than great riches. All I want to say about giving your family a good name is in the words of this little poem entitled, Your Name:

> Your name it came from your father
> it was all he had to give.
> So it's yours to cherish as long as you may live.
> If you lose the watch he gave you
> it can always be replaced
> But a black mark on your name
> son can never be erased.
> It was clean the day you took it
> and a worthy name to bear.

> When I got it from my father
> there was no dishonor there.
> So make sure you guard it wisely
> after all is said and done.
> You'll be glad your name is spotless
> when you give it to your son.

He gave them a good image. What did this boy see in his mind when he spent all that he had? He saw the father's house. The father's house looks different from the hog pen. When he looked at the father's house he saw plenty.

Thirdly, he was a loving father. Now we don't see the father going out looking for the son to bring him home. He watched and let him go. But we know that he waited some long, long hours for that son to come home. I can see this old father in the afternoon, pull the old rocking chair under the shade tree in the front yard and the sun set every evening and he sat there and rocked, with a tear on his check looking down the road. Watching the horizon, waiting to see if there is anything moving. No doubt praying God don't let anything happen to him till he gets home. I know he was doing that because the Bible says when the boy started home, the father saw him when he was a way off. He was looking for him.

There are many homes today who are looking for a son or daughter to come home. I've got this to say about some young folks away from home. When they get sick of the hog pen, they will come home. The reason a lot of sons and daughters are still away from home is because they are not sick of the hog pen yet. I know a lot of our homeless teenagers walk the streets, some of them have a home that is hell on earth. But let me tell you, a lot of them, are not sick of sin yet, and have not gone home. The father's house looked mighty good from the hog pen.

Then fourthly, he was a forgiving father. The young boy realized that the old man and the house and the chores weren't as bad as he thought they were. He was willing to go home and be willing to become a servant. He had all the marks of the hog pen on him when he went home. Sin was in his face, in his clothing and that father walked out there and put his arms around him just like he was. Before he had ever had a bath, stinking to the high heavens. The father walked out there and hugged him like he had a fresh shower and been in his house every day. He clothed him with the family robe. He said to his servants, let's have a little dancing and a little music and let's get happy. Let's have a celebration! He thought of his son as being lost and now he was found. The father didn't mention his sin. There is no mention of retribution here. What a beautiful picture here of God's grace to fallen man.

Each of us has taken our trip to the hog pen. We have each gone our own way. The scriptures says, while we were in the hog pen, Jesus died for us. You don't have to come to the Lord and say Lord how can I earn my way back. All you have to do is accept what he has already done for you. That's grace, that's God's grace. No retribution and this boy didn't request sonship. He didn't say father take me back as a son. He didn't have to, the father's grace provided it for him. That is exactly what the Father's grace has done for each of you. We didn't request sonship. It came as a result of the Father's grace.

There may be someone that would have to say with the prodigal, I have sinned against thee. I have sinned against heaven. I am no more worthy to be called thy son. Let me tell you there is not a one in this building today worthy. We are all prodigals and don't you ever forget it. Every one of us are prodigals. But listen, the son came back and he got a robe on his back and a kiss of forgiveness on his neck. I'm glad you can take that old robe, that's torn and tattered, dirty, filthy and you can come into God's presence and He will come over to you and put His arms around you and give you the kiss of forgiveness and as he takes his arms back, He will take that old robe off your shoulders and throw it in a pile with a lot of others. And the servants will come in and put on your back the family robe of righteousness.

Maybe you are here and you have not been the father that you ought to be. Maybe you need to come to this altar. Maybe you need to bring your child with you and pray a prayer of dedication- I am going to be the father I need to be to that child. Some of you are excellent fathers. I watch you and you do a marvelous job at being fathers. But maybe there is someone here who would say I have not been the father that I want to be and I want to be the kind of father my child needs. You know the one mark of the end time – father and son split, divided. Which one of them turns? The father's heart is turned to the child. Maybe you need to turn your heart back to your child.

Maybe you are here as a young son or daughter and you've not given your parents the love and respect that they deserve. Maybe you need to come to the altar and say forgive me. Maybe you are an older son or daughter and you've not loved and respected your parents as you ought to. Maybe you need to come and say, Lord, forgive me. Maybe there is a mother that needs to say, Father forgive me. You are in the father's house. You can come to the father's house and get that straightened out. You can be the kind of father and child you need to be.

Chapter 6
A Friend like Jesus
Acts 26: 24 – 29

We are going to pick up in the middle of an experience that the Apostle Paul is having after his arrest. We drop in verse 24 right in the middle of Paul's testimony. And then we will go back and look at some preceding verses in the message. Begin reading in verse 24: *"and as he thus spake for himself, Festus said with a loud voice, Paul, thou art beside thyself; much learning doth make thee mad. But he said, I am not mad, most noble Festus; but speak forth the words of truth and soberness. For the King knoweth of these things, before whom also I speak freely; for I am persuaded that none of these things are hidden from him, for this thing was not done in a corner. King Agrippa, believest thou the prophets? I know that thou believest. Then Agrippa said unto Paul, almost thou persuades me to be a Christian. And Paul said, I would to God, that not only thou, but also all that hear me this day, were both almost, and altogether such as I am, except these bonds."*

In our text, the Apostle Paul is standing before the king to give a defense and as Paul always does, he gives his testimony of how he was a Jew and how he was a Pharisee and Roman and how he followed the god of his fathers and the god of tradition. Those things which made it look like he had lost his mind was really an experience that he had with a man called Jesus Christ on the Damascus road. The king was moved by Paul's testimony and he said, 'almost thou persuades me to be a Christian'. Paul said, 'I would to God that you were a Christian. Not only you, but everyone who hears me this day'. Paul said, I wish they were as I am and that is a believer. Paul said, I don't want anyone to be in prison or in bonds as I am, but I wish everyone had the experience that I had and that is to know personally the Lord Jesus Christ.

As Paul talked, what was it that the king needed most? It wasn't wealth nor power, but as Paul talked to Festus, the one thing Festus needed among all other things, he needed a Savior. He needed a personal, intimate relationship with Jesus Christ. That's what that man needed. That was what Paul was trying to convince him to receive, as a free gift from God. Paul was wanting this man to become a Christian. What power this man could have had, if he had been a Christian! What power our political leaders, today, and what influence they could have, if they were all Christians! I mean born again Christians, real Christians. What a tremendous difference it would make with those who have influence. Paul wanted this man, who had power and wealth, to get the one thing he needed above all else and that was he needed a Savior.

A mother in a home, has to care for people, she has to prepare meals and she has to keep people happy and safe, warm and fed. What does that mother need? More than anything else in the world, that mother needs a Savior. What does a college student need? One thing above all else, is they need a Savior. They need Christ. A man who is in business and has all the cares of the business, he needs a Savior. That man today, in the darkest corner of our globe, who is bowing today before some wooden idol or involving himself in some far out kind of sacrifice to an idol, needs a

Savior. The richest man needs a Savior. The poorest man needs a Savior. He needs to know Christ as his personal Savior and there is only one who can save him. His name is Jesus.

How many of you have a special friend? Someone who means more to you, perhaps than anyone else. I suppose all of us have a special friend. I'm glad today that Jesus is my friend. I'm glad He was willing to be my friend before he became my Savior. He was a friend of sinners. I'm glad He is my friend. He called me to preach. He is my friend in joy, in sorrow and in sickness. He is my friend now and forever. He is the friend that everybody needs. He is the friend everybody can have.

Why does everyone need a friend like Jesus? There are three reasons: We need a friend like Jesus because of the past. We need him because of the present and we need Him because of the future. Everybody needs a friend like Jesus for those three reasons. We need Him because of the past. We all have sinned and come short of the glory of God. The scripture says for all have sinned and come short of the glory of God. That's true of preachers, deacons, Sunday school teachers, lay members of the church. It is true of everybody. In the past, we have all sinned and are sinners to this day. John said if a man says, I am not a sinner, he is a liar. Not only that, but John said, if a man says, I am free of sin, he makes God a liar. For God has said all have sinned. Now a young boy can go out and fly a kite and he can let it go out of sight, but as long as he's got that string, he can pull it back. But many times in our sin, we cannot call them back. We cannot recall them and pull them back in as if they never occurred. Sometimes when our sin is committed, there is no way to recall it. There is no way to get it back and undo it. Many of us, perhaps, envisioned a life in which we would spend our whole lifetime trying to cover up our sins. You can't cover them up. The scripture says, he that covers his sin shall not prosper but he that forsakes his sin and confesses his sin, God will bless him. We can't cover up our sin, so we have to do something with it. If all of us are sinners and if we can't cover up our sin, we must do something with them, mustn't we? That's why we need Jesus because of our past, our sin. He is the only one that can be a covering for sin. The old hymn says it more beautifully than it can be said and that is in these words: "There is a fountain filled with blood, drawn from Immanuel's vein and sinners plunge beneath that blood lose all their guilty stain". That says it beautifully and perfectly.

Sin is one of the most destructive and damning things that can happen in a person's life. Little sin, that begins quiet, even unnoticed, continues to grow. The scriptures says when lust is conceived in our hearts, it brings forth sin. In other words, we give birth to sin. It is conceived in our hearts, when drawn away by our sin of lust. That conception is sin. When we give birth to that, the scripture says, when it is finished it brings forth death. The scriptures says that sin left alone will cause our death. Jesus said those who try to cover up sin and act as though they have never sinned and try to go around with an attitude of who knows what, Jesus said they are like a grave, all painted white on the outside and look pure and good, but on the inside filled with dead men's bones. Jesus said all of our unrighteousness, he didn't say all of your filth and sin but he said all of your unrighteousness is as filthy rags. Even the good things in which we do when we are living in sin is as filthy rags unto God. So it has to be dealt with. There has to be some way which we can deal with our past. When we compare our lives with God, when we see ourselves in light of the holiness of the Lord Jesus Christ, we see how really far we are from the glory of God. We realize, if we are honest, that we do not even deserve the notice of God, much less His love. But Jesus says, come unto me and I will remove your sin, as far as the east is from the west. We need a friend like that. Everybody needs a friend like that. He says, I will cast your sin behind my back. God never turns around. He said, I will bury your sin in the deepest sea and remember it no more. We need a friend like Jesus, because of our past, because of that sin that all of us have to deal with. You can pay for your own sin. You don't have to let Jesus pay for your sin. The only way you can do that is to spend an eternity in hell. But you can let Jesus pay for it and spend an eternity in heaven.

Everyone needs a friend like Jesus not only because of the sin of the past, but because of the blessings in the past. We need to love and serve the Lord. The scripture says, God's blessing are new and fresh every morning. When God furnished manna for the children in the wilderness, he didn't give them a week's supply, he gave it fresh to them every morning. They went out every morning and gathered the blessings of God. There are 365 mornings every year and every 4th year, he gives us an extra morning. And there is a blessing every single morning. Do you ever get the feeling that you don't feel like God is doing anything for you? You might say, I don't know of anything in particular to be grateful to the Lord for today. Listen, you get out and go around a little bit. Get outside your own world and see what other people are doing and what's happening to other people. You can give praise to God for a lot of things. The song says count your blessings, name them one by one and it will surprise you what the Lord has done. You can turn it around a little and say it will surprise you what God wants done. God blesses us and His blessings are new every morning. Because of that, we ought to love and serve Him for the blessings in the past.

Not only because of the sin of the past, the blessings in the past, but the memories of the past, we ought to serve the Lord. Some of you can remember your mother praying for you. You can remember your father's good advice. You can remember those Christmas and Thanksgivings when all the family got together and it was a real time of joy and love. They are gone now. And to remember brings a tear to your eye. You miss them and you want to see them again. The scripture says, but if we believe on the Lord Jesus Christ, if our names are written in the Lamb's Book of Life, we will see them again. We need a friend like that. In the past, there are also resolutions we have made. You remember the time, the grand moment in your life, when you were convinced beyond a shadow of a doubt that you were a sinner and that if you died you would go to hell. You made your way to an altar somewhere and received Jesus into your heart. It was a grand and glorious moment when you walked out free from the burden of sin. You made a resolution, a vow to God. You said I will serve you all the days of my life. Some of us need to remember that, because not all of us have been faithful to the resolutions we've made in the past. Time and time again, people have come and made rededications in their life and we need to remember it. As we look at the past because of sin, because of blessings, because of resolutions, we see every reason in the world why we ought to be in love with the Lord and why we ought to be serving and following Him. He is our true friend.

We also need the Lord today and need a friend because of the present. You may think you are real smart. You may think you are able to control your own destiny and run your own life. But let me tell you, if it wasn't for Jesus, you'd be in a fog right now. Even if you do not know Him as Savior, he is looking after you. He is taking care of you. He has given you every opportunity to hear the gospel one more time and be saved. You can thank God, he is doing that today. We need Him because of the present. A man without Christ is living, but he is not living to the best of his ability. He is not getting the most out of life. We need the Lord Jesus who says, come and walk with me, I know about life. You know how we children are when mom and dad say let me give you some advice and we turn and say, what now. When we get a little older, we realize how stupid we were. Jesus says come to me, I know about life. Jesus says, I've been where you are. I have been tempted just like you have been tempted. I have lived life and can tell you about life. Come walk with me. Listen, we need a friend like that, someone who has been there and can tell us.

In the Russo-Japanese War, a Japanese colonel was captured by his Russian counterparts and he was condemned to die before a firing squad. This Japanese soldier, when asked if he had any last words to say, he said, yes, I want to take whatever money I have in my pocket and I want to give it to your Russian Red Cross. They asked him why he would want to give money to his enemy. He said, because some years ago, some missionaries came to my land and told me about the Christ. He told me how, that even in his death, he laid down his life for his enemies. I want to follow his example. Before he died he gave his earthly possessions to the enemy as an example of what Christ had done for him. He didn't learn that from the world. He learned that from the Lord. That is the Lord's spirit. We don't treat each other right until we learn it from Jesus.

I used to have a great deal of difficulty with folks that I had an offense against. Folks that I had some fault against. Some folks I couldn't really forgive until it finally dawned on me one time, and I wasn't in a church service, I was in a song service. I was in the Spirit, I guess. It really dawned on me that because Jesus had forgiven me. You know sometimes we feel like God forgave me, but why shouldn't he? We deserved it. But when we really get to thinking about it, we think about all the faults we have and it comes to our attention once and for all, he forgave us. That God really forgave us. He wiped our slate clean and if that's true, I can forgive others against whom I have an offense. After all, did not God forgive me? We never get to the place where we can forgive, until we get it from Jesus. He teaches us that. A man who will seek revenge does not have the Spirit of Christ. If someone has wronged you, leave it with the Lord. He can handle it. In fact, he can handle it a lot better than you can. Jesus, not only taught us the principal of how to live, he gave us the power to live it. Only a living Christ can give us that power to do as Jesus would have done.

We also need him in the present because we need a comforter. We act, sometimes, as though the sorrow that comes to us is undeserved or unexpected. Yet the Lord said, I'm sending you a comforter. The Lord must have known we were going to have times of sorrow. Why else would we need a comforter? Nobody in this world sees any more sorrow than a pastor. He is called into hundreds of situations where there is deep sorrow. Sooner or later, it will come to you and your house. Surely, as the Lord tarries, you personally are going to enter into a time of extreme sorrow, personal sorrow in your life. The only thing you can do is turn people's attention to the Lord Jesus Christ and to the Holy Spirit. Jesus said, I will send the Comforter.

In the present time, we also need an intercessor. I am glad Jesus is a friend that intercedes for me. When I was a young boy, I rarely ever had a conservation with my father in which I asked for something. My father rarely ever gave me anything unless I did ask him, but I refused to ask. But if it was something I just wanted and needed, I wouldn't go to my father I would go to my mother. I'd say, mother, would you ask daddy so and so. She was my intercessor. She could get more for me than I could get for myself. All of you know your mother served as some sort of condenser. On the way up to your father, she acted as an intercessor and on the way back down, daddy would say, momma, whip that boy. I was always glad he said that because by the time it got through her, it was condensed a little bit, you know, and you got slapped instead of hit over the head with a wagon standard. That's the way my father would whip you if he felt the urge.

Jesus is our intercessor with the Father. We go to the Lord with our petition because he is in that business of interceding for us. You pray to Him and He asks the Father for your blessings. Listen, life is difficult. Life is really difficult. We need a friend, brother. We need Jesus because he is with us every day. Do you know what he said? I'll never leave you. He is with us every day.

Finally, we need a friend like Jesus because of the future. You know what's waiting in the future? There is a lot of happiness out yonder in the future. There is a lot of graduations, jobs, promotions, a lot of goals reached. But, you know, somehow or other because of one thing that is out in the future other things lose their luster a little bit, and that is death. Death has a way of cheating us out of blessings, you know. We know it is out there, all of us, if the Lord tarries. Because it is out there for all of us, we need Jesus, a Savior. I'm reminded of death every day and you are to. Everything we look at is an object lesson of death. The trees get bare, the leaves fall off. Just look at yourself, some don't hear as good as you used to, you don't see as good as you used to and your steps are getting a little shorter. That is just reminding you, you are on your way to death. It is out there in the future. It is the last enemy. It hasn't been defeated yet, but it will be. Because it is still out there, we need a Savior who can take us and lead us through it onto the other side. Not only is there death, but there is judgment. In Polish cemeteries, they put the names of the deceased on their tombstones just like we do. There is a tradition among some of them and that is to leave the name off of them in hopes that they will be forgotten in the resurrection. In hopes that the resurrecting angel, who will bring them into judgment, will pass over that grave because their names are not there. That will never happen, by the way. God will bring us all into judgment. At the judgment, we will either rejoice to hear enter ye into the joys of the Lord or we will faint at the words, depart me for I never knew you. That's out there.

There is also an eternity. Death is not all that is out there. And judgment is not all that is out there in the future. There is an eternity out there. There are millions and millions and millions of years. You cannot count the drops of water in the ocean. You cannot count the grains of sand on the beaches. You cannot count the stars in the heaven and neither can you count the years of eternity. The question is where will you spend eternity? Eternity is either an endless heaven or an endless hell. Because of the past, present and future, we need a friend like Jesus. More than a friend, we need a Savior. We have a Savior, his name is Jesus. The scripture says, He is able to save to the uttermost those who come unto him, seeing that he ever liveth to make intercession for us, He is able to redeem us, he is able to set us at liberty to give us new life, take away the pains of death. A Savior like that is worth knowing. He is the best friend you ever had in this world. He will be the best friend you will have in the world to come, if you know Him as your Savior.

Chapter 7
We Would See Jesus
John 12:20-21

"And there were certain Greeks among them that came up to worship at the feast: The same came therefore to Philip, which was of Bethsaida of Galilee, and desired him, saying, Sir, we would see Jesus."

I suppose the last part of verse 21 has been used as a text for sermons more than any other scripture. "We would see Jesus". If you had been in Jerusalem on the day this scripture is describing, you would have seen a great multitude of people. You would have seen a great deal of chaos and confusion and an extra amount of activity around the temple area. People, from all over the country, had made their way to Jerusalem on this particular day that they might fellowship together. This was a very solemn day for the Jew. It was a day that was looked forward to and had great significance to the Jew. To understand the significance of that day, we have to go back in history just a bit.

God's people, because of their unfaithfulness and disobedience to God, had been carried away into captivity in the land of Egypt. While they were in Egypt, they were oppressed, persecuted; they were in bondage to a heathen people. God continued to add to their burden and they were very oppressed. In this oppression, God's people cried out to God for deliverance and God heard their prayer. At the same time, he was preparing a man named Moses on the back side of the desert. When God's people cried out and he heard them, God said to Moses, I want you to go down as my servant and I want you to appeal to Pharaoh to let my people go. You will be the leader that I have chosen to lead those three million or more people out of the land of Egypt and into the land which I promise to give Abraham, Jacob and Isaac, your fathers. Moses went down to Egypt and some very peculiar things took place under the watchful eye of God. The plagues and all of those things that transpired, when God was trying to get Pharaoh to decide in his heart to let his people go. Then God used the final blow – God used that which finally broke the resistance of Pharaoh, his army and people and allowed the Jew to leave Egypt. God said to those people of his, the Israelites there in bondage, I want you to kill a lamb and take a lamb without spot or blemish, one that is perfect. I want you to take that lamb, slay it and take the blood from that perfect sacrifice and sprinkle it upon the doorpost of your homes. For tonight, the death angel shall go throughout all of Egypt and the oldest child in every home will die except the home where the blood has been applied. He said when I see the blood, I will pass over you. That night, when God's angel came to Egypt and he noticed the blood applied to the doorpost by faith, God's people lived, but the oldest child in every home in Egypt died that night and Pharaoh said take your people and leave. They began their exodus and then entered into the land God had prepared and God said, from this day forward, for evermore, don't ever forget the Passover. Don't forget that night the death angel came to Egypt and passed over those people protected by the blood. From this day forward have a Passover Feast, a day of celebration, to remember a tremendous event in the lives of God's people. That is why they are in Jerusalem in this passage of scripture. They are there to celebrate the time God delivered them from oppression, through the applied blood of a perfect lamb. Jesus was there on this particular Feast of the Passover and he understood full well the meaning of the Passover Feast and he knew he was the Lamb. He knew he was the lamb without spot or blemish. He knew he was the one who would die and give his blood. He knew when his blood was applied to the sinful soul of man, they could be safe in Jesus for evermore. He understood perfectly what the Passover meant.

There were others there. The Greeks came, but the Passover meant nothing to them. They had not been delivered in such a way, but they were there to worship. Scripture says they came to some of the disciples and said to Philip, we have heard about Jesus. His fame has grown throughout the whole world. We have made our journey here to see Jesus. We would see Jesus. That has been the cry of the human heart ever since the dawning of history. We would see Jesus. We would see God's perfect redemption. We would see that one who can save us from our sin. We would see the one who came to give life and give it more abundantly. We would see Jesus. That is the cry of the human race.

Most of us, are like those people, who came to the disciples and said show us the Father and it will be sufficient. Just let us see God the Father. Let us get to know God. Let us know him in his love and his mercy to us and it will be sufficient for us. Christ said to those of you who have seen me have seen the Father for I have come to do that which he called me to do. Everything I do is because God told me to do it and God has given me the power to do it. There are times in our lives when we must see Jesus. There are times when no one else will do. There are times when we have to have our fellowship with the Lord Jesus Christ.

One of these occasions is when we are burdened with sin. I am talking about burdened. How long has it been since you felt a burden in your heart and a burden upon your shoulders because of your sin before God? How long has it been since you felt a load over lost men and women? How long has it been since you felt your own need before God and felt the burden or weight? In David's prayer in Psalm 51, perhaps my favorite passage of scripture, David is crying out in that Psalm in confession to God. He is a sin sick soul trying to get back into fellowship with God. He is saying, God wash me and cleanse me of my sin. He is saying blot out my transgressions, take away that sin that hides your face from me. He was simply a man guilty of sin who felt the weight and burden of his sin and he is crying out to God, I would see Jesus. That is simply what David was crying out. I would see that redemption of my soul. This man after God's own heart was humbling himself in confession and repentance and crying out to God to cleanse me and have mercy upon me and blot out my transgressions. When David felt the sin, he felt the pressure of the need he had.
The evil or sin in this world has been brought home to our doorstep. Much of the problems you and I face today, financially and socially, and in every other way, is nothing more than sin that has been brought home to rest on our doorstep. It is our own reward for our greed and corruption in high places. It is our own pay for not standing up and demanding that God and all that's holy and righteous and good be allowed to take its place in society, in our schools, and in our courts. We have gone to sleep. We have been lured to sleep by the devil. The devil has taken over this world. All the problems that we are having is nothing more

than a just reward for our deed. There is not one of us not guilty in some way for the sin this world is in today. Whether we are sinners or Christians afraid to open our mouths, we are receiving our rewards and God help us. I don't know if we are going to make it or not. That's the kind of burden I am talking about when we can see that sin and lust and all these things have been brought home to us. I don't know about you, but I am frightened to see the lowered moral standards that is threatening, not only our young people, but adults, but especially aimed at our young people. Sin has grown to the proportion in this country that sin is crouching at the very door of Democracy, brother. Our whole democratic system is being threatened and it was caused by sin. Sin is as real as cancer; as real as any other disease and when we see sin, we feel the burden of it. We cry out to Jesus, we would see Jesus. You might say, preacher, I don't know what you are talking about when you talk about the burden. Preachers are always talking about the burden of sin. How much does the burden of sin weigh, preacher? Ten, twenty, fifty pounds? I don't feel any burden. If you were to take 400 pounds and lay it on a corpse, how much would he feel? Nothing. Why? Because he is dead. The soul that does not feel the burden of sin is a dead soul, a dead spirit. We talk about the burden of sin. We talk about the weight of conviction. We want to see Jesus when we know our sin.

We want to know the Lord when we come to worship. I suppose that day in Jerusalem, at the great feast, there was a lot of confusion. I am sure there was chaos as everyone was trying to buy the perfect sacrifice and everyone was trying to get their offerings up to the Lord. I am sure after the Jews had gone through the whole day of ceremonies and those things that took place in a worship, they still went home with the feeling of guilt. They still went home feeling they were no closer to God than they were before. Folks can go to church Sunday after Sunday and never come face to face with Jesus Christ and have their sins washed away. I love the statement, I believe Billy Sunday said, sitting in church will not make you a Christian any more than sitting in a garage will make you an automobile. Just as those Jews came and worshiped and went home feeling guilty and empty inside, so we, today, can come to church, go through our calisthenics of worship and go home empty inside because we didn't see Jesus. We didn't see or feel Him. We want to see Jesus in our worship.

We want to see Jesus in the songs we sing. God deliver us and I know a way to draw a crowd is to have some singing, but God deliver us from singing where all you can hear are the voices of the singers and never hear the message of God. I had rather muddle through what we do sometimes than to have that. We want to see Jesus through the songs we sing. I am talking about songs that move, warm and bless people, because they came out of a heart experience. Like amazing grace, how sweet the sound that saved a wrench like me, written by John Newton. A man who was the scum of the earth. A slave trader who was guilty of fornication that the world would not even believe and God saved him and from that salvation experience, he wrote Amazing Grace. That's the kind of song that moves, warms and blesses people. The kinds of songs we sing tell us about the Lord Jesus Christ.

I don't know about you, but I wouldn't listen to a preacher very long that didn't tell me about Jesus, that didn't tell me about my sin and that didn't warm me that I'd go to hell if I didn't get saved. I wouldn't listen to a preacher, very long, that didn't present Jesus in his sermons. We want to see Jesus in our sermons. A young fellow got out of seminary and he was convinced that the way to draw a big crowd was to use all kinds of witty slogans in his preaching and too use high intellectual sounding phrases and words. So he worked on that and his crowd began to dwindle. One day he came to the pulpit and someone had left a note that said, we would see Jesus. He became angry in his heart and then he realized that he had not preached the Lord Jesus Christ. He began to preach Jesus, born of a virgin, died on the cross, as God's sacrifice for sin and the crowd began to come back. Then one day when he got to the pulpit, someone had typed this verse of scripture, then were the people glad when they saw Jesus in the midst. We want to see Christ in our sermons.

We want to see Jesus in our sorrows. There are times, we can be in the middle of living, sun shining and suddenly too quick for some to imagine, our lives are plunged into darkness and sorrow. What would we do, brethren, if in the midnight hour we could not see the light of the world, which is Jesus? We must see him in times of sorrow. When those sisters in Bethany lost their brother, they sent for Jesus immediately. They sent for him the very moment they knew Lazarus was dead. He came to them. We are like those sisters, when sorrow comes we would see Jesus. Sometimes, in the midst of sorrow, you see people beaten into the dust. Other times you see people have the peace of God written on their faces, even in the midst of sorrow. The peace of God is there. Why? What's the difference? They saw Jesus. It is only the darkness of night that teaches us how bright the stars are. It is only the darkness of sorrow that teaches us how full and sweet and wonderful the grace of God can be. If we never experienced sorrow, we would never know the grace of God was able to meet our need. We want to see Him.

I want to see Jesus in glory, don't you? He has promised to do that for us. He promised that beyond death and the grave and this old life, we would see Him. Now there are many others in heaven that we want to see. But as the song says, Jesus will outshine them all. We want to see him in glory. I want to feel the arms of Jesus around me. I want to feel him as he wipes away the tears. Scripture says, He will wipe the tears from our eyes. I want to be right in the middle of that. I don't even want to become too proud, too cold, too starchy, not to enjoy the grace and love that is experienced when two people come together to express their love and appreciation for one another. I love to have people put their arm around me. I love to be hugged and hug other people. I told someone before, that there is enough dog in me that I just love to be patted on the head every now and then. Want it be wonderful when Jesus wraps His loving arms around us and wipes the tears away from our eyes.

There was a father, one time, who was greatly troubled because a son of his had gone into the wrong life. The son had become ill and despondent. He wrote his father a letter. In the letter, he worded it as if to say, father is there any hope. The father sent the son a telegram that consisted of two words. Those words were 'home' signed 'father'. He said a lot to that boy who was lost and despondent and sick. He is saying to him, your hope is at home and your father welcomes you. The gospel of the Lord Jesus Christ is God's telegram to you and me. It's God's telegram to a lost and dying world; to a lost and despondent soul saying simple, 'home' signed 'Father'.

A man got on a train one day. Sitting in his seat, he noticed someone left a map. He picked up the map and it had all the tracks of the train, all those lines running through it. In one corner, someone had written 'Home' beside the name of one city. Someone got on that train one day, discouraged, blue and as he sat down to look at that map he saw home and out of his heart he took a pencil and wrote, 'home' beside a city that was many miles from where he was. As I pick up the word of God and search its pages, the roads lead like one scarlet thread through the scriptures. There is only one line, it's a scarlet line and it converges at the cross of Calvary. Every one of the lines or roads come together at the cross.

I have one desire and that is to present the Lord Jesus Christ. Whether it is done intelligently or emotionally is not important. The important thing is that I have the opportunity to take the name of Jesus and write it on your heart. I hope you have seen the Lord today through my words. I wish I had the gift of presenting Jesus in such a way that the whole world would come to know him. I wish I could find the words adequate to describe the Lord Jesus Christ. God has chosen not to give men that ability. He has chosen another instrument call the preaching of the word and the Holy Spirit. The Holy Spirit can come to your heart and can show you the Lord Jesus Christ. If you have never received Christ as your personal Savior, he died for you and to save you. If you will just come home today, kneel and receive Jesus Christ as your Savior, you would be on your way home. If you are a Christian and you have wandered away from God, why don't you come back home. Home is where Jesus is. He is waiting for you to come home.

Chapter 8
What is Sin?
Psalms 51:1-13

Psalms 51 is my favorite Psalm in all the Psalms. It is the six successive steps in renewing fellowship with God after sin has entered into your life. Though we won't be going through that, we will read a part of David's prayer. Psalms 51:1-13: *"Have mercy upon me, O God, according to thy lovingkindness: according unto the multitude of thy tender mercies blot out my transgressions. Wash me thoroughly from mine iniquity, and cleanse me from my sin. For I acknowledge my transgressions: and my sin is ever before me. Against thee, thee only, have I sinned, and done this evil in thy sight: that thou mightiest be justified when thou speakest, and be clear when thou judgest. Behold, I was shapen in iniquity; and in sin did my mother conceive me. Behold, thou desirest truth in the inward parts: and in the hidden part thou shalt make me to know wisdom. Purge me with hyssop, and I shall be clean: wash me, and I shall be whiter than snow. Make me to hear joy and gladness; that the bones which thou hast broken may rejoice. Hide thy face from my sins, and blot out all mine iniquities. Create in me a clean heart, O God; and renew a right spirit within me. Cast me not away from thy presence; and take not thy Holy Spirit from me. Restore unto me the joy of thy salvation, and uphold me with thy free spirit. Then will I teach transgressors thy ways; and sinners shall be converted unto thee."* One clear fact in the Bible, is that all of us sooner or later have to acknowledge that all men are sinners.

Romans 3:23 declares that all have sinned and come short of the glory of God. A lot of times, when you preach that, sinners think you are picking on them. But the scripture doesn't say, you are a sinner, it says we are sinners. All have sinned and come short of the glory of God. Galatians 3:22 has concluded that all are under sin. Sin is a poison of satanic origin that has entered into the bloodstream of the human race. It is that which runs through all our veins, all of us are contaminated and polluted with the fact of sin.

Men cannot live in that fact. So in order to rid their minds of the fact that all have sinned, they begin to play with the labels. They begin to fool around with the words. They begin to call sin all kinds of things instead of what God declared sin to be. To many people, sin is described as an unpleasant episode in man's upward climb to better himself. In man's upward climb to maturity, sins are the unpleasant part. Men try to minimize sin. But the Bible has some very serious things to say about sin. The Bible tells us what sin is, how it got started, what it will do and who have the problem. The Bible gives us all the details, but man wanted to call it something else. They wanted to begin to cover it up instead of saying today men are guilty of adultery, fornication and lust; we call it an affair. Instead of the horrible sin of sodomy, we call it a lifestyle change. Instead of drunkenness, we call it alcoholism. And on and on, we find labels to describe a problem all humans have and that problem is a three letter word called sin.

When you say the word sin you can almost hear the hiss of the snake that tempted Adam and Eve. Sin is man's problem. Men say sin is an accident; God calls it abomination. Men say sin is a blunder; God says it is blindness. Men say sin is a defect; God calls it a disease. Men say sin is an error; God calls it enmity. Men call it fascination; God called it fatality. Men call it luxury; God calls it leprosy. Men say sin is a mistake; God says sin is a madness. Men say that sin is just a trifle; God says sin is a tragedy. Men say that sin is a weakness; God says it is wickedness.

As you go through the entire Bible, God has exhausted the human language to tell us what sin has done to the human heart. I want to think about David's description of sin. I want us to get the definition once again for sin. Someone asked why are you always preaching on the same subjects? Why don't you get off the subject of sin and preach on something else? Well, when you get that down pat, we will move on to something else. I want us to look at the definition of sin by the words of David, a man after God's own heart. He was a man God loved and a man who loved God. Yet this man, who was close to God and had been given the responsibility of the kingdom, this man fell into sin. He realized the horror of sin. He got himself into a real mess. And God began to deal with David because of his sin. David confesses that sin and calls out to God for forgiveness. He uses three words. Notice he said, blot out my transgressions. He refers to sin as being a transgression. What is transgression? To transgress means to go beyond known limits. It means to step over the boundary line. David had read in the scriptures that adultery was a transgression of the law of God. John said in 1John 3:4, sin is a transgression of the law. Sin is to go beyond the known limits. Sin is to step over the boundary line that God has given us. God has given to us certain boundaries and he expects us to live within that boundary.

In the Garden of Eden, God put Adam and Eve in a beautiful paradise. He provided for them everything necessary for their happiness and well-being. Everything they could have desired, God provided for them. But he put a boundary. He said of everything in the garden thou shalt eat of except that one tree. That is my boundary, that's the line and I don't want you to step over that. I have all you need over here and there is a boundary. Adam and Eve stepped over that line and they transgressed the law of God and with that transgression, sinned and fell. That is what happened to David. David knew the commandment, Thou shalt not commit adultery, but David stepped over the boundary line, transgressed and sinned.

The second word that David uses in verse 2 is wash me thoroughly from mine iniquities. He refers to sin as iniquity. The word iniquity means to bend or to distort something from its original shape and design into something else. To twist and to distort. That is exactly what sin does – to distort from the original design. My wife had a spoon rest on the stove and it was plastic. It was a nice looking dish until it got a little hot and it ran all over the stove. It twisted and distorted to an ugly glob. That's what sin does. You can take something in its original beautiful shape and men take it and distort it into something ugly. David said wash me from mine iniquity. He said God please cleanse me thoroughly from my iniquity.

The third word he uses, he said, I acknowledge my sin. The simplest word and the word used most frequently by God is to describe man's condition is the three letter word sin. He has called it transgression, iniquity and now sin. It means to miss your mark. I remember a few years ago, when bow and arrows got to be big things. Everybody had to have a bow and arrow. I had watched Robin Hood enough to know it was a fairly simple thing to do. So my wife bought me one. I was even going to be a deer hunter. After about three months of trying to get the string on it, I finally got it strung. I borrowed four bales of hay and made a big target on that hay. I made a bull's eye. I stepped back and I took that arrow and pulled it through the bow and aimed straight for that bull's eye. I let that arrow go and I guess a strong gust of wind or something came by and the arrow went up and fell 30 yards away from the bale of hay. I just put it back in the closet and it has been there ever since. Sin is to miss the mark. God has a bull's eye and something he wants us to go to and we miss the mark. That is what David said he had done. I've stepped beyond the limits, I distorted and twisted and I used something God intended to be beautiful and made it ugly and I have missed the mark. I have sinned against God.

There is something else about sin that I want you to notice in David's prayer. Notice how many times David uses the personal pronoun me or my. Blot out my transgressions. Wash me from my iniquity. My sin is ever before me. Purge me. David's sin was a personal thing. He recognized that he could no longer be judged as a general sense with the nation of Israel, but he himself stood before God as one individual. He said it is my sin, my transgression and my iniquity. When I stand before God, I won't have to tell God someone else was to blame for my sin. I won't be able to say, it was because of this or that. Sin is a personal thing. The Bible says the soul that sinneth, it shall die. Sin is a personal thing.

Something else I want you to notice is where the sin was. David said thou desirest truth in the inward part: and in the hidden part thou shalt make me know wisdom. Sin was a matter of the heart. The Old Testament said, thou shalt not kill. Jesus, on the Sermon on the Mount, said he that is angry in his heart is guilty of murder. The Old Testament said, thou shalt not commit adultery and Jesus said, he that looketh after a woman to lust after her hath committed adultery in his heart already. Jesus was saying sin is basically and fundamentally an attitude of the heart. It is a personal and inward thing. Regardless of what your sin causes you to do, basically it is what you are inside. Out of the heart flow the issues of life. As man thinketh so is he. It is a matter of the heart.

Another thing about sin is that it is a very serious thing. Notice that David said, against thee, and thee only, have I sinned. His sin was serious because it was against God. Now when David committed adultery, he sinned against his own family, he sinned against the family of Uriah, he sinned against the kingdom that God had made him overseer. But basically, David had sinned against God. He came to realize, in the final analysis, that his sin was rebellion against God.

Then we notice the deceitfulness of sin. Hebrews 3:13 says, lest we be hardened through the deceitfulness of sin. If there ever was a deceiver, it is sin. It is sin's design to cause us to sin. The ultimate purpose of sin is to dethrone God. In the meantime, its short range project is to deceive us until we are destroyed. Sin is a deceitful thing. Ever notice how sin never shows its victim the true colors of sin. How that Satan appears to be an angel of light. In reality, he is a roaring lion seeking whom he may devour. But he projects himself as the angel of light. Let me give you an example of the deceitfulness of sin. You are driving down the road and there is this billboard on the side of the road. There is a man on it, not just any man, but he is a hunk (as they say today). Little mustache, hat on side of the head, tanned, built and eyes that look right through you. Around his neck is a woman, not just any woman. In the background is a beautiful brook flowing through a valley with the goldenrods blooming. Above the sign it says, where there is life, there is ….. And you know what's in the blank. A famous beverage. I saw that and said to myself, sin why don't you picture the real picture. Why don't you put the real picture of a man, so stupefied that he has lost his baring and run head on into a family and killed six? Why don't you show the suffering of that wife? The disbelief of those children? Why don't you picture that financial disaster of all of that? Why don't you show a man that can no longer hold a job? Why don't you show your victim the real thing? Sin is deceitful. It will not show its victim the real thing. Beware lest we be taken in, the scripture says, by the deceitfulness of sin. Sin is a destroyer. The Bible says, sin, when it is finished, brings forth death. It deceives, but when it is finished, it brings forth death. The Bible says it bites like a serpent and stingeth like an ader. To put it in spring creek terminology if you eat the devil's corn, you'll choke on the devil's cob.

There is the destruction of sin. If I could carry all of us back to Jerusalem to that time when Jesus of Nazareth was held prisoner. We would have seen him work miracles, we would have seen him lay his hands upon those who were blind and deaf and lame. We would have heard him say things like, he that hath seen me, have seen the Father. All that the Father giveth to me will come to me and he that cometh unto me, I will in no wise cast out. But we see this man standing trial accused of crimes he did not commit. We stand there and say sooner or later someone is going to step up and the truth will be known. As we watch the trial progress, we realize that here is a man that is going to be railroaded to crucifixion that is not guilty. And we hear him as they pluck the beard from his face. We hear the judge saying, I find no fault in this man. The people say, crucify him! And the judge, to wash his hands of the sentence, says if you just will crucify someone, I have a prisoner who is guilty and if you did have one man released and one crucified, which of these would you have. Surely, they are going to say, crucify Barabbas. But they say, give us Barabbas and crucify Jesus of Nazareth. We watch him as they blindfolded him, smack him and say to him, if you are the Son of God, prophesy and tell who it is that hit you. We watch him as he stands beneath the whip. The Bible says, he didn't look like a human being. We see him after those days of weakness, pick up that heavy cross and make his way to Calvary and we see the people on the road spitting upon the Son of God. When they reach the mountain, they lay him down on the cross and nail him to the cross and put him in that hole.

They say, if you be the Son of God, come down from the cross. I say, surely God you are going to come down and destroy these who treat you so bad. But he doesn't come down, why? Remember, David's prayer. Why doesn't Jesus come down from the cross? He was wounded for our transgressions. He was bruised for our iniquities. David's prayer – cleanse me, blot out my transgressions and wash me of mine iniquities. The reason, Jesus didn't come down from the cross, is because of sin and his love for us.

What does man need for the remedy of sin? What can wash away my sin, nothing but the blood of Jesus. What can make me whole again, nothing but the blood of Jesus. As they crucified the Lord, there were two men crucified with him. One on the left and one on the right. One of those men rejected the Son of God and died in his sin. The other recognized him as the Son of God and died to his sin and became a child of God. In which are we today? Have we died to sin or would we die in our sin? If you have not received Christ as your personal Savior and the Holy Spirit is speaking to you today, I invite you to come and receive the Lord Jesus Christ as your own personal Savior. Whatever you need today, Christ is waiting for you.

Chapter 9
A Good Man
Acts 11:19-24

I want to talk about a good man. What does it take to make a good man and what are some characteristics of a good man. Acts 11:19-24: *"Now they which were scattered abroad upon the persecution that arose about Stephen travelled as far as Phenice, and Cyprus, and Antioch, preaching the word to none but unto the Jews only. And some of them were men of Cyprus and Cyrene, which, when they were come to Antioch, spake unto the Grecians, preaching the Lord Jesus. And the hand of the Lord was with them: and a great number believed, and turned unto the Lord. Then tidings of these things came unto the ears of the church which was in Jerusalem: and they sent forth Barnabas, that he should go as far as Antioch. Who, when he came, and had seen the grace of God, was glad, and exhorted them all, that with purpose of heart they would cleave unto the Lord. For he was a good man, and full of the Holy Ghost and of faith: and much people was added unto the Lord."*

You can go to the library and find volumes about the life of some individual you have never heard of in your life. They have book after book about people's biography. In this text, Luke writes a biography of Barnabus in one sentence; containing twenty-eight words that tell you more about a man of God than a whole volume could tell you about an unbeliever. Listen to the words is verse 24: *"For he was a good man, and full of the Holy Ghost and of faith: and much people was added unto the Lord"*. What a wonderful, glowing, beautiful description of a good man. I might add, it is a well-deserved tribute to a man of God. All of us would, therefore, know more men like Barnabus. All of us would like to be neighbors to a man like that. We would like to go to church with more men like that. Barnabus was a good man.

Who was Barnabus? Barnabus was reared on the Island of Cypress and he moved to Jerusalem. While he was in Jerusalem, God called Barnabus to preach the gospel. Barnabus was a preacher called of God to preach the gospel of the Lord Jesus Christ. Then sometime after Barnabus was saved, the Holy Spirit came to the disciples and to the church and said to the church separate unto me, Barnabus and Saul, for a work that I have called them to do. They became the first missionaries. First, Barnabus was called to preach, the Holy Spirit spake and they were called to be missionaries. The whole life of Barnabus was a useful life. A life that was clean and used by God and much people were added unto the Lord because of Barnabus. His whole life is marked with good works. He was a good man.

What do we mean when we say someone is a good man? Sometimes we call a fellow a good man and he is not a good man at all. If some guy is a real good sport or spends his money freely or if he makes a good impression on you, we say he is a good fellow. But he may not be good fellow. You remember reading about the Dark Ages when people were fanatical in some areas. There was one particular man I read about in history. He built himself a tower fifty feet high and four feet square at the top and he went up there and was going to live his entire life on that four foot by four foot fifty foot tower. Have his meals brought up with a rope. They asked him what he was doing on top of the tower, he said, I am being good. I am separating myself from the world and living above the world being good. He lived there his whole life. What was he good for? Absolutely nothing – the whole world was around him was going to hell and he was sitting on a fifty foot tower being good, but good for nothing. And so when we refer to people today as a good man, he may not be good at all. A man can live his whole life doing nothing bad and yet still not be good.

Luke did not mean that when he was talking about Barnabus. If a man does nothing bad, if he never steals, if he never commits adultery or murder, and he is perfect in his own personal moral makeup and never does anything good for his fellowman and never stands for anything good, then he is not a good man. A man, you can truly say is a good man, is a man who not only refrains from that which is bad, but he is that man that separates from evil and gives his life to God. Most people think that a good man is someone who is a negative person, in that, he doesn't do things that are considered bad. But a man who is a good man is not only negative, but he is positive. He separates from things that are bad and does things which are good. That is exactly what Barnabus did. He not only refrained from evil and from every appearance of evil, he gave his whole life as a positive thing to God. Therefore, the scripture says, he was a good man.

One of the ways you and I can know Barnabus was a good man is to look at verse 24 and see the words 'Holy Ghost'. How do we know he was a good man from that statement? You know he was a good man because the Holy Spirit will not fill an evil heart. The Holy Spirit will only fill that heart which is good and dedicated to righteousness. Before the Holy Spirit will come into a man's heart, the bad has to be cast out, doesn't it? The Holy Spirit will not abide in an evil heart. Who is going to be the boss of your life? Are you are going to cast out the evil or allow the evil to stay in your heart and the Holy Spirit on the outside.

There was a colored man who was riding a horse and the horse began to buck. As horses will do he began, what we refer to as the fence row buck. Where he draws up in the back and his legs are stiff and the man was beginning to be jarred loose from the saddle and with all the twisting and turning the horses hind foot came up and got into the stirrup on the saddle. The man looked down and saw the horse's foot in the stirrup and he said, 'Look here horse, if you are going to get in, I'm going to get off'. That is pretty much the way God is with us. If Satan is going to ride in the saddle, the Lord is getting off. But if you are going to let me in the saddle, the Lord says, then get Satan off. That's what it takes to be a good man. That is what it takes for the Holy Spirit to fill a heart. It must be a good heart. We are too much prone to think negatively only. If we do not do things that are considered bad, then we are a good person. Let me tell you this, if you are a preacher, a deacon, or if you are a layman in the church, just a Christian living in your community, your testimony is not going to make any difference at all, unless your testimony, commitment and your profession of faith is backed up by a good life. Unless people can look at you and say your life is good, not look at you and say I never once saw him get drunk, I never saw him gamble or be unfaithful, I never saw this or that. But they can look at your life and say it was backed up by a good life. He lives what he preaches. He lives what he believes.

Barnabus was a good man. The Bible says he was a godly man for he was filled with the Holy Spirit. The reason we know he was a godly man is because the Holy Spirit is God and God was living in him, possessing Barnabus. God lived in his heart. Jesus had promised that the Holy Spirit would come and live in the believer's heart. Jesus said, if I go away, I will send unto you another comforter and when He is come. Then he begins to tell all that the Holy Spirit would do, and one of the things was he would possess you, h would live in you. Barnabus was a believer. And that Holy Spirit that God promised would live in the heart, was living now in Barnabus' heart because that heart was fully surrendered. So God lived in it. Every thought Barnabus has was guided by the Holy Spirit. Every action was guided by the Holy Spirit. On the day of Pentecost, souls were saved. Why? Because the preacher, the disciples and apostles were filled with the Holy Spirit. That is why three thousand souls were saved.

If it could truly be said of me on a Sunday morning or a Sunday night, that Terry Boyd is filled with the Holy Spirit and it could truly be said of every member of the congregation, he or she is filled with the Holy Spirit, what a difference there would be in our services. What a difference there would be in the outcome of our services, if it could truly be said of the preacher, deacons, trustees and every member of the church that they are all filled with the Holy Spirit. Great things would happen. Therefore, we ought to pray that each one of us be surrendered in our own heart so that God could fill us. Surrender ourselves to God's will. When God wanted Barnabus to go a certain way, he went that way. If God wanted Barnabus to preach over here, that is where he was preaching. When he wanted him to come back he came back home. He was completely guided by the Holy Spirit, because his heart was fully surrendered to God. Not only that, but he was a man of faith. One of the things that stands out about Barnabus was the he had faith in the Lord. He had faith in whatever God wanted him to do. God would take care of all the details surrounding him. He had complete faith that if God said to go on that missionary trip with Paul, God would take care of lodging. God would take care of food and God would take care of all the necessities. God would go before them and prepare their hearts for the gospel and therefore he had implicit faith. He was a man of faith, the Bible says, that whatever God wanted him to do, he did it and left the results to God. That kind of faith is the kind of faith you and I ought to have when we live our lives today in this storm tossed life. We need to pray, Lord, I am weak, but thou art strong. I put my faith in you. Barnabus had that kind of faith.

Barnabus had faith in God and faith in his fellow man. Paul was converted, you remember, after a rather unusual life. Paul was that man who personally undertook the responsibility of killing all the Christians and wiping the name of Christ off the face of the earth. He believed that Christ was an imposter. He believed God would be well served by the death of Jesus Christ and by the death of all Christians. He was dedicated to God and he loved God. He was doing God a favor by ruining Christianity. Now that man was saved. How would you feel if the fellow who had shot at you about a dozen times, all of the sudden got saved and came and knocked on your front door? Would you go out, throw your arms around him and say, Brother, it's good to see you? No, you would stand behind a locked door with a shotgun and if he took one step out of the ordinary, you would shoot him.

You heard about the fellow who got saved and was quite a character. When he got saved, there was such a change in him that when he came home his wife fell at his feet and wept. His children ran and hugged him because of the change. His old hunting dog began wagging his tail but kept one eye on him. He watched that rascal. That is the way we would be. Now Paul was that kind of fellow. They were afraid of him because he had murdered so many of the Christians and then all of the sudden he got saved. The church was dubious of Paul. They didn't trust him. The word got out that this enemy of the church got saved. They thought he was professing to be a Christian so he could get into the church and run wild with his havoc. There weren't going to let Paul in. If they did, they were going to watch him like a dog.

Barnabus had another spirit within him. He wasn't quite ready to turn Paul out. He wanted them to trust him. Barnabus said to the church, Paul is a good man. Paul is our brother and he has been saved like the rest of us. It opened the door in the church for the apostle Paul. Barnabus was a man of faith; a man of faith in God and a man of faith in his fellow man.

Later Barnabus was preaching a revival in Antioch. It was a great revival with many being saved. Barnabus was the preacher and that was the way to get recognition and a good way to have a good reputation is to have a great revival. In the midst of that, so many were getting saved, Barnabus knew he couldn't handle it by himself so he sent for Paul. You come do the preaching, this thing has gotten too big for me. Paul came and preached and Barnabus gave up the glory of that great revival. They worked together in that revival. Two years winning many to the Lord Jesus Christ.

There was another incident that showed how good he was and a man of faith in his fellow man. Paul and Barnabus started out on their first missionary journey and they took John Mark with them. When the going got rough, John Mark turned and came back, he gave up. When they started the second missionary journey, Barnabus said let's take John Mark with us. Paul said no. Barnabus insisted. Barnabus was so sure of John Mark, he left Paul and John Mark went. His faith in John Mark was justified because John Mark wrote the second gospel. He didn't quite make it the first time, but with a little help from Barnabus he did. He became a great man of God. He was used of God because someone had faith in him.

That is the kind of life that makes up a good life. What are the fruits of that kind of life? First, he was a liberal man. Have you ever met a good man and a godly man that wasn't liberal? A godly man is a liberal man. When the Jews were first being saved in Jerusalem, they were being cast out of the temple, they lost their property and everything they had by the other Jews. Barnabus sold his property and gave it to the church. He sold all that he possessed and gave it to those Jews who were losing their property because they believed in God.

Secondly, he was a mission minded man. Those first Christians thought the gospel was just for the Jews and nobody else. I think sometimes the Christians of today are so prejudice and so bigoted in their feelings toward the other race that it makes me sick. But it is nothing compared to the first Christians, for they believed the Gentiles were like dogs without a soul. So when the first Jews heard the gospel they were sure it was for Jews and no one else. That only a Jew could be saved. When the news came to them that some Gentiles were getting saved, it wasn't good news at all to the church. I know a young man who just left the ranks of the Free Will Baptist because he wanted to build a church to minister to the colored race. He wanted to build a Free Will Baptist church in the colored district. He went to some of our more enlightened and educated Free Will Baptist for help and you know what they told him? Brother, you are just going to cause trouble. As soon as you start a church they are going to want to join the association. Now let me ask you? Do you think God is pleased with that? I don't think God was pleased with it at all. I think it makes God sick at his stomach. I think God is sick at his stomach with a lot of people and their feelings towards those of another race. These first Christians felt the same way toward the Gentiles. We don't want them in our church, we don't believe, in the first place, they can be saved. So when they got the news, they sent good old Barnabus to investigate and put a stop to it. When Barnabus got there and saw the Spirit of God on the faces of the Gentiles, Barnabus began to rejoice in God. And rejoiced that salvation had come to the Gentiles and he began a mission work among the Gentiles. Man of faith, a liberal man, mission minded man, he was one of the first missionaries of the cross. Since Barnabus, many people have followed in his footsteps. I thank God that he is still calling those to the mission field, just like he called Paul and Barnabus.

Another fruit in the life of a good man is that he has a consoling spirit. Barnabus means, son of consolation. Wherever Barnabus went, he must have been a blessing to people. He must have had a way of just consoling or just being a blessing to those people. He had a comforting spirit. Perhaps the disciples had seen him many times as he ministered to people and blessing them. They said that is his character, he is the son of consolation. I imagine he was the kind of man who could stand in church meetings when everybody else was negative and down in the dumps and about ready to walk out and he could get everyone back to their senses. There are some people that God gives a gift for that. When everybody is going in every direction, they can speak and exhort and get people back to their right minds. Another characteristic I wish I had is a man free of jealousy. It just makes me mad when someone brags on our music director and they don't brag on me. I'm just kidding. That is a problem among preachers and Christians, jealousy of one another. When you first read about this missionary enterprise, it is always Barnabus and Paul. Now when it gets to being really good they change the billing and it's Paul and Barnabus. Ever notice that in the word of God? The Holy Spirit came first and said separate me Barnabus and Paul. Then when Paul became so famous, they changed it to Paul and Barnabus. He played second fiddle, but it suited Barnabus. He didn't mind walking in the shadow of Paul, as long as he could do something for God. It was alright to play second fiddle, if it gave glory to God. He was free of jealousy.

Last of all, he was a soul winner. I guess all of us would have to say, oh me to that one, rather than amen. The scripture says much people were added unto the Lord. Through the life that he lived, through his testimony, through his preaching, many received the Lord Jesus Christ and were saved. How many do you suppose have turned to Jesus because of you? Can you think of some people who are Christians today because of your influence in their life? That is a good feeling. We can't all be a Barnabus, but we can all be good. We can be faithful to God and to his church. Then surely the good things will begin to flow from our lives, people will be saved and people will be blessed and the name of Jesus Christ will be glorified because of us. Let's all try to be good men and women, so that when they say of us, he is good that it can be said he is truly a good man. I would like to be able to think that someday that could be my epitaph. That it could be said on your tombstone, here lies a good man or here lies a good woman. Let's dedicate ourselves to being good in God's sight.

Chapter 10
Degrees from God
John 3:1-8

There are a lot of people who have just started back to school; some in elementary, middle, high school and college. It is the hope of everyone entering college to get a degree. Some may get a higher degree than others, depending upon their own motivation and desires. All of them are seeking after a degree. I decided a few years ago that I wanted a degree. I decided I was going back to college. I thought that since my brother was the only one in my family with a degree, he would be excited about it. I said to him, "I'm going to go back to school". He said, "Why?" I said "I want to get a degree". He said, "I'll give you mine". So if it didn't mean any more to him than that, I would rethink my decision to go back to school.

I want to talk about several degrees that are higher degrees than you can receive from man. Degrees which come to you from God, the Father. Degrees that the world may think unimportant and may laugh and scoff at, but in the economy of God and in God's economy of things, these are high degrees. Let's talk about a few degrees God gives.

The first degree is a BA, born again. It is the degree every person receives from God when he receives his Son as the Lord Jesus Christ. God cannot give us another degree until this first one is earned. You have to have the BA degree before the others. In Jerusalem, there was a man named Nicodemus and he had a lot of honors. He was a Pharisee. He was a ruler of the Jews. He was a political man. He had power, intelligence and social standing. But none of these things made him happy. These were the honors man had placed upon him. The things most men craved and work for, Nicodemus had earned. He had received the applause of man and degrees of man, but he was still hungry in his heart. Isn't it amazing how we want and once we get them, we still feel empty. We are not yet fully satisfied. And Nicodemus was such a man. He had done all he could do, as far as, man was concerned, but he was hungry in his heart for something. He heard that Jesus Christ was in Jerusalem. He heard that this man Jesus was giving wisdom, peace, joy, and understanding. He went to see this man who just may have the secret to the longings of his heart. Under the cover of darkness, Nicodemus made his way to where Jesus was to talk with him. A lot of people made fun of Nicodemus for coming to see Jesus under darkness. He had to slip and hide and make his way to Jesus. I am grateful that he came and I don't care when it was. I am glad Nicodemus had this interview with Jesus Christ, because we have learned some of the most beautiful truths from this interview of Jesus and Nicodemus. Nicodemus was a shrewd man and as was the custom in those days, he began his interview with Jesus with a compliment. He said, we know thou art a teacher come from God because no one could do what you do except God with you. Jesus stopped him right there and he read the hunger in Nicodemus' heart. He knew the one thing Nicodemus wanted was not to talk about miracles and he was a teacher come from God. Jesus knew that Nicodemus wanted assurance in his heart. He stopped him short in his compliment and said, except a man be born again, Nicodemus, he cannot see the kingdom of God. Nicodemus was taken back and asked Jesus, what do you mean born again? Don't you know it is impossible for a man to be born the second time. You can only have birth one time. How can these things be? "Except a man be born of the water and of the Spirit", Jesus said, "He cannot enter into the kingdom of God". Now we know what he meant, when he said spirit. We know that meant the spiritual regeneration that a man receives when he receives Christ as his Savior. What did he mean when he said, 'except a man be born of the water and of the Spirit"? What did he mean? Was he talking about baptism, as so many people have said? No, he was not talking about baptism. Baptism was not even under discussion. He was talking about a physical birth which is a water birth. He was also talking about the spiritual birth.

1 Peter 1:23 says, *"Being born again, not of corruptible seed, but of incorruptible, by the word of God, which liveth and abideth forever."* Simply means that a sinner learns all that he knows about salvation from the word of God and from the Spirit of God. Everything you need to know about getting in the right relationship with Jesus Christ, the Spirit of God will show it to you through the word. A sinner listens to the word of God. The Holy Spirit comes and brings the word of God and applies it to the sinner's heart and he sees himself as lost. But at the same time, he sees the Lord Jesus Christ dying for his sin and so he trusts him as his personal Savior. All of what he learned was from the word. And so he says, being born again not of corruptible, but of incorruptible by the word of God.

The sinner's part in salvation is an active part; but at the same time God does all that needs to be done. All a sinner has to do is turn from his sin, confess his sin, to repent of it, which means turn away from it never to go back, and trust the Lord Jesus Christ with all of his heart. That is saving faith. God does all the rest. John 1:12 *"But as many as received him, to them gave he power to become the sons of God, even to them that believe on his name:"* Not to as many of them that were baptized, not to as many of them as repented, but as many as received him. Salvation is not in creeds and doctrines, but it is in a person. A man must receive a person in order to be saved. So as many as received him to them gave he the power to become the sons of God. No name is saved, nowhere in the Bible is there a precedent for anyone being saved until first he has received Christ as his personal Savior. First, not last, he must receive Christ, who is able to save to the uttermost them that cometh unto him seeing that he ever liveth to make intercession for us.

Jesus was teaching one day and the Pharisees were a little upset. And they said to Jesus, God is our Father. We are of the family of Abraham and Jacob and Isaac and we are God's children. Jesus said, No, you are not. Your father is the devil and you are doing the devil's work right now. One of the things we need to learn and apply to our hearts daily is the fact that not all of us are children of God. We are only God's creation, but we are not children of God until we have been born into the family of God. He said, you are not of God, if you loved me and if God were your father, you would love me. Salvation means more than just forgiveness. If any man be in Christ, he is a new creature. It is a wonderful thing to know that your sin has been forgiven and that the burden and the weight of knowing that you're lost is gone. What is even greater than that is the fact you become a new creature. Old things are passed away behold all things have become new. Isn't it wonderful to wake up every day to a new day? It is a wonderful thing to be in the newness of life – to know that God is on the throne and you are his child and you have been forgiven, it a wonderful thing to know that. And to know you are a new creature and the whole world is new. One of the things he warns us about is the fact that sinners cannot understand that. He said, Nicodemus, I cannot explain to you the new birth any more than I can explain to you the wind. You don't see the wind, but you hear it. You don't know where it came from; you don't know where it is going, but you can see the trees moving. You can hear the sound of the wind, but that is all you can tell about the wind. So is everyone that is born of the Spirit of God. How much did you know about the spiritual things of God until you were saved? Very little. The only thing a sinner knows is that he is lost and Jesus can save him. Then after he is saved, God imparts a knowledge to him that he can understand now spiritual things. A sinner can no more understand the things of God than a dog understands why some folks wear glasses. They are just blind to it. It is a wonderful thing to know God can take a poor, miserable sinner like us and make us fit for the kingdom of God. That's receiving the BA degree. That is the only degree God gives you. There are some more but you have to earn them.

The second degree that comes from God is the SF degree – Spirit filled. We do not make enough of the Holy Spirit. We do not talk enough about the Holy Spirit because a lot of folks have gone to seed on the doctrine of the Holy Spirit. So we tend to stay away from the doctrine of the Holy Spirit. Let me tell you something, you don't have to be a fanatic on fire nor a high brow sitting on the iceberg to understand the things of God and the Holy Spirit. You don't have to be to one extreme to the other. It takes a little common sense to receive the spirit-filled degree from God. When a man is saved, the Holy Spirit comes into his heart that moment to dwell with him. Now you can pray, be baptized seven times, you can have someone massage your Adam's apple and speak in all kinds of tongues, but brother, when you got saved all that there is of the Holy Spirit came into your heart to live and to dwell within your heart. I want everyone to understand that when a man gets saved, the Holy Spirit, the third person of the trinity, comes into that person's heart to live. He don't move in one suitcase today and one next week. All that there is of the Holy Spirit comes to live in your heart now. After he comes to dwell in your heart, he comes many times to fill you for service to God. Just like you're baptized once, you receive the Holy Spirit once. There are many, many fillings. You wouldn't have any power except through the Holy Spirit. The Holy Spirit comes to fill you to do service to God. Now that is fairly easy to understand. Without the filling of the Holy Spirit, we cannot do service for God, because it is that which gives us the power to do it. A lot of folks have a misunderstanding about the Holy Spirit. They say in order to be filled with the Holy Spirit, I have to empty myself. So I'll empty my heart of every evil thought and deed. I will clean my heart completely of all negative things. You know what you've got? An empty heart is all you have got. The Holy Spirit comes to fill your heart. You don't need an empty heart. As the Holy Spirit comes and fills your heart, he purifies and cleanses your heart. A lot of folks look on this side of salvation and think if I get saved, I'll have to quit this and that. So I think I'll wait awhile to get saved. They don't understand that once you are saved, you don't want to do those things. God takes it away. You have a whole new heart. You are a new creature. It is not hard to give up strawberries once you get sick of them. You may think, I would never give up strawberries, but if you ever got sick on them you would never want another one. So it is with the things of the world, once the Holy Spirit comes into our heart, you just don't want those things. You think differently. You live in a whole new atmosphere. It just took one night to get Israel out of Egypt, but it took forty years to get Egypt out of Israel. So the Israelites remembered, after they got into working with God, leeks and onions. They wish they had never left. A lot of Christians are that way. They become a Christian or join the church and say after a while, I wish I could go back. When you find a Christian that is always laughing and talking about the evil things he did before he got saved, he wishes he could go back, remember when God takes you out of Egypt, He takes Egypt out of you. You don't want to go back. Some folks have the wrong idea about being spirit-filled. The scripture says, if ye then being evil, know how to give your children good gifts, how much more will your heavenly Father give them who ask of the Holy Spirit.

There is another degree, the CF degree. The CF degree is the constant faithfulness degree. Just before the Apostle Paul died he said these words, "I have finished my course, I have kept the faith". I have finished my course. He got on that course when he met Jesus on the road to Damascus and he never took a short cut, he never took a detour. When Paul said, "I've finished my course", he was talking about that course that God gave him the moment he got saved and he never left it. Constantly, was he faithful to God. Paul didn't follow God for one day and go back to the world the next. From the moment he got saved until the day they chopped his head off, he was constantly faithful to God. There was no partial thing to him, no wishy washy. He was saved, he knew it and he glorified in his salvation and he lived his life out for God. He was constantly faithful in God's service. God wants us to be faithful constantly. He doesn't want us one day playing golf on Sunday and the next Sunday praying in church. He wants you to be constantly faithful. You know what your duties are as a Christian. You know you ought not to forsake the assembling of yourselves together after the manner of some is. You know you ought to be in church and prayer meeting. You know you ought to witness. You know all those things that God expects us to be faithful constantly, He takes no pride in wishy washy Christians. God wants you to be faithful and He gives you a degree to those who are. The great men of the Bible were faithful. Moses talked to God at the burning bush. God gave him some orders and Moses never laid them down until God took him home. Constantly was he faithful. He made some mistakes along the way, but he was constantly faithful to God. We have a lot of troubles, worries, discouragement and so did Moses. He put his hand to the plow and didn't look back, until God took him home. Some church members are flashy, some are flighty, some are fidgety, and some are fussy, but God wants us to be faithful.

Another degree is the TO degree. This degree means tithes and offerings. God says they are mine. Malachi says, a man who does not tithe will rob God. There is the LO degree. That is loving obedience. There is a difference in being obedient and lovingly obedient. I can tell Christi to do something and I can tell if it's obedient or lovingly obedient. Tell a child to do something and they walk around and stall. They get it done, but you wished you had never asked them. When God tells us to do something, there is a joy in doing it. That is loving obedience. Because the love of Christ constrainth us to do the will of God. There are things that a person ought to do – get saved, be filled with the Holy Spirit, be baptized, and partake in the Lord's Supper. Just as the cross points two ways, so does the communion table. Just as the cross points back to our sin and forward to the coming of the Lord Jesus, so does the Lord's Supper point back to the cross and to the coming of the Lord Jesus. You will never be happy as a Christian until you are an obedient one. Do you have that degree of loving obedience? Jesus said, "if you love me, you will keep my commandments.

The WD degree is the well done degree. If we are faithful, the scripture says, we will hear the Lord say, well done, thou good and faithful servant. Now that is going to be some wonderful words to hear. To hear the Lord himself say well done, brother. Well done, sister. You have done a good job. It would be great to hear that. Notice he didn't say, be thou good and brilliant or talented. He said, be thou good and faithful. You may think, at times, you are a failure in the world's eyes, but if you are faithful, you are a success in God's eyes. You know who keeps the church going? You know who keeps the bills paid at the church? You know who keeps the missionaries on the foreign field from our church? Not the rich, no the talented, but the faithful. They are the backbone of the church. One day just as we can depend on them now, they will hear God say, well done, thou good and faithful servant. Not that there is anything glamorous about being faithful, but its Godlike, to be faithful. In 1 Corinthians we are told we will be rewarded for that. You may go to church every Sunday. You may teach a class. You may sing in the choir and pay your tithe, you may preach and serve. Many times we do that for our own sake and for our own glory. But the judgment fires will burn up all that work as hay, stubble and wool and all that is left will be precious stone. If we work and give to the glory of God and for the love of God, our works will be like precious stone that will abide forever.

I have told you some degrees in God's economy. One is given to you, the others you will have to earn. What is our motive in receiving a degree from God? Again, the scripture says, the love of Christ constrainth us. We love him and we want to accept the degrees of God. I work as a salesman part of the time. Have you heard about the salesman who met the preacher? The salesman said, I'm a travelling man. The preacher said, so am I. Salesman said, I am in the jewelry business. The preacher thought of that verse in Malachi which says, they shall make up my jewels, talking about the children of God. So the preacher said, so am I. The salesman said, my father took me in as a partner. The preacher said, so did mine. The salesman said, I am working to receive a good report from my father. The preacher said, so am I.

How many degrees do you have today? Have you received the BA degree? Have you been born again? Have you accepted the Lord Jesus Christ as your personal Savior? God waits to confer upon this day, the BA degree. If you are saved, do you have the SF degree? Are you spirit filled? Are you serving Him with loving obedience? Are you constantly faithful?

Chapter 11
In the Book
Revelations 20:11-15

I want to spend a few minutes on a very interesting topic. I want to talk to you about the books and in particular the phrase, 'in the book'. Revelations 20:11-15 reads, *"And I saw a great white throne, and him that sat on it, from whose face the earth and the heaven fled away; and there was found no place for them. And I saw the dead, small and great, stand before God; and the books were opened: and another book was opened, which is the book of life: and the dead were judged out of those things which were written in the books, according to their works. And the sea gave up the dead which were in it; and death and hell delivered up the dead which were in them: and they were judged every man according to their works. And the death and hell were casts into the lake of fire. This is the second death. And whosoever was not found written in the book of life was cast into the lake of fire."*

I want to share with you some of the things we think about heaven, and some of the things that are in heaven. It is a beautiful place. Notice in Revelation 21:18-23, *"And the building of the wall of it was of jasper: and the city was pure gold, like unto clear glass. And the foundations of the wall of the city were garnished with all manner of precious stones. The first foundation was jasper; the second sapphire; the third, a chalcedony; the fourth, an emerald;*

the fifth, sardonyx; the sixth, sardius; the seventh, chrysolite; the eighth, beryl; the ninth, a topaz; the tenth, a chrysoprasus; the eleventh, a jacinth; the twelfth, an amethyst. And the twelve gates were twelve pearls; every several gate was of one pearl: and the street of the city was pure gold, as it were transparent glass. And I saw no temple therein: for the Lord God Almighty and the Lamb are the temple of it. And the city had no need of the sun, neither the moon, to shine in it: for the glory of God did lighten it, and the Lamb is the light thereof." The holy city of New Jerusalem is a beautiful place. The Bible tells us of the pure stones, gold and all those things I can't even pronounce. Must be pretty if it is such a word you can't pronounce. The beauty is not the subject of concern. The beauty of heaven is not what we should be interested in, but rather, what will enter the holy city, or perhaps, who will or will not enter into that holy city.

There is a song out that says when I get to heaven don't bother to stop and let me see the jasper, pearly gates or golden streets, just take me straight to Jesus. That is probably going to be our feelings when we get to heaven. We leave what heaven is going to look like and we begin to deal with the subject of who is going to be there and who is not going to be there. Notice in chapter 21 verse 8, he tells us who will not be in heaven. *"But the fearful, and unbelieving, and the abominable, and murderers, and whoremongers, and sorcerers, and idolaters, and all liars, shall have their part in the lake which burneth with fire and brimstone: which is the second death."* So we know who is not going. We learn from the scripture that those who are unbelievers will not go, those who are unrepentant, such as murderers, will not inherit that eternal city. So who will go to heaven? Notice in chapter 20 those who will inherit the eternal city are those written in the Lamb's Book of Life. They are those who will go to heaven.

I want to ask you a question. Is your name written in the Lamb's Book of Life? Do you know for sure that your name is recorded in that book God keeps which is called the Lamb's Book of Life? The scripture tells us that those who are born from above, and those who have received Christ as their own personal Savior, become a part of the heavenly family. God is our father, Jesus Christ is our elder brother and you and I are joint heirs of God with Jesus Christ. We become a part of a heavenly family.

Just like here on earth, there is a family register, there is a family register in heaven. Those people who make up the family of God have their names recorded in the family register. The question is – is your name written in the family register? You remember the book of Ezra, when Israel had been taken into captivity in Babylon and they were finally free and brought back to Jerusalem. Not the temple in Jerusalem, the different tribes who ministered in the temple, had been gone for some time. There were only those special people who had been recorded as priest could minister in the temple. So when they came back from captivity, they went to the temple to take up their place in the temple of God. To begin as priest again in the temple of God. So those in the temple asked for the register. Bring forth the register of the tribes. Those who were not written in the register, who names were not recorded, were put out of the priesthood because they were polluted. Now these people were Jews. They were among the nation of God. Israel was God's people. That was God's nation and family. These people were very much involved in everything God's people were involved in yet when they got to the temple they fully expected to enter into it. They fully expected to take up their ministry. They fully expected to go in, but their names were not found in the book.

Now suppose you were to die and you were a good church member and you were a good neighbor and you had tithed and worked hard and witnessed and you lived a certain moral standard that you believed to be acceptable of God and in your community. Your name is on the church roll and you fully expect to enter into the heavenly city. When you arrive in heaven, the angels bring forth the book and begin to scan the pages and your name is not recorded in the book. You ask them to search again and they did not find it. It was a tragic thing for those Jews who had been in captivity to go back and expect to go into the city and yet they were rejected because their names were not written. It will be even worse for those today who fully expect and whose name are not recorded in the Lamb's Book of Life.

I have often thought how bad it would be to go to hell. And the only thing I know worse than going to hell is to go to hell expecting to go to heaven. I can't think of anything worse than that. To be numbered among God's people, to be a member of the church, to live a moral standard, to be a good neighbor, to work and fully expect to go to heaven and not go because your name had not been recorded in the Lamb's Book of Life.

So I ask the question again, are you registered in the family register? Is your name written in the Lamb's Book of Life? Notice verse 11 and 12 of chapter 20. These are very interesting verses: *"And I saw a great white throne, and him that sat on it, from whose face the earth and the heaven fled away; and there was found no place for them. And I saw the dead, small and great, stand before God; and the books were opened; and another book was opened, which is the book of life: and the dead were judged out of those things which were written in the books, according to their works."* Did you notice the difference in the book? There are books in heaven and there is A book in heaven. And there is a great difference in the books and THE book. So there is one thing we want to be sure of and that is that our name is not in the books but our name is in THE book. This book is not like any other book, it is separate from the rest; it is the book of life. It is interesting to me that the dead, that is the unsaved, are recorded in many books. The redeemed of God are recorded in THE book. What does that tell you? It tells you that there are few who will be saved. That there will be many who will be lost eternally perhaps multitudes fully expecting to go to heaven, fully believing that their name is written in the book, but their name is in the books and not THE book.

There are so many dead without Christ. So many who have rejected Jesus Christ, that it took many books to record their names. Yet there are so few who receive the Lord Jesus Christ. There are so few in comparison that it only took one book to record their names. There was a sermon preached by a Roman Catholic priest. The title of his message was, 'The Few Who Shall Be Saved'. To read his sermon, you would think he was an Independent Baptist. All through time, people have fallen for this thing of cheap, easy believism that as long as you believe in Christ, you will be saved. Multitudes of people have fallen for that, believing that their names have been recorded in the Lamb's Book of Life and fully expect to go to heaven because some preacher told them that is all they have to do. They are going to die and stand before God and discover that their names were never recorded in the book. Because they never believed and trusted in the Lord Jesus Christ. There is not going to be a worldwide revival where everybody is going to be saved before the end of time. Few people are walking the road to heaven. There will be fewer of them as time runs out. There will be a multitude of those who will not go to heaven. Verse 15 of Chapter 20 says, *"And whosoever was not found written in the book of life was cast into the lake of fire"*. I like to underline that in my Bible and get you to underline it in yours, because we are going through a stage of changing our morality. We are going through a state where theologians are changing the word of God. And in a few more years, we are going to have some kind of star wars force to take the place of God. I got a card from a friend of mine, when I was sick last summer. In the card she said, may the light be with you. To her that is God. As we get older, and as the world stands longer, God will be reduced in the minds of theologians and in the pews until God will be some kind of fixture between a vending machine and Santa Claus. And everybody is everybody else's brother and everyone is a child of God and everyone is going to heaven when they die. Read verse 15 again, *"And whosoever was not found written in the book of life was cast into the lake of fire."* That settles it. That is the absolute fact and truth. That is what God said, that is what God recorded in his word and that settles it. That a man's name has to be recorded in the book in order for him to go to heaven. There has to be an experience in which your name is recorded and written in the book. If it is not written in the book, you will be cast into hell, and that is God's word. No theologian will ever change that.

The books were open. Who is the bookkeeper? If you know your name is being recorded and someone is keeping books on you, it is good to know who the bookkeeper is. You know who the bookkeeper is – Jesus. Because is the book not called the Lamb's Book of Life? Jesus is the Lamb and keeper of the books. Why is Jesus the keeper of the books? When you were saved, did you ever ask the question, why? Why was I saved? Why did God design to bring me salvation? Why did it ever cross God's mind and why did God bring the word and the Holy Spirit together to get me saved? In Ephesians it says, God, for Christ's sake, has forgiven you. In the book of Revelation it says, for his name sake. We are not saved for our sake, but we are saved for his sake. God, for Christ's sake, hath forgiven you and for his name sake. We are saved for his glory. If we are saved for him and his glory, he keeps the books. It is only fitting that he does. I will tell you for sure God knows who are his.

The books are also kept on the wicked. Again, who's the bookkeeper of those who are wicked? It is not the devil. The wicked are his, but he doesn't keep the record. The reasons are obvious. Just like if we belong to Jesus, he is keeping the books. The wicked belong to the devil but he doesn't keep the books. Other sinners don't keep the book. There would be no justice in that kind of thing. And the saints of God do not keep the record of the sinners because that would be unfair. Aren't you glad some other Christian isn't keeping the book on you? God keeps the record. When the world is judged out of the books, for their works, it will be based on his records. And we can learn from that, that death can be death or it can be a gateway. The scripture teaches us that the wicked just keep on dying and dying, but the saved rest. When we die, we stand before God. We will not have to give God a list of what we have done and haven't done. We won't have to give him a list of all the good and bad things we've done, because he already knows. He will not have to ask anyone and he will not have to depend on our memory, because he is keeping the book.

To have our names written in the book, we must believe on the Lord Jesus Christ, we must repent of our sin, we must confess him before men. The bookkeeper is right and the bookkeeper is righteous. We cannot have our names recorded in the Lamb's Book of Life and then walk the way we want to walk. We cannot come to Jesus and be saved, have our names recorded and live our lives the way we want to. If the keeper of the book is righteous, and he is the standard of justice, then we have to walk as he walks. If you are in Christ, you are in the book. If you are in the book, you are in the family. If you are in the family, your name is recorded in the Lamb's Book of Life and you will have your part in heaven.

Not only is the bookkeeper right, righteous, holy and just, but, Praise God, he is our advocate. That is the only part of the books being kept. The fact that the keeper of the books is our advocate. Hebrews 7:25 reads, *"Wherefore he is able also to save them to the uttermost that come unto God by him, seeing he ever liveth to make intercession for them."* You know if Christ did not love us and if Christ had not died for us and we sinned and made a mistake and he would mark it in the book, and that would be the end of it. Then when we die all of those things which are recorded in the book would be brought against us. But because he loves us and ever lived to make intercession for us, when we sin and fail the keeper of the books takes that sin to God and says to God the Father, Father, he has sinned, but I have come to you to make intercession for him. And the scripture says the blood cleanses us from all sin. Not only does he cleanse us, he keeps on cleansing us. So he is right and righteous, but he is also our advocate.

Is your name written in the book beyond a shadow of a doubt? You may be a good church member, but is your name in the book? Have you been born again, washed in the blood? Have you been cleansed from sin, have you witnessed the Holy Spirit in your heart? Do you know beyond a shadow of a doubt that your name is recorded in the book? You can have your name recorded the instant that you pray and receive Christ as your personal Savior.

From The Shepherd To His Flock

Chapter 12
What will it Take?
Acts 22:20   Genesis 19:15

I have come to realize something very important. It is something I have known all the time, but haven't really had to rely on it as much as recently. There is nothing in this world that is stable. There is nothing in this world you can count on. The only thing you can count on is outside of the world. I'm like the colored preacher who was talking to a man about his problems and suddenly there was an earthquake. He said, brother, you can't even depend on the grounds you stands on. I fully believe that God works all things together for good to them that love the Lord, who are called according to His purpose. I believe all things, somehow, some way, to those who really love the Lord, will work out for their good and God's good. But isn't it strange the things we go through before we turn to God? Isn't it strange how we use that tremendous power, that power that created the universe and brought it into being, how we put all that in the background and use it as a last resort. I think sometimes, if I were God, I wouldn't listen to anybody. If they were going to use me as a last resort, I probably wouldn't listen. Aren't you glad I am not God?

I want us to look at some of the things it took to bring some people to God. I want to ask you the question, if you have never received Christ as your personal Savior, what will it take to bring you to God? What is going to happen in your life, when you say, Lord, I give up? Lord, I surrender. What would it take to bring you to God? To those who know the Lord, but you also love the world and you are miserable when you are in church and you are miserable when you are in the world, you are a mess. What will it take to bring you to God? What will it take to bring you to a place where you say, yes, Lord, have your way in my life?

This is the way it usually happens. We begin to experience sin, it is tantalizing, it is interesting and fun. But the whole time, we are engaged in sinful processes, our conscience seems to tell us we would be happier if we weren't doing that, yet we continue to do it. The Holy Spirit continues to make us miserable. Maybe after all the fun is over and your lying alone with the head on the pillow and there is no one else there, something tells you, I'd be a lot happier if I'd quit this mess. The Holy Spirit keeps working with you, you keep living for the devil, and keep trying to serve the Lord and make the devil happy too and you are miserable inside and out. The Holy Spirit is convicting you. Then you have a crisis and you can do one of two things. You can soften your heart and receive Christ as your Savior and let God have his way in your life and be happy, or you can harden your heart, reject the Holy Spirit, and say no to the Son. God withdraws his spirit from you and you go on your way to hell. That is the way it happens. God never lets anyone go that far without doing everything short of taking over your will to bring a man to heaven. God is not willing that any should perish, but that all shall come to repentance. God is not willing for anybody to go to hell. Not only is he not willing for a man to be lost, but he will do all he can short of taking over your will. We are Free Will Baptist. You can decide to accept or reject the Lord Jesus Christ. He will not force you. Short of taking away that freedom of your will, he will do all that is possible for him to do to influence you to accept the Lord Jesus Christ as your personal Savior.

Let me tell you a true story. A true story about my family and growing up. We were associated socially with a congregation, but we had gotten to the point none of us went to church. No brothers, mom and dad, no one went to church. I had a beautiful blue-eyed sister, twelve years old at this particular time. Sunday morning she would get up, she would get herself ready, rain, sleet or snow, she walked out that country road to the highway. She caught a ride in the back of a pick-up truck with Mr. Denton Reeves to go to church every Sunday morning. She would come in from church and begin to tell us at the dinner table what she had learned in Sunday school, to our great embarrassment. She would talk about Jesus. She wanted to say the blessing and we were embarrassed. She wanted to pray at night, we were embarrassed. That went on for a while and one day, as quick as you could snap your fingers, her life was snatched away from her. I watched her die. Brother, suddenly, everybody in the Boyd family got religion. We got religious in a hurry. Everyone started going to church and you would have thought we had been there every Sunday for the last fifty years. You can go into my mother's house and look above the door and there is a little school picture, the only one we had, of a beautiful little blonde haired blue-eyed girl smiling down at you as you sit in your chair. The whole family, with the exception of one, is involved in church, but brother, what a price we had to pay. She was the only one ready to go to heaven. She was the only one who could have died safely. And God took the one ready to get the rest of us. I am responsible for her death. Everyone in my family is responsible for her death. God took her because she was ready. What will it take to bring you to

God? What will it take to bring you to a place to say, Lord, here is my life?

Acts 22:20 says, *"And when the blood of thy martyr Stephen was shed, I also was standing by, and consenting unto his death, and kept the raiment of them that slew him."* It took the death of a godly man to bring Saul of Tarsus to the Lord. Saul of Tarsus never could get out of his heart and mind the scene of watching a man who was godly die. It shook him to the very foundation. The more he thought about it the more he came miserable in his heart until finally he surrendered to God. It took the death of a godly man to bring him to the Lord Jesus Christ just like it took the death of a godly little girl to bring the Boyd family back to God. What would it take to bring you back to God?

Did you know that God's people are expendable? Will it take a death in your family to bring you to God? Could you die as peaceably as that little child of yours? Are you as ready to go as he or she is? That is cold isn't it? That's hard for a preacher to say, but suddenly, they are gone, why? To point you to God. To remind you that it is appointed unto man once to die and after that the judgment.

It took an uncle's prayer to bring about a special intervention of God's grace to save a nephew. In Genesis 19:15 Abraham was a godly man. Lot was in the city that was wicked. Abraham began to pray. Even his wife didn't make it and years later the physician Luke would write and say, remember Lot's wife. It took a burning city, the loss of personal property to bring Lot to a place of salvation. It took the thread of bankruptcy to bring Jacob to God. Jacob had worked his tricks one after the other, he had tried everything and all that he owned was in jeopardy. He was about to lose all those flock that he had cheated for and tricked for. Suddenly, everything he had was stripped away from him and now he can pray. Now he can quit his conniving and turn to God and he can pray. Oh God, the God of my father, Isaac, deliver me I pray thee from the hand of my brother for I fear him. And Jacob was left alone. There was some wrestling to do and he spent the night with the angels of God. God touched him and he became the Prince of Israel. Jacob called the name of that place a word which means, for I have seen the Lord, face to face and my life is preserved.

Did you know God can get you in a corner? Did you know that God can, through the very circumstances of life, get you in a corner? Isn't it strange how, I remember it well, when I came to know the Lord, miserable in my heart and soul. God was after me, the Holy Spirit was convicting me and Jesus Christ was following me down every street and every alley and finally he got me into a corner and backed me against the wall, threw me flat on my back and put his foot at my throat and I said I surrender, Lord. I went to prayer meeting the next night and said I found the Lord. Brother, he found me. There was no other way out, God had me in a corner. The only thing I could do was die or accept God.

There are some things in this world you cannot lick without God's help. Joseph's brothers found out the chickens come home to roost. They found out that sin no matter how carefully covered has a way of being uncovered and suddenly brought to life. They sold their brother into slavery. They said, we are through with that dreaming rascal. We are through with that fellow who is always telling us one of these days' boys, I am going to be your ruler. They threw him in a pit and covered it. They lied to his father and said that the biggest lion you ever saw ate Joseph and he believed it. It was covered up beautifully, but God intervened and Joseph was sold into slavery and little did the brothers know, that one day they were going to face him and say as Judas said, thy servants have dealt with thee wrongfully and committed iniquity. They thought they had planned the perfect crime. They had covered their tracks. There was no investigation. They were shocked to find out their sin was still alive.

If there was a newspaper in Jericho, it took the headlines of that paper to bring Rahab to God, who was Jericho's most famous madam. When Joshua's spies went in to Jericho to spy out the land before they destroyed it, she said something like this to them. We have heard about your God. We have heard how your God opened the Red Sea and how you crossed on dry ground. We have heard how you have killed the two kings of the mighty enemy of our neighbors. We have seen the Jordan River, we've seen God work these miracles before you and she said, and because we have seen it there is not a man left in Jericho with any courage. Our hearts melt within us and our courage is gone. Then she began to turn to God.

The headlines in tomorrow morning's paper ought to be clear enough to all of us. The headlines we have read in the past week, the past month are clear enough to turn us to God. I think the headline could very well read for all practical purposes to an intelligent individual, Get right with God! That is what all the news is spelling. Whether front page or middle section it is all spelling one thing, get right with God. God is about to bring this thing to a halt. God is about to wrap it all up.

It took blindness, torture, brainwashing, insult and misery to bring Samson to God. Samson was a man God wanted to use mightily, but he wanted to be a spiritual playboy. He liked all the ladies. He was a man of muscle and good looks, but no sense. He kept trifling with his soul, he kept tantalizing the ladies with his strength and finally he went to sleep in Delilah's lap and she gave him a haircut he never forgot. And when he woke up his eyes had been gorged out with a hot iron and he was tied to a gristmill and he was pulling it like a donkey grinding corn. God wanted to use him. Finally, when they brought him out, they wanted to have a little fun. When they began to laugh and mock him, he prayed Lord help me this one last time. I confess my sin, I've erred, and my life is gone. It's over Lord, just give me strength to die with my enemies. It took all of that to bring Samson to God.

The most touching story in the scriptures took the prayers of a little boy to bring a backslidden preacher back to God. Eli was backslidden. The scripture says during that time there was no vision in Israel. He heard nothing from God, he didn't know what was going on. When he heard that little boy pray, he went to the boy and said son, tell me what God said to you. One day as that boy began to pray, something tugged at Eli's heart. He said, I pray thee, tell me, and don't hide it from me. The scripture says the Lord appeared again in Shiloh. What will it take to bring you to the Lord?

Have you ever heard your child pray? Isn't it touching? Don't you wish you could pray as confidently as they pray? God bless momma, God bless daddy, etc. If they are mad at somebody you will notice they leave them out of the prayer. A little boy was scorned at the supper table and sent to bed early. The mother said she'd be up to say prayers later. She finally came up, he got down on his knees and said, God bless daddy, God bless Johnny, and God bless Suzie. Amen. He got up and looked his mom straight in the face and said, I reckon you noticed I left you out. Ever heard that little girl or boy of yours pray? It would get some of you if you went to Sunday school class and heard those little fellows pray for you. It would break your heart. What will it take to bring you to God?

It took the aftermath treachery, lust, blackmail, and murder to bring David to God. Two people fell into sin and a whole nation staggered under it. Then after that sin was committed, a little baby lay dying, the baby born out of that elicit relationship. He was sick and about to die and David is praying. It took all of that to bring David to God. Listen to David pray in Psalms 51. If you can read that and not have chill bumps run up your spine, there is something wrong with you. He is praying as a man brokenhearted. Watching a little baby dying and he is praying to God. God have mercy on my heart, wash me thoroughly from mine iniquity and cleanse me from all my sin. To what depth will God have to plunge you?

It took seven insane years when a man's hair grew long, his beard matted, and nails grew like they were beast claws to bring Nebuchadnezzar to God. The scripture says, Nebuchadnezzar, telling his own story, at the end all of that, I lifted up my eyes to heaven and my understanding came back. He said, I am blessed. I praise the most high and I honor he that liveth forever and whose dominion is from everlasting unto everlasting. He had to learn the hard way, will you?

It took an earthquake to bring the sheriff of Philippi to God. It took a hungry heart to know the meaning of God's word to bring the treasurer of Ethiopia to God. It took the torment of seven devils to bring Mary Magdalene to God. It took a pig pen to bring the prodigal son to God. It took the crucifixion of the Lord of glory to bring the thief to God. What will it take to bring you?

Let me tell you plainly that what I've said is hard. Preacher, don't tell me God might take someone I love. I didn't say He would, I said He could. That is not God's way or desire. He doesn't want to do that. God is not willing that any perish, but all come to repentance. You just need a nudge now and then. I know in my heart and in my mind, I could guarantee it, God is reaching out to you today. You can feel his hand on your shoulder right now. God is after many of you. You have felt this convicting. It gets better. If I go to the links people do and cause things to happen, why not have, as the scripture says, the good sense to apply our hearts unto wisdom and heed his call and receive Christ as our personal Savior. You know God's after you and dealing with your heart. You know perfectly well what you need to do. You are waiting for something to hit you and brother, it will.

You are going to do one of two things. You are going, by your attitude, determine right now how far God's going to have to go to get you. God wants you and he is going to get you. Your attitude, right this minute, will determine what God has to do to touch your heart. He is going to do whatever is necessary. What will he have to do for you? Will you grit your teeth and swell up and say he'll have to kill me? I won't do it. As I said before, that's not the way God wants you to come to him. God wants you to hear the gospel message and be convicted of your sin and accept

Christ as your personal Savior. That is the easy way. We, sometimes, want to go the hard way and force God's hand. Paul could never erase the memory of watching a godly man die. David could never erase seeing his baby die and I could never forget the impact of that truck hitting my little sister and watching her die in the highway like a dog. I never could forget that. What it took to bring me to God? What will it take to bring you?

Chapter 13
Is It Finished?
Luke 14:28-30

We are living in a time of imitation. A time of instant things, a time of labor saving devices that are hitting the market. People's jobs are becoming easier as far as time is concerned. Yet with all of that, it seems that which we do for God; that which God claims of our time is beginning to be less and less. We have a gospel presented in many different ways. I sometimes get in trouble because I'm not easily put in a notch somewhere. That's not very popular among some Free Will Baptist, they like to know exactly where you are at all times and what you stand for. We hear the modernistic gospel preached which is basically love thy neighbor. Then we have some fundamentalist who preach love the Lord and hate everybody – don't trust anybody. Somewhere in between all of that seems to be the love of God which speaks to us and uses us, thrills us and blesses us. One of the things that seems to bother me, at least, is the fact that Christians, a lot of times, don't really realize that which they are building with their lives. From the time they are saved until God calls us home, is a time of building. Far too many of us believe that you walk the aisle, give your heart to the Lord and just wait for the bus to come by and take you to heaven. That you hold out till the end and you get folks to pray for you that you will hold out till the end. There is not much joy in that kind of Christian living. Many of us don't realize that we begin our Christian walk by being saved. That is the very beginning. We have not gone anywhere. We just got to the place we can begin to build. Far too many of us, I'm afraid, do not sit down and count the cost of a Christian life. We do not take the time to say this, "if I am going to let the Lord Jesus Christ save me from sin and hell, I'm going to serve and live for him. I'm going to be faithful to his church and his word. I'm going to fellowship with God. I'm going to walk with him and surrender my life to him as Lord and Master". It doesn't do much good to ask the Lord to save you and then not fellowship and become connected with a New Testament church. Then not let your life count for God and most of all, not to be faithful. Everybody can be faithful. In the scriptures, Luke 14: 28-30 *"For which of you, intending to build a tower, sitteth not down first, and counteth the cost, whether he have sufficient to finish it? Lest haply, after he hath laid the foundation, and is not able to finish it, all that behold it begin to mock him, Saying, this man began to build, and was not able to finish."* That certainly would have been a time of embarrassment to begin to build something and not have the ability to finish it. It would be a mockery. I feel the same way about the Christian life. It is a shame to begin the Christian life and not be able to do what God asks us to do. And not to be identified, in the community, as a man or woman of God. To begin to build something and then have the world steal your affections away until you are not able to finish is mockery.

We, as Christians, are building something. We are building a life message. We are building something that the whole world can identify. Therefore, we must not only lay the foundation, we must finish the building. We must count the cost and see if we are willing to pay the price of what God expects of us as Christians. To see if we really are dedicated enough to do what God has asked us to do. Count the cost before building.

When I received the Lord Jesus Christ as my personal Savior, I built my foundation upon him who is the rock. No other foundation can man lay than that which is laid and that is Jesus Christ. So if I'm counting the cost of the Christian life, it is only fitting that I count the cost of that which I've based my life upon. What did Christianity cost? What did salvation cost? What did the foundation on which I'm building my life cost God? What did it cost the Lord Jesus Christ? I say it cost him everything to purchase my salvation.

Let's just think for a moment. Let your mind, if it is capable, of visualizing what heaven is like and what God and his Son is like. But let's try and visualize the foundation our salvation is built on. If I see heaven and I see God and his Son, and I see the angels flying back and forth throughout heaven to do the bidding of the Son of God, and I hear those angels cry out, Holy, Holy, Holy, Lord God of Host. I see the Lord Jesus Christ as the central figure in heaven. I see him in the bosom of the Father. I see him enjoying heaven and fellowship with God the Father. Then I see him turn aside all of that. I see him withdraw from the Father and withdraw from being the central figure of heaven. I see him withdraw from the angels doing his bidding, withdrawing from the choirs of heaven singing, Holy, Holy, Holy. I see him turn aside and I see him leave all of that and come to a sinful earth moved by the greatest love known to man. What a love he had for lost sinners. Then when he came to earth, I can visualize him as he walked the dusty roads of Jerusalem and Israel. I see him doing nothing but good and always for someone else not for himself. I see my Lord as he walks by that little child and take that child and hold it up to his bosom and see the very peace of heaven come over that child's face. I see him reach down and touch the cripple and I see the cripple roll up his bed and walk away praising God for his deliverance. I see him touch the eyes of the blind and they began to rejoice in all the beauty they see for the first time. I see him lay his hand on the ear of the deaf and I see that individual with a smile on his face because he is hearing again. I see the Lord as he walks among men doing nothing but good.

I hear the hosts singing out Hosanna, Hosanna, blessed is he that cometh in the name of the Lord. Then I hear that same multitude crying, Crucify Him! Crucify Him! I see the Lord of glory as he begins that journey from Pilate's hall to Golgotha. I see him as they slap him and as they beat him and spit upon his face. They plucked the beard from his chin. I see them as they take that crown of thorns and mockingly put it down over his brow and I see the blood begin to trickle down his face. I see him fall beneath the cross. When he reaches Golgotha, I can hear the ring of the hammer as it drives the nails in his hands and feet and I can hear the thud of the cross as it falls into the hole prepared for him. I can hear him and see his lips begin to move and I wonder what he is going to say. And he prays, Father, forgive them for they know not what they do. Only the Son of God can pray like that in a time like that. Then a little later, I see him cry, It is finished! And I say, yes dear Lord Jesus, it is finished. You have given your last ounce of energy and your last bit of love and you have paid for my salvation upon a tree. That is what it cost for me and you to be saved. It is expensive.

To see our Lord kneel in the Garden of Gethsemane and pray with such inner torment that he sweat great drops of blood. For me it was in the garden, he prayed not my will but thine. He had no tears for his own grief, but sweat drops of blood for mine. That is what it cost the Lord of glory to purchase our salvation. I want to ask you a question. Seeing that it cost so much, can you and I go through life just picking up the blessings of God like a sponge? Shall we just float around on a bed of ease? The song says, there is a cross for every man and there is a cross for me.

So what does it cost to be a Christian? What does it cost for us to walk with God? First, it costs us a separation from the world. It was from the world of sin that God saved us and it is from this world of sin that you and I must separate ourselves from. When a man or woman is converted, the first thing you ought to see in their lives is not perfection, not maturity, not generosity, but you should see a difference. His life is different from the rest of the world. He has been delivered from the world. People can look at him and say something has happened in this man or woman's life, they are different now. The scripture says, if any man be in Christ, he is a new creature, old things are passed away, behold all things have become new. There ought to be a difference. We are not perfect at all. 1 John 3:9 says, *"whosoever is born of God doth not commit sin; for his seed remaineth in him: and he cannot sin, because he is born of God."* Yet John says all of us have sinned and we lie if we say we have not sinned. That scripture is simply saying whosoever is born of God, who has been delivered from the power and penalty of sin, who has been set free from the pull of the flesh does not practice sin. He no longer walks in the old paths. He no longer continually sins. He is free from that and he is different.

I believe with all my heart there are people in hell today and there are going to be folks in hell simply because of the influence of a so-called Christian. Brother, I've talked to them. I have begged people. I have pleaded with children of church members to come to church. They say if that's what my father has, I don't want it. I'll live without God and without the church. I don't want anything he has got. Now they may be unfair and they may be stupid, but someone is responsible for that person's philosophy. And God help us if it is a Christian or someone who has said they were a Christian. There ought to be a difference. There are some places that a king's son cannot go. There are some things a king's son cannot do. Come out from among and be separate, saith the Lord. Now I'm not for one minute saying that we ought to distrust everybody and that we ought to isolate ourselves. I don't believe in that. But there ought to be a difference. We ought to be visible Christians. There ought to be a gap between us.

Secondly, it cost us separation. You may say, people are not persecuted today. Oh, yes they are. A true born again child of God will be persecuted. If they hated your master, they will hate you. Paul and Silas are the best examples of that. They were beaten unmercifully. They were beaten with the whip until their backs looked like hamburger. They were locked in an old musty dungeon in an inner prison with their hands and feet in stocks. Because of their faith in God and because of their testimony concerning the Lord Jesus Christ they are being persecuted. On one particular incident, about midnight, Paul says to Silas, let's sing a song. I'm sure Silas must have said, Paul that last blow took all the singing out of me. I don't feel like singing, Paul. I don't feel like praising God. Paul tells Silas to not be downhearted. All things work together for good to them that love the Lord, who are called according to his purpose. And I am persuaded that the sufferings in this present time are not worthy to be compared to the glory that shall be revealed in us, Silas. They began to sing. The glory of God filled that jail. The glory of the very presence of almighty God came down and filled that prison cell and in a few moments Paul is gonna walk out. He is going to have that jail door under one arm and the jailor under the other and take him right on to Jesus. He is introducing his whole family to the Savior. No one is going to do that to you today. No one is going to shoot you for being a Christian. No one is going to beat you for going to church. But if you mean business for God, when you go to work and they find out you went to church twice on Sunday, they are going to say you're crazy. What do you mean going to church twice on Sunday? Why didn't you play golf, why didn't you go out on the lake? Why would you go twice on Sunday? Then when they find out you tithe, they are going to turn you over to somebody. What do you mean you give ten percent of your income to the Lord's work? Look at all the things you could buy with that ten percent. That's the kind of persecution we have today. People lose their families because they identify with Jesus Christ. Their families turn against them. People lose their best friends. There was a deacon who lost a very good job for the simple reason he would not drink with his boss. He was fired because of it. Persecuted for being a Christian. Persecuted for saying, I belong to Jesus. And if you are a born again child of God and you identify yourself with Jesus Christ, it will cost you something. Christianity is not cheap. Jesus had a lot of evil things said about him. They lied about him and said all manner of evil against him. But he wasn't listening to what they said. He was listening to another voice, he was going to hear one day that would say, well done, my good and faithful servant. Brother, I'll tell you something, I want to hear that voice one of these days. I believe whatever comes my way in this life will be worth hearing Jesus say, well done.

It cost us surrender of our time. It may seem trite for me to say this, but do you know it costs us a little time in the matter of the culture of our souls. It costs us a little time. Becoming a Christian is the only thing I know that people have the mistaken idea that you just join and that is it. It costs you time to pray and fellowship with God and with other Christians. There has to be some time given to this thing of living a Christian life. I wondered what it would be like if God treated us the way we treat him. Suppose I were to come to God and say Father, give me my daily bread and he say, I'm too busy to fool with you today, do the best you can. But Father, I'm hungry. I need my daily bread. I'm sorry I've got other appointments today. Suppose God treated us the way we treat him. Suppose God made us as sick as we say we are on Sunday morning. Brother, we would have an epidemic if God said alright I'll make you sick. Suppose God made us as poor as we say we are when we are asked to contribute. We'd all be in the soup line. It costs us something to be a Christian. What if I said, Father, I am a sinner, I am lost in my sin, and I want to be saved. Father, I want you to come and take me to heaven. He'd say, there is a lot of folks in front of you. That would be about the way we would treat him.

I was talking to a friend who was moving a washing machine. I said you know everybody has all these labor saving devices. Women used to wash on Monday, they would have to build a fire under a black kettle. They would wash clothes in a black kettle and run them through an old hand wringer and it would take them all day to wash. They made their own soap. Most would work in the field tell just time to quit, go to the house, and cook for the man. And yet they always found time to go to prayer meeting and Sunday school and church. Today, we push buttons, give something a sling and go out the door and it does the work while we are gone, but we don't have time to go to church. If you are going to let God save you, God expects you to give him some time. Your excuse won't hold up, by the way.

It pays to be a Christian. There is a heaven to gain and a hell to shun. It pays. It is wonderful to have peace in your heart and joy in your soul because you know the Lord Jesus Christ as your personal Savior. It pays to have that fellowship with God. It pays to be a Christian when we come to the last hour of our lives. Then we begin to look back and realize that the only thing that counts now is what we have done with Jesus Christ and for him. He doesn't care how much money you made. He doesn't care how many houses you built. He doesn't care how successful you were in your business. The only thing that matters is what you have done with Jesus Christ. At a time like that it pays to be a Christian. It will pay in eternity. Lost man will be in hell throughout eternity to nash his teeth and cry out if only I had listened. The saved man will be in heaven forever rejoicing and singing, Oh Happy Day!

Do you know him today? Do you know him as your own personal Savior? If you do, do you love him? Do you love him because he saved you from sin? Do you love him because he walks with you and fellowships with you and he is closer than a brother? Are you willing to do service for him? Are you willing to surrender your life to Him, not as Savior, but as Lord and Master of your life? How much do you owe God this morning? How much of your time do you owe God? How many of you could say, if I am supposed to be doing something for God then I owe him an awful lot of time that I haven't given him? How much time do you owe God in prayer and reading the Bible? How much do you owe God in cold cash? How much do you owe God?

It cost Him everything. Do you love him? Have you obeyed him? Have you publicly confessed him? Someone says, preacher, I'm a Christian, I believed on the Lord but I just haven't publicly confessed it. Are you sure you are a Christian? Listen to the scriptures, thou shalt confess with thy mouth the Lord Jesus, thou shalt be saved. Have you done that? Have you been baptized? If you haven't, you need to take care of that. Get it done. You are building something and that which you are building is built on something expensive and is going to cost you something. Do you love him enough to finish the building?

Chapter 14
What is a Christian?
Romans 6:1-13

"What shall we say then? Shall we continue in sin, that grace may abound? God forbid. How shall we, that are dead to sin, live any longer therein? Know ye not, that so many of us as were baptized into Jesus Christ were baptized into his death? Therefore we are buried with him by baptism into death: that like as Christ was raised up from the dead by the glory of the Father, even so we also should walk in newness of life. For if we have been planted together in the likeness of his death, we shall be also in the likeness of his resurrection: Knowing this, that our old man is crucified with him, that the body of sin might be destroyed, that henceforth we should not serve sin. For he that is dead is freed from sin. Now if we be dead with Christ, we believe that we shall also live with him: Knowing that Christ being raised from the dead dieth no more; death hath no more dominion over him. For in that he died, he died unto sin once: but in that he liveth, he liveth unto God. Likewise reckon ye also yourselves to be dead indeed unto sin, but alive unto God through Jesus Christ our Lord. Let not sin therefore reign in your mortal body, that ye should obey it in the lusts thereof. Neither yield ye your members as instruments of unrighteousness unto sin: but yield yourselves unto God, as those that are alive from the dead, and your members as instruments of righteousness unto God."

The whole argument that Paul is presenting in Romans chapter 6 is the fact that we have been buried in the old life. We are, in fact, dead as far as sin is concerned. Now Paul is pleading with us as Christians on the basis of our burial with Jesus Christ. We are to be dead to the life of sin and alive now to walk in a new life. So he says, how can we sin when we are already dead to sin? How can we live and fulfill the lust of the flesh because that is what we died to? When we were buried with Christ in his resurrection, we symbolized our being dead and buried to the old life and therefore rising to walk in newness of life. There is a kind of newness of life that all of us have experienced. All of us, at one time or another, have been sick and in great pain. When the pain left us it was almost like a new lease on life. When I put on a new suit, I walk like a new person. There is a kind of new life that is peculiar to the Christian.

Paul takes about this man who is walking in a new life. Now the apostle Paul was just such a man. There was a time in Paul's life when he hated Christ. When the very mention of the name Jesus Christ would make him fall into a rage. He hated everything Jesus stood for. He literally thought he was doing God a favor by murdering and having put to death all of those who were following this new kind of religion, this Galilean had started. There was no real feeling in his heart that he was doing anything wrong. He thought he owed it to God to wipe Christianity off the face of the earth. So he hated Christ and all that Jesus Christ stood for. Then we see the same man giving every ounce of his energy trying to win men to Jesus Christ. Giving up everything he had and giving his life away for the cause of Jesus Christ. Something happened to this man. He no longer walks in the old life. He has had an experience with Jesus Christ and now he is walking in a new life. And now he is a different individual all-around and a whole new person. It is called the newness of life and he talks about that newness in Romans 6.

In our church we have had some people who have recently been saved. They are beginning a new walk. To some it is very difficult; to some they have been delivered from so much. Because they have come from so far to this knowledge of Jesus Christ, sometimes it is rather difficult for them. They are trying to walk in a new way. Now we do not need for those of us who have been Christians for years to stand back and wait until they fall, so we can say, I told you so. Our responsibility to God and to each of these new converts, is to watch over them, pray for them, spend time with and share our testimony with them that they may grow in knowledge and in grace. It is thrilling to see young people and adults who are saved encounter Satan after they have been saved and see them bounce back and see them gain in faithfulness as we go along. There is that newness of life as far as they are concerned.

That is the definition of a Christian? The scripture says they were called Christians first in Antioch. That was sort of a mockery. They would laugh at them and call them Christians because they were listening to the preaching and teachings of this Galilean peasant. Today, there is no greater badge of honor than the word Christian. Even though it started as mockery, today it is an honor. It doesn't matter to me if folks call me rich or poor, brilliant or ignorant, but I want people to call me a Christian. I am willing to give up all the other titles, if I can be known as a Christian. There is something about being a Christian.

A Christian is anyone who has:
1. Come to God as a lost sinner,
2. Taken the Lord Jesus Christ as their personal Savior,
3. Have surrendered to Him as Lord and Master,
4. Confessed Him publicly as being their Lord and Master, and
5. Strives to please Him day to day as they live. Let me talk about each of these five elements of a Christian.

First of all, a Christian is a person that has come to God as a lost sinner. The scriptures teaches us that all have sinned and all have come short of the glory of God. The scripture says because we are sinners, the wages of sin is death. Without Christ we are lost. Without Christ we have no hope. Without Christ we are going away from God turning each to our own way. We recognize the fact that we are sinners. We are arrested by the Holy Spirit of God and we do an about face, and come to God. Not because we have any merit, but we simply realize we are lost.

Second, we accept the Lord Jesus Christ as our personal Savior. There is more to becoming a Christian than believing that Jesus died. More to it that knowing there was a historical man names Jesus who was born at a certain time and lived for a certain number of years and did certain things and was buried and resurrected. It is not enough to believe that. There are two elements of faith – belief and trust.

We must believe, in order to be a Christian that Jesus Christ was born of a virgin. We must believe He went about doing good. We must believe that at about 33 ½ years he was arrested, tried, sentenced to death and was crucified on a cross. We must believe He was dead, buried and resurrected again. We must believe all of that in order to be a Christian. And secondly, we must believe that all of that was God's will for Him. All of that was His paying for our sin. After we believe He did all of that, we trust Him. We say, Lord Jesus, I believe that you died for me. I believe I am lost without you, therefore, I trust you with the salvation of my soul. I believe and I trust.

Next, we must surrender to Him as Lord and Master. Many of us, I'm sure, were first convicted of sin, came to a point in our lives when we wanted to believe yet we did not want to give up anything. We wanted to make sure, if we died, we would go to heaven, yet we didn't want to live what we thought was a Christian life. When we came to know the Lord and we loved Him so much, we realized that which we feared was not existing at all. Jesus is so real and so rich that He is worth all that we have to give up in order to be a Christian. But we have to make Him Lord of our lives, as well as, Savior. We have to do his bidding. We have to surrender to Him as our Lord and Master.

Then we confess Him publicly before the world. How many secret disciples do you suppose the Lord has? In the New Testament, there were a couple of people who served the Lord Jesus Christ rather secretly because they didn't want the Jews to know. But I don't believe Jesus Christ today, has any secret disciples. The very plan of salvation includes in it a public confessing in order to be saved. The scripture says if a man believes in your heart that God hath raised Him from the dead and shall confess with your mouth, the Lord Jesus thou shalt be saved. It is a very intricate part of the plan of salvation. Believe in my heart, trust in my heart and then whosoever shall confess Him with the mouth shall be saved. Jesus said, whosoever shall confess me before men, him will I confess before my Father which is in heaven. Whosoever shall deny me before men, him will I deny before my Father which is in heaven.

One of the most important things to a Christian is to know that Jesus Christ is standing at the throne of God interceding for us. We cannot stand to think that we do not have Him there to plead our cause. To know we have the Lord Jesus there in God's presence interceding for us. When we pray in the name of Jesus, He goes to the Father with our petition and says, Father, this is one of mine. I died for him. He has believed on me and trusted me. Just to know He is there. The scripture says if we do not confess Him here on earth, He will not confess us before our Father. So if we come to Him in prayer, having denied Him, before men, He simply ignores our prayer. He will not intercede.

And final element of a Christian is that we strive to please Him. Before I came to know the Lord Jesus Christ as my personal Savior, I was lost. I was lost as anybody could be. I was on my way to hell outside of the Lord Jesus Christ. But in His love for us, He made it possible to hear the plan of salvation. He made it possible for the Holy Spirit to give us faith to believe and He saved us from our lost condition and hell. How can I but serve Him? How can we go on ignoring everything Jesus Christ has done for us? To walk in newness of life. To walk, you have to be born first. So it is in the Christian life, you have to be born again to walk in the newness of life.

What are the duties of a Christian? First, there is baptism. In every instance in the New Testament, when someone came to know the Lord, they were baptized and baptized immediately. There is no reason for us not to follow that principle. Regardless of what we believe about the error that is being preached about baptism, we have no right to turn side from the principle of the New Testament that is immediately being baptized upon believing in the Lord Jesus Christ. Jesus walked miles to be baptized by John the Baptist. It would have been a glorious sight to have witnessed the Lord being immersed in the water, watching Him come froth and watching that dove come down and light upon the Lord Jesus Christ and to hear the voice of God say, This is my beloved Son, in whom I am well pleased. It would have been a glorious moment. Not only did He set the example of baptism, he said, Go ye into all the world and preach the gospel to every creature, baptizing them in the name of the Father, the Son and the Holy Ghost, teaching them to observe all things whatsoever I have commanded ye and lo, I am with you always even to the end of the world. Jesus set the example and then He commanded us to do it. If a man has believed in the Lord Jesus Christ and has not been baptized, he is disobedient to God. He is disobedient to all the teachings of God. I believe that salvation is absolutely essential unto baptism, I do not believe the other way around. I believe an individual has to be saved before he is baptized. I believe he has to be a believer and that's the only way you can be a fit candidate to be baptized. But I believe it is the essence of obedience. Paul says it is a symbol. It is a picture of something real. It is a picture of the death, burial and resurrection of Jesus Christ. When we are baptized, it pictures our death to the old life. It pictures our resurrection with Jesus Christ. It pictures our newness of life. And it pictures our resurrection in the last days.

Secondly, there is the Lord's Supper. This is a symbol and another picture of something real. Jesus said, this is my body, when He took the bread. When He took the wine, he said, this is the blood. This do in remembrance of me. And as often as you do this, you show forth my death till I come. I do not believe there is any salvation in the Lord's Supper. But it causes us to remember, that which saved us. To remember He who saved us. Remember His death to save us. Some take the Lord's Supper every Sunday, some every month, some take it once a year. There is no principle for that in the New Testament. The Lord simply says as often as you do this, do it in remembrance of me. As often as you do it, you do show forth my death until I come.

Then, we believe as Free Will Baptist, there is the duty of washing feet. We believe that if you read the book of John you find a strong command in fact, a stronger command to participate in the washing of feet than to participate in the Lord's Supper. In the Lord's Supper, he said as often as you do this, you do so in remembrance of me. In the book of John, after He took the Lord's Supper, he washed the disciples' feet and said, I have given you an example and ye ought to do it. He didn't say as often as you do it, He says you ought to do it. It is a stronger command. We believe it is an ordinance of the church. We do not believe there is any salvation in it. But we do believe, as John said, if you know these things, happy are ye if you do them.

Then there is the matter of giving. There is one prescription in the Bible for giving and that is a tenth. The place to bring it is the storehouse. The storehouse is the church. Then joy comes when we are able to give over and above that our offerings unto the Lord. God has made a promise to the tither. God said, I will open the windows of heaven and I will pour you out a blessing. Those of you who tithe know that

God's plan is better than yours, and you have been blessed by it and it is all a part of God's will for your life.

There is the joy of serving God: singing in the choir, teaching Sunday school, teaching little children, visiting, etc. Folks say I can't do those things. I can't give that much time to the church. Let me ask you a question. The things that you do, that keep you from doing things for the Lord, how important are those things which take up all your time? Then let me ask you the question the Lord asked Peter, lovest thou me, more than these? When you look at all the things that take up your time and those things you use as an excuse not to be doing more for the Lord, ask yourself this question. Do I love these things more than I love the Lord?

Then there is the privilege of prayer. It is a comforting th ng to know that God has everything you need. Everything you need, God has it. Therefore, we need to pray. The only way to get what God's got is through prayer. A lot of folks think God is like a vending machine. You go out through the day and all the sudden you realize you are hungry, so you put money into the vending machine and pull the lever and out comes some goodies. Some people do God the same way. They go about their lives, master of their own fate. All of the sudden a problem arises and they drop to their knees and pray. They say, God do something. I believe it is God's good pleasure to give us all things we need. I believe my God shall supply all your needs according to His mercy. But I believe the only way to get it is through prayer. Therefore, we have a great joy and happiness in prayer.

Another thing is the matter of studying the Bible. The Bible is God's love letter to the Christian. If you love Him you are going to read about He had to say. The more you read what He had to say, the more you love what He had to say and the more you will enjoy it.

We have discussed the definition of a Christian, the duties of a Christian and then we are going to discuss the delights of a Christian. One of the things that makes it all worthwhile, are the delights that come to us by living for Jesus Christ.

First, there is peace in your heart. A peace which passeth all understanding. I don't know what's going to happen in the future. I could worry myself to death like my dad did. One of the things that comes to the Christian by knowing God is peace in his heart. I don't know about tomorrow, but I know who holds tomorrow. It is a wonderful thing to know your sins are forgiven. The sin problem has been dealt with. You may have trials and tribulations, but you don't have a sin problem because God has forgiven you for that. There is peace in your heart because the sin problem has been settled. This peace is not the absence of hurtful feelings. It is not the absence of going through trials and tribulations, but it is peace in the presence of all that. There is a story about two artists competing in a contest. They were offered a prize for painting a picture which most beautifully portrayed peace and tranquility. One artist painted a beautiful valley with green grass and a mirror smooth lake. A picture of perfect peace. The other artist painted a picture of a tumbling waterfall. Just a huge waterfall coming down and underneath that waterfall he painted a bird's nest and a mother bird feeding her young. That won the prize for peace and tranquility. In the midst of turmoil, there was peace. In the midst of that tumbling rushing waterfall, there was a bird living in perfect peace. That is the way the Christian ought to live.

There is the happiness of the daily companionship with Jesus Christ. Jesus said, I will walk with you. I will never leave you or forsake you. The closer we walk with Him, the closer He gets with us, till you can reach out and touch Him. The scripture teaches that when sorrow comes He will be there to comfort us. When troubles come, He will be there to help us. When doubts come He is there to give us assurance. And when death comes, He is there to take us home. The joy of walking with Him.

Then there is the commendation and the crown. Jesus will say in those days, well done, thou good and faithful servant. Those are sweet words. At the judgment seat the rewards will be given for the deeds done, whether they be good or bad. He not only saves us but He rewards us. We need to live for Him that our rewards may be full and rich. There are two words that give us the whole secret of the Christian life. Those two words are "Be faithful". Those two words make all the difference in having your name on the roll and being a real Christian. The only thing God asked of us is that we be faithful. God doesn't ask us to move mountains. God doesn't ask us to give great sums of money. All men can be faithful.

I read a story not too long ago about an old medical missionary in India. He had been in the mission field for 47 years. He had a young assistant with him. The old medical missionary was quite ill and they thought he was going to die. In fact, they were sure he was. This young assistant was trying to comfort the old missionary in his last days. The old missionary noticed some problem or something in the heart of the young assistant. He asked the young man what was troubling him. The young assistant, I received two letters from home. One is an offer to become the head of a hospital and the other is to become the head of our Home Mission Department in our denomination. I've been praying what I need to do. He said you have been here 47 years working among these people and you have nothing to show for it. You have no money, no position, no fame and you've just given your life away. I am thinking seriously about going back to one of those jobs. I don't want to live here for 47 years and nobody know I existed. He asked the old man's advice. The old man said, I couldn't tell you what to do but I'll tell you how I feel about it. He said, in a few days, I'll be gone. I'll go on to my reward. I fully expect when I get to heaven to be met by some little dark skinned Indian boy or girl. They are going to run to me and I won't recognize their name because there are so many. This little girl will say, you were the one that introduced me to the Lord. You told me about Jesus Christ. Now let me be the one to take you to the Lord. Let me introduce you to Jesus here in glory. The young man bowed his head and said, I'll stay.

The definition of a Christian, the duties of a Christian, the delight of a Christian. To live our lives for Him and at the end of the way, hear Him say, Well done, thou good and faithful servant.

Chapter 15
Look at Him!
John 19:1-4

"Then Pilate therefore took Jesus, and scourged him. And the soldiers platted a crown of thorns, and put it on his head, and they put on him a purple robe, and said, Hail, King of the Jews: and they smote him with their hands. Pilate therefore went forth again and saith unto them, Behold, I bring him forth to you, that ye may know that I find no fault in him."

I want us to take that one sentence that has become the theme of artists, poets and theologians through the years. That one exclamation, Behold the Man! Which means simply look at him. That exclamation by Pilate on the balcony before the howling mob has become a focal point for those artist who would portray to us the suffering, crucified Savior. History will say that no small part of the death of Jesus Christ was caused by the Roman soldiers. For it was the custom of the Roman soldier to take those who were sentenced to be crucified and almost beat them to death before the crucifixion.

The first verse said Pilate took Jesus and had Him scourged, which means they beat him until he was a bloody mess. And they took a bunch of thorns, platted a crown and put it on his head and pushed it down into his forehead until the blood began to run down his face. And the Lord stood there with a robe that the soldiers, perhaps, found somewhere in the building and wrapped it around his shoulders. They bowed before him mockingly saying, Hail, the King of the Jews. There was absolutely no limit to what they would do to show their hatred for this man Jesus. They would go to any length to further ridicule this man who had been rejected by his own people. While the mocking was going on, while they were going through all this insult to Jesus, Pilate must have walked again through the judgment hall and looked at Jesus, and saw him standing there with that purple robe and thorns on his head and blood running down his face and for some reason, I believe Pilate was moved with compassion and he sought to release him. He wanted, from that moment, to release Jesus. He was saying to himself, we have done enough to this man. He is innocent in the first place. He was moved with some kind of compassion and I believe Pilate thought if he could take this Jesus and present him to the people, if he could take him to the balcony and let the multitude see him suffering and see the agony, they crown of thorns and blood on his face, they crowd would feel as he did and say they had done enough. Surely they would say it is over. So Pilate took Jesus to the balcony so all the people could see him and said to the crowd, look at him! The people all the more began to cry out crucify him, crucify him. They were like a bunch of dogs. Have you ever noticed how a pack of dogs react? If one of them ever tastes blood, they go mad. They have to kill and when they smell blood it turns them on fire. That is exactly what happened in the minds of these people when they saw this man who was beaten and bloody. They were set on fire to continue to mutilate him and ridicule him. But Pilate thought they would be moved to some kind of compassion, so he took him out and said, Behold the Man!

I would like for us to do that today. To behold the man and look at him as the crowd looked at him. Look at him as a man who had been beaten and mutilated and mocked standing before you with blood on his body. I want you to picture that in your mind and look at him for a moment. The Prince of Glory, the Prince in heaven before the world was created, this Jesus that is standing before you today on the balcony of Pilate's judgment hall beaten wearing a purple robe and it is nothing else than the manifestation of God himself. That is God himself standing before you. That is almighty God in the flesh standing on that balcony presenting himself to the crowd.

The scripture says, in the beginning was the word and the word was God and the word was with God. All things were created by him and without him was anything made that was made and that word was made flesh and dwelt among us. And we beheld his glory as the only begotten of the Father. Tell of grace and truth. That was God manifest in the flesh. That, who you are looking at in your mind, and that's who the multitude was looking at that day. The word of God became flesh and dwelt among us. Paul, later said, in him dwelt the fullness of the godhead bodily. It was God. The scripture says, he made himself of no reputation and he took upon himself the form of a servant and became obedient even to the death of the cross. Behold the Man! Think of him for a moment. The prince of heaven standing on a balcony in Pilate's judgment hall beaten, prepared for his execution. Behold the Man!

Do you every think about the contrast there is between that scene of Jesus Christ and the nativity scene? Just think for a moment, the night of all nights, the first Christmas night when the angel choir came down from heaven; when the shepherds saw the star; when they announced to them behold we bring you good tidings of great joy which shall be to all people for unto you is born this day in the city of David, a Savior which is Christ the Lord. And all of heaven is singing. What a beautiful night. The whole world is alive because that word has now become flesh and it's laying in a manger in Bethlehem and all of heaven knows it. Contrast that with him standing on a balcony. The Son of God beaten, ready for execution, Behold the Man!

When he was brought to the temple, as a little child, Simeon said to Mary, Mary the sword pierce thine own soul also. When he was just a little baby. Just after the whole heavens had been awaken after the shepherds heard the message and the wise men had come and all we know about the wonderful Christmas. Mary brings him as a little baby to the temple and Simeon told Mary the sword is going to pierce through your soul and standing at the foot of the cross, Mary watched him crucified. Behold the Man! What a contrast.

Pilate looked at him for that few moments and then he evaded what he saw five times. So typical of the way we look at Jesus. I ask you to look at him and picture him in your mind. All of you saw him. All of you have come to one or more conclusions about what you saw. I would like to tell you what Pilate did about what he saw. As he wrestled with the problem, what am I going to do with Jesus Christ, no matter how he tried it kept coming back to him just as it will keep coming back to you? Once you behold the man, once you hear the message, you have to make a decision, you have to wrestle with what will I do with this man called Jesus? Pilate ask the question, what shall I do with him, this man called Christ? And you will have to personally decide what to do with him. No matter how you try to evade the issue, it will come back to you.

Pilate, in the first incident, learned that Jesus was from Galilee. That he was from another part of the Roman Empire and was under someone else's jurisdiction. Herod was the man who had to decide whether Jesus would die or not, so Pilate said, carry him to Herod. Whatever Herod says, I'll do. If Herod says free him, I'll free him. If Herod says, crucify him, I'll crucify him. That was his first evasion. He himself knew that Christ was innocent, but he could not come to the conclusion to set him free. He tried to shift it off on someone else, so he said, whatever Herod does, I'll do. I see that very often in people saying, I'll do whatever he does or I'll do whatever she does. Whatever they do with Jesus, that's what I will do. Whatever is acceptable in my age group that is what I'll do with Jesus Christ. If the crowd laughs at him, if the crowd uses his name in vain, I'll use his name in vain. If I am with someone who is a godly man, then I'll act godly. I'll do whatever the crowd does with Jesus. I'll swear like a sailor or pray like a preacher. I'll do whatever the crowd does because it make no difference to me.

A man, who was a good friend of mine, came to me and said he was going to join the Shriners. I said have you investigated it? He said, no, but I found out all my customers belong and I can increase my sales at least tenfold by joining. I thought how silly is that for a man to go into something he knew nothing about, go to all those meetings, put out all that money, wear those silly looking hats, so he could sell more. Excuse me if you belong, I think the hats really look nice. Folks join the church for the same reason. Folks profess Christ for the same reason. It is acceptable and expedient that I do it. You know it will always come back to you. Just as you breathe for yourself, you will die for yourself and you will stand before the judgment by yourself. Then the question will be, what have I done with Jesus?

The second evasion that Pilate made was let's compromise on this thing. Let's not do either one. Let's not decide to crucify him or not crucify him just let's scourge him and let him go. So we don't have to make a decision either way. I see that a lot as well. People say, I'm not really going to give my life to him, but I'll do this. I will forsake this sin. I'll quit doing that. I won't really live for him. I won't give my life to him, but I will make some compromise. I'll quit chewing tobacco on Saturday night; I'll do something to compromise with Jesus. That way I don't have to accept him in my life. I'll just do a little something.

The third thing was the most foolish thing in the world. Pilate tried to reason with the crowd. He took him out on the balcony and said I've scourged and mocked him surely this is going to be enough to satisfy them. I'll go out and say to them, look at him. Look at what I have done to him and be satisfied. You can't reason with Satan. Satan has no sympathy for Jesus Christ. Satan demands that he be crucified. Satan demands that there be no compromise. Just as Pilate tried to reason with the crowd, we try to reason with the devil. You can't do it. Satan is too big for anybody in this congregation. You can't argue with him. You can't stand up to him. You are not big enough and you certainly cannot reason with him. He has no sympathy for God. You can come to church on Sunday morning, hear the gospel preached, you hear the invitation, and you have a desire in your heart to go forward and give your heart to the Lord, the devil will give you twenty reasons why you ought not to go. And he will give you ten thousand reasons why you ought not to go on a particular Sunday. You cannot reason with him.

The fourth evasion Pilate made was substitution. He said to the crowd I have a man locked up who has been tried and convicted and proved that beyond any shadow of a doubt he is guilty of murder. Take him and crucify him and let your blood thirstiness be satisfied. Substitute a man who we know is guilty and to crucify him. Take Barabbus, he is a murderer. He has been rightly convicted. I can't find any fault in Jesus Christ and I know Barabbus is guilty so let us crucify him. How many times have you heard people say that? I will not accept him as my Savior, but I'll substitute something else. I'll live a good life. I'll pay my honest debts. I'll be a good citizen and I'll even join the church. A man will substitute everything under heaven instead of humbly, prayerfully and preciously receive Christ as his own personal Savior. Substitute everything – works, living, membership, baptism – whatever they can think of they will substitute.

I heard a terrible story about a man who was a chain smoker. There came a little sore on his lip where the cigarette dangled. It got pretty sore and he went to the doctor. The doctor in this little community said, sir, you need to go to a specialist and need to go quick. You need to go immediately and have that sore looked at because it is a cancer. The doctor gave him the name of a specialist. He can take care of this before it goes any farther. The man went back home. His neighbor began to talk to him and said it's going to cost money to go to a specialist. They charge you a lot of money and the hospitals charge a lot. The neighbor said, I have a tub of medicine that if you put it on your lip it will heal it in no time. The man thought about all the money he was going to save. He took the neighbors medicine and dabbed it on his lip. A few weeks passed and it got worse. He went back to his doctor and the doctor said, I told you to go to a specialist. Why didn't you go? My neighbor told me I could take this medicine and save money. In a few weeks, the cancer had eaten all the man's lower face off. That is not a very pretty picture, but that is exactly what Satan does to us. That is exactly the way he works. You have a little bit of conviction in your heart, you begin to feel a need to make things right with God, Satan says to you, I can save you a lot of embarrassment. I can save you a lot of time, why don't you just put a ten dollar bill in the offering plate and your conscience will feel a whole lot better. Why don't you go to church Sunday night and everybody will faint? Why don't you just show up for Wednesday night prayer meeting? Or why don't you go to your neighbor and help him strip tobacco? You will feel better about this thing in no time. You won't have to go to the altar. You won't have to confess any sin before people. Let me tell you how to substitute something else for it. That conviction begins to grow and you put a little salve on it to cover it up and first thing you know, your soul has been destroyed in hell forever. Brother, we need the great physician.

Finally, the worst one of all is when Pilate called for the basin of water and a towel. Symbolically, he wanted the basin and the towel placed on the balcony for the world to watch as he washed his hands of the whole mess. I am going to wash my hands, dry them and be free of this forever. If you want to crucify him, then crucify him because I find no fault in him. He washed his hands of the whole thing, yet he delivered Jesus Christ to be crucified. He thought he was being neutral. He thought he was saying, I don't have to make a decision. I can straddle the fence. I don't have to fall either way. There is no neutrality with Jesus Christ. If you have not accepted him, you have rejected him. You are not in the process of deciding, you have already decided. If he is not living in your heart today, then you have rejected him. You have rejected the Son of God. There is no neutrality. No man can escape the question. When Christ is presented to you, you can ask yourself these questions: Will I crucify him or will I crown him as Lord of my life? Will I love him or will I reject him? Will I serve him or will I turn my back on him? Behold the man.

Jesus Christ has been presented to you many times. He has been presented to you and you have painted a picture of him being born in a manger and you've looked at that. You have been presented a picture of Jesus hanging on a cross. You have seen him preach the Sermon on the Mount. You have seen him, in your mind, as he walks on the water, as he fed the 5,000. Today, I presented him to you standing before you to be executed and crucified. And I say to you, as Pilate said to that mob that day. Look at Him! Behold the Man!

What will you do with Jesus?

Chapter 16
Fatherhood
Ephesians 3:14-15

"For this cause I bow my knees unto the Father of our Lord Jesus Christ, of whom the whole family in heaven and earth is named".

Do you notice where the family originates and where the family gets all its principles and organization? The example is from the fatherhood of God. Just as God is the head of Christ and Christ is the head of the church, the family is likewise organized. The father is to be the head of the family, the wife being the heart of the family and the children in submission to mom and dad. But the whole fatherhood concept, the whole family concept, is aimed after the fatherhood of God. We need to concentrate on first of all building New Testament families and then we can build New Testament churches. We need to listen to what God has to say about fatherhood. Don't think about what we have come to accept as being normal. I don't appreciate the jokes about "the old man". I don't appreciate jokes about "the old lady". The family is a sacred unit. The family is the unit that God gave its name and organization. One of the worst things that could happen to our nation is for the family to be scattered or broken. The one thing we are suffering from now is the fatherhood of the family not taking the responsibility that God gave fathers. For this reason, other people have had to take on those responsibilities. You can accept what's normal and make jokes about "the old man" or you can have God's best.

What is God's best for fathers? God has put a tremendous responsibility upon the man who is the husband and the man who is the father. No one wants to fail as a husband or as a father. If you knew life in its true perspective, if you knew and understood your family as God sees it, and you don't make a success of that position, it doesn't make any difference what you do in life, you are a failure. If you are the President of the United States, the kind of some country, a multimillionaire – if you don't make a success of being a husband and the success of being a father, then you are a failure. I don't want to fail. God has had to show me some things in my own life. I don't speak to you as an expert as a father, because you know what an expert is – any man out of town with a briefcase. But the test for every ministry is in the home. I don't want to fail at that particular ministry. If I were to come to you and stand in this pulpit and try to preach to you about the family and my own family was in disarray, I would be a hypocrite. If it doesn't work in your home, then you are a failure. Some reason or another, I cannot sit and listen to preachers who are preaching when I know that their homes are out of order. How can someone tell me how to please God, when he himself has failed in the most important ministry that God has given to him? In my life, being a preacher is not my most important job. Preaching is far easier than being a husband and being a father and those are the most difficult jobs I have.

In both the Old and New Testaments, God has given to every man, two divinely appointed offices in the home. God appointed man to do two things. He appointed him, first of all, to be a prophet in his home and then be a priest of his home. A man is a prophet in his home when he relates to his family things of God. He is the priest of his home when he brings his family to God in prayer, when he intercedes for his wife and children. He is talking to God about his family. When he talks to his family about God, he is the prophet in the home by declaring the truth of God. God expects every one of us in the New Testament covenant to be both prophet and priest of our home. One of the reasons why the father has not accepted his spiritual responsibility as being the leader of the home is because wives will not give it to him, or he does not have interest enough in the things of God to assume the responsibility that God has given to him.

In Genesis 7:1 *"And the Lord said unto Noah, Come thou and all thy house into the ark; for thee have I seen righteous before me in this generation."* I want you to notice that it was on the basis of Noah's righteousness that his whole family was admitted into the ark. Can God say that of you? Can God look at you as a father in your house and say to you, "Come thou and all thou house into the ark for thee have I seen righteous before me in this generation"?

In Genesis 18:17-19 *"And the Lord said, shall I hide from Abraham that thing which I do; seeing that Abraham shall surely become a great and might nation, and all the nations of the earth shall be blessed in him? For I know him, that he will command his children and his household after him, and they shall keep the way of the Lord, to do justice and judgment; that the Lord may bring upon Abraham that which he hath spoken of him"*. We find why God chose Abraham to be the head of a new nation. We know why he chose Noah, now we understand why he chose Abraham. God said of Abraham, "I know Abraham". When God chose

Abraham, his choice was not arbitrary, his choice was not by default. God was looking for a man that could do one thing above all else. In order to begin a new nation, the head of the new nation had to meet this qualification and that is a man who command his children and his household in the ways of God. Not who could get the biggest army, not who had the most political charisma, not the one who could inflame men's heart to fight and to defend their country, but a man who could be a father. The man who could be a good husband was chosen to be the leader of this great nation. The one thing that was necessary for Abraham to inherit the promise of being a great nation was that he command his children and his household to keep the way of the Lord. Command is the right word. You have got to see to it that God's way is kept in your home. You are not a man, if you give that responsibility to someone else. That is the problem in the world today. Eighty percent of all the men are not keeping that responsibility; they are giving it to their wives or to someone else. Wives are doing a good job, but it is not divine order. It is second best. God's command is not to the wife, but to the husband. That means father, on Sunday morning, you get up and you command your children to get ready to go to church. Men may say, well, preacher, I don't want to influence my children, and I don't want to force religion on my children. Satan is influencing your children, Satan is out to get your children. Satan will command your children, and Satan will have them if you do not command them in the ways of God. We have heard it said that if folks make me go to church, when I get older I will not want to go. The majority of those made to go to church, when they were young, are still in church. Children will not hate being made to go to church if we live it at home.

No nation on the face of God's earth can become mighty and remain mighty when their family life is not in order. God destroys countries through families that are distraught. We will not have another generation of greatness in this country of ours, until the family is restored. Until spiritual leadership is given back to the one God gave it to. Until fathers pick up and take their own responsibility and not be under the foot and thumb of their wives, but be a man. Paul said be a man, be a man of faith, be a man of courage, be a man of love, but be a man and command your household in the ways of the Lord. There will not be any excuse when you stand before God for not having done it.

Notice in Deuteronomy 11:18-21 *"Therefore shall ye lay up these my words in your heart and in your soul, and bind them for a sign upon your hand, that they may be as frontlets between your eyes. And ye shall teach them your children, speaking of them when thou sittest in thine house, and when thou walkest by the way, when thou liest down, and when thou risest up. And thou shalt write them upon the door posts of thine house, and upon they gates: That your days may be multiplied, and the days of your children, in the land which the Lord sware unto your fathers to give them, as the days of heaven upon the earth".* Have you ever heard the expression 'heaven on earth'? That phrase comes from the word of God when he was speaking about families. A family is heaven on earth. Is your family a heaven on earth? Or is your family, like a number of families, just a filling station? Folks are just passing through filling up and going somewhere else. Is your home a heaven on earth? If it is not, whose fault is it? Primarily, it is the father's fault. God said to these fathers under the law to feel their homes with the word of God and it was not enough to hear the priest. The priest had problems of his own. The word was to be the theme of the home. Do you want to know why children are against religion? I will tell you why — not because they were made to go to church when they were little. I can tell you what makes children quit going to church. Because religion will always seem artificial to a child, if we act one way in church and another way at home. It will always be artificial to a child. Young people say to me, religion doesn't mean anything to my parents. It has been said that most Christians lead a cat and dog life. They purr at prayer meeting and growl at home. Religion, to a lot of people, is like an old suit hanging in the closet. You hang it up when you get home from church, and then next Sunday you put it on again. That kind of religion will be false or artificial and will be sickening to a child and he will grow up to hate it. Parents, today, act quite differently at home than they do at church. Did you hear about the farmer with his mules and wagon that stopped and picked up the preacher? He didn't get home till midnight. His wife said, "What in the world have you been doing?" The farmer said, "Well, I stopped and picked up the preacher and after I did that the mules didn't understand another word I said." Parents talk differently at home. It is bad for church members to go to church on Sunday morning, go out to the Country Club on Sunday evening, miss the ball and throw the club in the creek and cuss. That is bad. It is breeding a generation of rebels. Children do have split personalities today. Children have split personalities because they see their parents living differently at home than they do at church.

There is another word that has to do with fathers and that is faithfulness. Many people come to me about children that belong to someone else. They are a problem. Did you ever notice in the New Testament that every time the Lord dealt with a child or a question concerning a child, he dealt with it only on the basis of either one or both of the parents, because it was the parent's responsibility? He did not just deal with the child, except in the presence of either the mom or dad. Do you remember the story of the epileptic child? The man said to the Lord, "Lord, if you will, you can heal my child and make him well." Jesus said, "No, not if I can, because I can, not because I will, but if thou believes, I can heal thou child". God held that father responsible for the healing of this child by faith. God said, "No if you believe I can heal that child". The father had the responsibility for the religion, for the spiritual life of that child. We are required to exercise faith on behalf of our children.

In Psalms 112:1-2 *"Praise ye the Lord. Blessed is the man that feareth the Lord, that delighteth greatly in his commandments. His seed shall be might upon earth; the generation of the upright shall be blessed."* If you fear the Lord and delight in his commandments and word, your offspring will be blessed. That is a promise of God. That is a promise like, 'Train up a child in the way he should go and when he is old he will not depart from it'. Notice what God said, if you train up your child. It doesn't say if you take him to Sunday school every Sunday, when he gets old he will come back to it. But it says that if you train up a child, train him in the ways of God, he will not depart from it.

In Isaiah 49:24-25 *"Shall the prey be taken from the mighty, or the lawful captive delivered? But thus saith the Lord, Even the captives of the mighty shall be taken away, and the prey of the terrible shall be delivered: for I will contend with him that contendeth with thee, and I will save thy children."* If a man fears God, and lives for God and is keeping his responsibility, God said, I will fight with you to save your children. That is a promise of God. Not only is it a promise, but it is the privilege of every father. You can't give that privilege to the preacher or to Uncle John, or someone else. Every father on earth derives his authority from the fatherhood of God in heaven, God the Father, God the Son, and God the Holy Spirit. And every father on earth is called after the fatherhood in heaven. Its name, pattern, and sanctity is derived from the fatherhood of God. Every child born into this world starts out life picturing God in a very special way. If you were to ask a little child, what God looks like, he will tell you that God looks like my Dad. Every father is a child's picture of God. Is there any wonder why some children have a warped sense about God? If their picture of God is the same as their picture of their father, there is no wonder that children grow up hating God. The fatherhood on earth is a sacred thing. The reason people have a horrible picture of God is because they have a horrible picture of their father. It is kind of hard to have a good image of someone who is selfish or covetous.

I talked to a young person a couple of years ago, who was a preacher's kid. This child hated preaching, hated church, hated religion, hated God and hated everything. His father was a preacher and the reason he hated everything was because he had come to hate his Dad. The only thing important to Dad was being a preacher. His family didn't mean anything to him. The preacher saw his responsibilities to build a church and preach the gospel. In the meantime, his family was going to hell. God never intended for a father to do that. There is nothing as important to a man as his wife and his children. Not his job, not his future, nothing takes the place of a man's wife and his children. God will hold men responsible for them. That young person had grown up to hate God and his father was a preacher. His father never came home, he travelled all the time, was mean in his spirit. "Get your hair cut, lower your dress, slapped them away from the table, mean as the devil. This man was building a reputation for being a preacher and losing the only thing that means anything to a man in the process. There is no wonder God did not bless his ministry. If it don't work at home, brother, don't export your confusion.

The child's complains was, "My father has no time for me". There is another principle in the word of God and that is fellowship. One complaint that I hear of children is that my parents never listen to me, they talk to me, but they never listen to me. The complaint I hear from preachers whose children have grown up with this, I wish to God in heaven that I had spent more time in just simple non-religious activity with my family. Just more time in simple fellowship. Fellowship is eternal. Every young person I know, wants love, fellowship and understanding and if they don't find it at home, they will find it somewhere else.

Ephesians 6:4 *"And ye fathers, provoke not your children to wrath; but bring them up in the nurture and admonition of the Lord"*. Admonition means education of the Lord. I have got one complaint with the Lord and that is by the time you learn how to raise children, you are too old to have them. It is a learning process. I failed, but I didn't fail intentionally and I am learning, with God's help. I have learned to know that when folks suffer in the name of anything long enough, they grow to hate it. We need grace to be good fathers. We need all of the grace of God we can have to be good husbands. We need wisdom. James said, "if any man lack wisdom, let him ask of God." We don't have the wisdom, because we don't ask God. We don't intercede for our families, because we are not priests and prophets in our homes. Bring them up in the nurture and admonition of the Lord. That is education of the Lord and that is the father's job. That is the opposite of most homes today. Who reads the Bible? Who prays? Who gets the kids ready? Mother does it all. When the child gets older, he says he wants to be just like daddy. Daddy's have an idea that religion is an occupation for old ladies and little children. Education of the Lord, if they know it, will make a difference. It doesn't make any difference what the teachers tell them, if you tell them. If fathers raise their children in the education of the Lord, it will make a difference.

In the last chapter of the Old Testament in Malachi, we have the great problem of the end of time. Malachi 4:5-6 *"Behold, I will send you Elijah the prophet before the coming of the great and dreadful day of the Lord: And he shall turn the heart of the fathers to the children, and the heart of the children to their fathers, lest I come and smite the earth with a curse"*. Why is the earth cursed? Why are we having so many problems? Because of homes, fathers against children, children against fathers. The great end time problem is that the father and son are not reconciled. The greatest need we have today is reconciliation. If we don't get reconciled, we will undergo the great curse. But did you notice who is to turn first? The father is to turn to the child. The father takes his son outside and says, I have something to tell you, I have been a failure. Son, let me tell you this, I have not been the kind of father God wanted me to be to you and the kind of husband I ought to have been. Fathers need to apologize to their sons and daughters for the way they have lived and be reconciled to their children and both reconciled to God. If we don't do that, we will lose the battle. If we do that, we will win the battle. Let them make some silly rule about prayer in school. It won't make any difference, if our homes are right. The reason that is causing such havoc is because parents depended upon that little bit of Bible reading and prayer for their children's spiritual education. I don't really know why parents care one way of another. I don't know why church members care whether they have prayer or Bible reading in school or not, if they don't' have it at home. Why should they be concerned about it? Why sign petitions, why make speeches? It is just being hypocritical. If we organize the family and the father takes his rightful place and the wife gives it to him, we can bring this nation back to God.

Let's unite in prayer, today, a prayer of faith. We can stop some of the things that are happening in our school systems, in our government and in our land. Not by negative attitude, but by our positive one based upon the promises of God's word.

From The Shepherd To His Flock

Chapter 17
Why Did Jesus Die?
Romans 5: 8-16

Have you ever heard someone ask this question: Why did Jesus have to die? They are not questioning that he did. They are not questioning what happened when he died – that he brought us salvation. But the question is an interesting one and a fair one to ask. Why did Jesus have to die to do it? God is all powerful. God can do anything. God holds the whole world and our lives in his hand and there is nothing that God cannot do. And if God is all powerful and he can do all things, why did not God choose some other way to bring salvation than the suffering and the agony and the bleeding and the dying of his own Son? Why was it necessary for God to choose his Son to die for sin? Jesus left his home in glory. He came to this sinful world. He was persecuted, beaten, humiliated and rejected. And he finally died on the cruel cross. Why did not God save him from all of that? Perhaps Jesus was asking that question when he cried out on the cross, "My God, my God, why has thou forsaken me?" That question was never answered.

Salvation has always come at the result of suffering. There has never been any kind of salvation that did not involve suffering and sacrifice on the part of someone. You may say, I will not accept salvation on that basis. Let me ask you a question. You accept this country you live in, don't you? Brother, our forefathers bled and died to give you this country. There is suffering involved in this country that we have today. You accept food that you eat knowing all the time that some foul, fish or beast has given his life in sacrifice that you might have nourishment. Salvation always comes at the hand of suffering. The scripture teaches us that you and I have sinned. We accept that because God said it was so and you and I know it is so. If God hadn't told us, we would still know we are sinners. You and I have sinned and we have come short of the glory of God and every one of us, the Bible says, "all have sinned and come short of the glory of God. There is none righteous, no not one." Jeremiah 17:9 *"The heart is deceitful above all things, and desperately wicked: who can know it?"* All have sinned and come short of the glory of God. And the same word tells us that the wages of that sin is death. Therefore, someone has to suffer, someone has to die to give us life. Now the glorious truth is that there was someone who was willing to die to give us that life. That is a glorious truth.

When Jesus said to his disciples, "I must go up to Jerusalem and die", don't you know that was a heartbreaking thing for Jesus to say. When he said I have to leave you now and go up to Jerusalem and be placed in the hands of the priest and the rulers and die. I have got to die. Then as he hangs on the cross of Calvary, they laughed at him, they scorned him, they spit upon him and they said he saved others, but he cannot save himself. That is exactly right. He saved others, but himself he could not save. Do you realize that Jesus make a choice. Jesus could not save both himself and us. Therefore, he had to choose, who will I save myself or them? And the blessed truth is that he chose to die that he might save us. So in dying, Jesus carried out God's plan for eternity past. The scripture says, "That Jesus was a lamb of

God, slain from the foundation of the world". So when Jesus died, he carried out God's plan from eternity past.

Now, why did he die? He died to show us first of all, God's great love for us. God's overwhelming love for us. A man loves a woman, a woman loves her child, and a patriot loves his country. But nowhere in heaven nor in earth is there a love found like the love of God for you and me. No love has ever been found nor even can we comprehend that kind of love God has for us. What's the climax of that love affair that he had with us? Here it is: "For God so loved the world that He gave His only begotten Son, that whosoever believeth in Him, should not perish but have everlasting life". Jesus died, first of all, to show us how much God loved us. Jesus did not die for us because we loved him. The scripture says, "While we were yet sinners, Christ died for us". While we were yet his enemies, while we were yet rebelling and turning against him, then in the midst of sin, he died for us. What love! And Jesus died on the cross to show that love to us.

Did you ever try to give a definition to God's love? Have you ever heard a man, who has been blessed greatly, say God has been good to me. He has given me good health, He has given me a fine family, a good home and job. God has been good to me. Have you ever heard a drunkard, who has been converted give this testimony: I was bound hand and foot, I was a slave, my life was worthless and I was on my way to hell and God saved me? Took away the burden and gave me a new life. Have you ever heard someone say, my father or my husband, who was cruel and so rebellious and so angry all the time, God touched him and he was saved. You ought to see our home now, it is like a paradise. That is a little bit of God's love. And when we see Christ hanging on the cross, then we really see the love that he had for us and how much he really cared.

The second thing is, Jesus died to show us how much God hates sin. God knows sin. And God knows what sin does to people. God knows what sin did to Adam and Eve. He knew what he created man for and he knew what man could attain. He knew the blessings that were there for man and he saw sin ruin all that and he saw what sin did to Adam and Eve. He saw what sin did to Aken. He saw what sin did to David, Peter and he hates it. He hates it because he knows what it does to people.

God loved all those people, but he hated the sin that ruined them. In the last six months, I have looked into the casket of people who died quickly, who died in the very youth of their life and I have said to myself, "I hate death". As I looked into the casket of a young blonde haired blue eyed little girl that leukemia had stricken, I said, "I hate death". Because of what it did to someone I loved. God says the same thing about our sins. I love you with an everlasting love, but I hate sin because I know what sin can do and what it does do to people. When I look at the cross and I see Jesus dying, I see the heavens are dark, and the sun refuses to shine and the whole world is shaking and quaking. I ask the question, why is it so dark? God comes back and says, I want to show you how much I hate sin.

He died to satisfy a violated law. One of the things we have never accepted is that God has laws. God is not some old grandfatherly figure, some Santa Claus, that you finally get your way with, but God is God and God has laws. When those laws are broken, they are unchanging, they are unmerciful and many people break themselves on the laws of God. But when they are broken, someone must suffer to satisfy the broken law. Now who is it going to be? No one on earth will qualify to satisfy the broken law. We read in the Old Testament, that the animals who died to satisfy the law had to be without spot and blemish. They had to be perfect. And taking that same thing and coming into the New Testament, and even into our day, who is going to die for us to satisfy the broken law? There is not a man on earth that can do that for us. And in the host of heaven, there is no one who qualifies. The Son of God, the Messiah, God's only begotten Son is the only one who qualifies to die to satisfy the broken law. His blood is the only blood that will do. His blood is the only blood that is pure. He is the only sacrifice without spot or blemish. So he says, Father, I'll die to satisfy that broken, violated law. God, if he just pardoned us or overlooked our sins, wouldn't be fair, he wouldn't be just, he wouldn't be God. Someone must pay and there is only one who can and he did. He died to satisfy the violated law. He died to put us on a new way of life, a whole new system of living. Jesus did not come to patch up our old garments, but the scripture says, he came to give us a new garment, a robe of righteousness to cover our sin. In the Old Testament, the religious ceremonies involved ceremonies and creeds and the workings of man and the law. And when Jesus came he did not come to say, I have come to improve the law, I have come to amend the law, or I've come to add some things to the law. He said, I have come to fulfill the law and give you a whole new economy, a whole new way of living. And when Jesus brought that new life to the religious people of his day, their religion was not leading them to God and they hated his teachings. They hated him so they killed him because he was teaching a new way.

We have a lot of roads in the county that are in terrible shape. And the county is doing all it can do and that is going around and patching the potholes, so they can jump out tomorrow and you can tear up a spring tomorrow. What needs to be done and we can't afford it, but what needs to be done is not patching the roads, but we need new roads to be built. That is the way it is with God. We don't need to patch up our old garments, we need new garments. We don't need to patch up the old way, we need a new way and that is what Jesus came to do, give us a new way. When we get on the new way, we find it is the way that leads to heaven. People, today, who are trusting in their goodness and in their creeds and in their ceremonies, will miss heaven by a thousand miles. There is only one way and He died on Calvary.

Jesus died for you and me:

1. To show God's love for us.
2. To show His hatred for sin.
3. To satisfy a violated and broken law.
4. To give us a new way of life.
5. That repentance and remission of sin might be preached in His name.
6. To make atonement for us.
7. To reconcile us to God.
8. To conquer death and to conquer the grave
9. To save us from hell.

Jesus died that repentance and remission of sin might be preached in his name. Jesus said on one occasion that it is right that he die and that he be raised from the dead and that repentance and remission of sin be preached in his name among all nations. They tell me that teaching repentance is almost a lost art. In almost every pulpit, in days gone by, use to ring forth with the message of repentance. Preachers used to shout and preach the word of God, to those who were listening to them calling upon them to repent and turn back to God. I remember one particular man who used to preach in a church and he said he preached repentance, repentance, repentance and he said the amazing thing was that no matter what sin he preached on almost everyone in the congregation confessed it and repented of it. He just preached repentance and that seems to be a lost art in some churches. But Jesus died to give us the message of repentance and remission of sin. That is why he died, that's why he called me into the ministry and I cannot imagine anyone preaching any other message except that message that Christ died to give us. He died that repentance and remission of sin might be preached in his name to all nations.

I have prayed time and time again that I could preach in such a way that those who were listening to me would say the same thing that they said to Peter on the day of Pentecost, "Men and brethren, what must I do to be saved". Wouldn't it be a wonderful thing to so speak the word of God and to be so anointed by God that men would respond to the gospel message by asking the question, "What must I do brethren?" It would be a shame and a disgrace for any member of any church not to know how to be saved. It would be a shame upon the church, the minister, the deacons, upon anyone who had any leadership in the church. It would be a disgrace if any member of a church could not tell someone how to be saved. We preach the message of salvation. I have heard those who have been members of churches all their lives, who could not tell you how to be saved. That is a shame. The message of salvation ought to come from the pulpit so often that every member of the church can tell you how to be saved. That ought to be our message. Jesus said, I must die and be raised from the dead in order that the message of repentance and remission be preached in my name. No one can repent of my sin except me. I am the only one that can repent of my sin. I cannot repent for your sin and you cannot repent for mine. And to repent from sin means to turn away from it, to do an about face. To be done with sin. And no one can remit our sins or put them away, except the Lord Jesus Christ. I will tell you what a thorough job he does of putting away our sin. The scripture says that he would remove our sin as far from us as the east is from the west. As the country preacher said, "that is a fer piece". That he would put them into the deepest sea and no power, not even Satan with all his power can get to our sins, which are buried in the depths of the sea. We are the only ones that can repent our sins and he is the only one who can remit our sins and he does a thorough job of remitting them. He puts them away never to be remembered against us again.

He died to make atonement for us. Napoleon, when he was out to conquer the world, looked at a map which had a little red dot on it that represented England. Napoleon said if it wasn't' for that little red spot, I could conquer the world. The whole map that I hold in my hand could be mine, if it were not for that little red dot. If it were not for the red spot of Calvary's cross, Satan would and could conquer our souls. Jesus died to make atonement for our sins. All of the blood that was ever shed upon the Jewish altars, and it must have been millions and millions of animals that were slain upon altars in the Old Testament days. But all of that blood and all of that ceremony of the priest offering up the sacrifices never remitted one sin, never atoned one sin. They rolled the people's sin forward until the perfect ultimate sacrifice could be made for sin - period. When Jesus came and went to the cross, the blood of Jesus Christ went backward and forward. When he died on the cross and shed his blood, his blood went all the way back to the first sinners this side of the Garden of Eden and went all the way to the last soul on this side of eternity. His blood made atonement for our sin. Now, I don't mean that everyone in that period of time was saved. But atonement was made – a covering was made for our sins. And every person that ever believed on the Lord Jesus Christ and called out to him for remission of their sin – their sin was atoned because he made atonement when he died on the cross. Atonement means a covering for sin. This winter when you are lying in your bed and you begin to shiver because you are freezing or cold and there is a blanket hanging in the closet, but you don't bother to get up and get the blanket and you freeze to death, whose fault is it? You have no one to blame but yourself. And in the same sense, Jesus Christ shed his blood to cover our sins, but if we refuse to come under the blood and have it cover our sin, then we have no one to blame but ourselves. So he died to make atonement to mean that everyone who would believe could have their sin covered by the precious blood of the Lord Jesus Christ.

He died to reconcile us to God. 11 Corinthians 5:19 *"To wit, that God was in Christ reconciling the world unto himself, not imputing their trespasses unto them; and hath committed unto us the word of reconciliation."* God was in Christ, reconciling the world unto himself. That when Christ was here upon the face of the earth, that was God. God was using Christ, working through him to reconcile an alienated world unto himself. To reach out and reclaim man that had been lost through sin and bring them back together. What do we mean by reconciliation? There was a man who had a fight with his son and the fight reached such proportions that the son left home. There was alienation between him and his father. They would not speak and the son would not live in the same house, so he left home. In the years to come, the mother was stricken and was dying and the telegram was sent to the son to come home because his mother was on her death bed. When the son arrived at his home, his mother was lying in the bed, the father was on one side of the bed and the son was on the other side. She reached and took her son by the hand and took her husband by the hand and brought those two hands together across her dying body and in her death she reconciled the father and son together again. When Jesus Christ went to the cross, in his dying, he reached up and brought God down and he reached down and brought man up and over his dying form, he joined God and man together, reconciling the world unto himself. He died to make reconciliation.

He died to conquer death and to conquer the grave. Jesus was the only one to ever put any light into death. Before Jesus died, death was eternal blackness. Before Jesus died, those who lost loved ones, lost them without any hope. They were gone forever and they would never see them again. Death had no hope to offer for any future life. Death was just like you know someone today and they are gone tomorrow. But when Jesus came he gave light to death. He went into the tomb and he came back from the tomb. He said there is life on the other side. He came back to life and the scripture says that because he lives, we shall live also. We owe all of our faith and our hope for eternal life to Jesus Christ because he died to gain victory over the grave and to pass that victory on to us. There was no knowledge before Jesus died. Job said, "If a man die, shall he live again?" And as I said, Jesus went to the tomb and came back to answer

Job's questions and said there is life on the other side. He conquered death for us. D. L. Moody said one time and it would be a good slogan for you to adopt for yourself and me also. He said, "One of these days you are going to hear that I am dead. Don't you believe a word of it, because I will just be alive forevermore!" We owe the death of Jesus Christ for that kind of hope and assurance in our lives.

Finally, He died to save us from hell. Jesus knows about hell. He knows about sin and what it does to people and he hates it. Just as I hate death for what I have seen it do. Jesus knows about hell and he died to save us from hell. He knows that hell was prepared for the devil and his angels. He also knows, as he looks down, that the whole world is rushing toward that awful place. Though it was not prepared for man, though God has given every possible escape from hell, men are still rushing toward it and Jesus sees that. He died to save us from that terrible place. He desires to save us from hell. That is what he does for all of those who come to him.

Romans 8:1 *"There is therefore now no condemnation to them which are in Christ Jesus who walk not after the flesh, but after the Spirit"*. There used to be a lot of street preachers who would stand on the corner and preach. I suppose they would get laughed at and I know that in North Carolina, it is still a common sight to drive through town and see young men preaching. One particular street preacher was preaching about hell and as all street preachers do, every once in a while, they had a bunch of hecklers in the crowd. They began to laugh at him and throw comments at him. One particular heckler said, "You have been talking about hell, preacher, tell me where is it?" The preacher looked him in the face and said, "Hell is at the end of a Christ rejected life". Jesus came to save us from that but it is not enough to know that he died to save us from hell. We are not saved automatically. The scripture says that we must repent of our sins and we must come in faith. The scripture teaches us that he doesn't save us in sin, he saves us from sin. If we could ask a godly righteous mother, what to do about Jesus Christ, I am sure that mother would say, "You take and trust Jesus Christ as your Savior, as I did". If I could ask some converted sinner, what to do about Jesus Christ, he would say, "I was lost and under the penalty and wrath of God and on my way to hell, and I received him as my Savior and he lifted me up and put my feet on solid rock. He made life worth living." That man would say, I beseech you to do the same as I did with Jesus Christ, accept him as your personal Savior. If we were to ask the angels from heaven, what to do about Jesus Christ, they would say the smartest thing you could do would be to trust him as your Savior. And if we could, today, ask the redeemed host that John saw around the throne what to do with Jesus, they would say to us, "We came through the great tribulation and he washed us in his own blood and brought us home to heaven where he wiped away all our tears. If we were to ask the rich man in hell what to do with Jesus Christ, he would say, "Receive him as your personal Savior and don't come to this place of torment. Receive Christ as your Savior".

There was recently a fire in one of our northern cities. A theatre was on fire and a young teen-ager went into to those flames a number of times. He brought from that burning building, fifteen people who had lost themselves in the smoke. He was burned so badly himself that he died a few days later. That's a little bit of what Jesus Christ did for us. Jesus saw us in sin, he saw us going toward a literal hell, so he rushed to the cross and he snatched us like brands from the burning. It cost him his life to do it. He died to save us from hell. Can you reject a Savior like that? Can anyone reject a Savior like that? A Savior who died to show us love, to show us God's hatred for sin, to show us a new way of life, to make atonement, one who died that repentance and remission of sin be preached in His name, one who died to conquer death and the grave, and one who died to save us from hell. How can you reject a Savior as that?

The reason Jesus died was to take the love of God and bring it into the reach of man to take by his Holy Spirit and breathe upon our hearts the message of redemption and to save us from a tragic loss of life in this world and a loss of life throughout eternity. How can we reject that Savior?

Chapter 18
Casting Bread
Ecclesiastes 11:1

"Cast they bread upon the waters: for thou shalt find it after many days". I am sure that many of us have heard that phrase from time to time – cast your bread upon the water. Maybe we didn't know that it came from the scriptures. We may not know where it originated. I am sure that those of you who have studied Ancient History are quite familiar with the Nile River and the valleys surrounding the Nile River. In the years that it was so popular and fertile and all of life seemed to come and the waters would cover all of the rich farming land and the farmers would get in a boat and get in the flood waters and would throw their wheat, the seed out upon the water. The seed would sink to the bottom and then when the flood waters receded, it left a thick rich silt on top of those seed and then in the spring those seed would spring up and in a few months there would be a golden harvest.

Surely the writer of Ecclesiastes was thinking about that practice when he wrote this scripture. That would certainly seem to us today to be a very foolish practice. Why not wait until the flood waters went down and prepare the soil as we do here today and sow the seed and wait for the harvest. Why take the chance of what seems to be a wasted practice of throwing seed on the water and yet it was a very useful time to sow seed. They had good harvest and the seed were not wasted. There always came forth with a rich harvest from that practice. Things that we do today, in the spiritual rim, are much like that. We cast our bread upon the waters in what may seem to be a waste of time. I'm sure a few months ago, none of us would have ever realized that there would have been any success to a tape ministry, especially when my preaching was on the tape. In fact, I heard some snickering from several people when they suggested carrying a tape with my message on it for anybody to listen to. But that ministry has grown. There are several people in our town that listen to the tapes first thing Monday morning, they look for them to come. They are carried to the hospital. I have visited patients who play the tapes while I visit. We may ask ourselves, what good is that going to do? I don't know that it will ever do any, but it is casting bread upon the waters and we shall find it after many days. It will be a blessing. There are many things we do in the spiritual rim that may seem to be a waste to us, but God knows about and surely, if we are faithful to cast the bread upon the waters, God can take that and use it and perhaps it will return to us, perhaps in the salvation of souls, perhaps in the encouragement of someone who is discouraged, in helping someone to decide their goal in life, or perhaps just being a blessing to other people. But God takes that which we do for good and uses it to work out his purposes in all the earth.

The command is "Cast thy bread upon the waters". Cast thy bread – that signifies a willing, voluntarily casting forth of that which we have. Not being forced from us, not someone having to take it away from us, but we willingly cast our bread upon the waters. Galatians 6:10 *"As we have therefore opportunity, let us do good unto all men, especially unto them who are of the household of faith."* As we therefore have opportunity let us do good unto all men – not because it may profit us, not because we hope for a reward, but simply because the occasion has presented itself.

You would be surprised how God deals with other people through our opportunities to minister to them. We never know how what we say will affect someone. Never know whether we are going to accomplish anything or not. But God knows. There is several illustrations in the Bible of men and women who cast their bread upon the waters, in return expecting no reward. But they found it after many days. It came back to bless them. I think of one particular experience that has always been tender in my thinking and that was the widow of Zarephath, who had an only son and she lived in a time of great famine and her husband was not there and she was a very poor woman. Her son was with her and they were in dire circumstances. One day she got down to the very last portion of meal in the barrel and the last drop of oil and prepared to make one last cake for her and her son. We may refer to them as fritters, cornbread and water fried in a skillet or maybe mush. She intended to prepare one last meal and the prophet of God, Elijah, came by and said to her, "Fix me first something to eat, a little cake." Why should the widow fix him a cake? Why should she take the last bit of food that she had and share it with a stranger? And she said to the prophet of God, "I was about to prepare one last meal and then prepare to starve to death with my son. Elijah said, "Fix me first something to eat". And without knowing and without expecting reward, she fixed the prophet of God that last little bit of meal and oil that she had and that prophet of God sat down to eat it and the meal barrel never ran empty. Every time the widow went to the meal barrel and oil it was always full. God just kept replenishing that barrel. That widow cast her bread upon the water, not knowing that they would come back to her, but she found them after many days. It came back to bless her. So many of us, in fact all of us, have a selfish streak. Many times, because of our selfishness, we rob ourselves of a great blessing. Not being willing to cast our bread freely upon the waters that it might come back and bless us.

Another very tender story that is a prime example of giving without hope of reward and God taking it and using it and blessing it, is the story of David. David was anointed. David was predestined by God to become King of Israel and because God had withdrawn his spirit from Saul, Saul became filled with an evil spirit and began to seek David's life. Saul's son, Jonathan, realized that his father was in error and he became the closest friend David ever had. He warned David many times, when death was sure to come David's way. David escaped because of the friendship of Jonathan. Jonathan died later and David became King and Jonathan had a poor crippled boy and King David went and brought Jonathan's son into the palace and he lived with David while he was King and he cared for him the rest of his life. Jonathan helped David without any hope of reward, without expecting anything in return, yet it came back. He threw his bread upon the waters and he found it many days after. It came back to bless him a thousand times over, by his son being cared for by the King.

How can we as Christians, cast our bread upon the waters? One way we cast our bread upon the waters is through kind words. How many people have been blessed simply because of some kind word spoken in due season? How many times have there been people working in Christian work who have become so discouraged and despondent over not having any success in the ministry and almost ready to resign and someone would speak a kind word. Again that hope would renew in their hearts and they would go forth to burn themselves out for God, simply because someone spoke a kind word. You walk down the street of any town, a man meets you with a smile but behind that smile his heart is breaking. When we give him a kind word, we never know how much we bless him. Nothing hurts me worse than a harsh word spoken to me. I had rather someone curse me, I'd rather someone hit me. I had rather someone slap me than, in some haughty spirit, say some unkind word. We ought to radiate the sunshine of God. Every Christian ought to. You see, every Christian knows Jesus Christ, every Christian trusts God, every Christian is on his way to glory and the scripture says, freely have you received, freely give. If the Christian knows the Son of God, if he trusts God, if he is on his way to glory, he has received abundantly, then he ought to give freely. When we walk into a place of business, the sun ought to shine because we radiate the Spirit of the Lord Jesus Christ. How many of you have a friend that is lost? Maybe a few kind words might do much to win him to the Lord. Perhaps, if we quit rebuking people for not coming to church, perhaps if we would quit fussing at folks and simply say a kind word to them, it would win them to the Lord. At any rate, there are those who you have witnessed to for years and haven't seen them yet come to the Lord. But every time you have said a kind word, every time you have talked to them about the Lord, you have cast your bread upon the waters and ye shall find it after many days, is the promise of the scripture.

We cast our bread upon the water through preaching the gospel. In London, one morning, there was a young lad who went in to hear someone preach. That particular Sunday, the preacher wasn't there and some layman got up to preach. He took his text from the scripture about Moses lifting up the serpent in the wilderness and he said, "Look and live" and pointed his finger at that young man. That young man did – he walked out of that pew and came down the aisle and looked to the Lord Jesus Christ and he became the greatest preacher of modern times. He was Charles Haden Spurgeon. Sitting in a little church, lost among the parishioners and a layman was speaking, not a preacher. He heard that message and God took that bread that layman cast upon the waters and it came home to him.

A preacher changed his message one morning, changed his text for some strange reason. When he got into the pulpit, he just said God has laid upon my heart another text. He turned to it and began to preach. After the service, there was a man in that audience, who was at the point of taking his own life and God knew what he needed and God changed the mind of that preacher. He preached another text to save that man's life. All of us can make it possible for the gospel to be preached. Not all of us can preach, but all of us can give, all of us can send missionaries so that the gospel might be preached.

So, the command is to "Cast thy bread upon the waters" and then the compensation is "for thy shalt find it after many days". That means nothing good is ever lost. No good deed that you ever perform is lost. Nothing good that you stand for, nothing good that you speak, nothing good that you mean for your neighbor, nothing good is ever lost. Did you ever think about the fact that God is not a waster? God doesn't waste anything. Remember when Jesus fed the five thousand, he had them pick up the fragments, he wasted not even the fragments of feeding the multitude. God wastes nothing and everything good is never lost.

We sing about America and about that man who stood aboard that ship and wondered whether we had won that battle and wondered whether Old Glory would still be there in the morning. When we were fighting that battle, General Lafayette of France came to America and without any hope of reward, without any request for reward, he came and fought beside America. He fought with the colonists to win our independence. Not for reward, but for 141 years later, France is fighting for her life against the German hordes and America helps her win her freedom. A nation casts its bread upon the water and found it many days later. God's word has a lot to say about giving to the poor. Deuteronomy 15:10-11 *"Thou shalt surely give him, and thine heart shall not be grieved when thou givest unto him: because that for this thing the Lord thy God shall bless thee in all thy works, and in all that thou puttest thine hand unto. For the poor shall never cease out of the land: therefore, I command thee, saying, thou shalt open thine hand wide unto thy brother, to thy poor, and to thy needy, in thy land"*. Proverbs 19:17 *"He that hath pity upon the poor lendeth unto the Lord; and that which he hath given will he pay him again"*. Giving is a good investment. The scripture says that whenever we go out and help someone who is in need, we are not giving to him primarily, we are lending that money to God. How does God intend for the poor to be fed? Through you and me. How does God intend for the poor to be blessed, and to be housed, and to be fed? He intends for me and you to do it. God said don't walk up to someone and say well God bless you, be ye warmed and filled and walk off. God wants you to give to that man's need and God says when you give you are lending every dollar of it to me and I will repay. That is a good investment. Luke 6:38 says *"Give and it shall be given unto you; good measure, pressed down, and shaken together, and running over, shall men give into your bosom. For with the same measure that you mete withal it shall be measured to you again."* All of the Bible says give in the name of the Lord and he will multiply it again unto you.

Everyone knows the story of Helen Keller. How Mrs. Sullivan took Helen who was deaf and blind and through her years of toil, Helen became one of the world's greatest women. Then Mrs. Sullivan lost her eyesight and Mrs. Keller cared for her the rest of her life. She cast her bread upon the waters and she found it many days after.

On a lonely hill outside of Jerusalem, the Lord Jesus Christ is hanging on a cross, his life is ebbing away and all is lost it seems. His enemies have captured him, his enemies have killed him and once and for all it seems that they have quieted the voice of Jesus. But Jesus casts his life upon the waters and it came back to him in resurrection. And because he lives, you and I live also. This is an encouragement to every Christian worker. Preachers, sometimes, regardless of what some think, do spend hours in preparation and in prayer. He pours his heart out week after week. People come and listen and it seems that it has no effect. What does he do? Just keep preaching. God said my word shall not return unto me void. It shall accomplish whatsoever I have sent it to do. I know some Sunday school teachers who put up with a lot of wiggly little boys for many years. Years later that Sunday school teacher sits back and watches a young man live a good life for God, lives a life in Christian service, it has all been worthwhile. She casts her bread upon the waters and she found it – it came back to her again. We sometimes give to the poor wondering whether or not we wasted. Many times, people come to the parsonage or church and have asked for help. We wonder, if we give, if we have been taken advantage of or not. We wonder if that poor man or woman is worthy of what we give them. Some of us get taken, but when you give, not because you ever expected a reward, but you give because it is your nature to give, you give because Christ saved you and blessed you and you wanted to share with others. You are lending it to the Lord and he will repay.

One day a preacher got up to preach and he saw a woman and three little boys come in and sit at the back of the building. The woman was obviously a very poor woman for she was not dressed well, neither were the three boys. She got out of church that morning before the preacher could speak to her. The next Sunday she was back and moved up a little closer with her three boys. That week the preacher found out where they lived and he went to visit them. Come to find out the husband was a drunk, he had deserted his wife and three boys and they were in desperate need. They continued to come to church, they began to hear more and more of the gospel of the Lord Jesus Christ and one by one those four were saved. The mother first and then the boys were saved. They did not look like much of a prospect, especially on that first Sunday, but that preacher preached the gospel to them, said kind things to them, helped them and all four got saved. Later, one of the boys walked down the aisle and surrendered his life to full-time Christian service. He knew God wanted to use his life for something. He went to Bible College, seminary, and went on to pastor a rather successful church. The other boy during that time came and surrendered his life to the service of God and became a missionary. The last boy came and said he was willing to do whatever God wanted him to do. I don't feel that God is calling me to preach. I think we may have ruined some good full-time Christian workers by making preachers out of them. But he said, I don't feel God wants me to preach, but I'll do whatever he has for me to do. He became a Christian lawyer. That first Sunday, neither of them looked like they would amount to anything, but he preacher just ministered to them, he casts his bread upon the waters. The scripture says we are not to grow weary in well doing, that we get to the point that we say, well it is not doing any good, I'll just quit. Don't grow weary in well doing for we shall reap if we faint not. Cast thy bread upon the waters, talk to that lost friend about Jesus Christ, say that kind word to your neighbor, give to him who needs and ye shall find it again after many days.

Chapter 19
Jesus Spoke
Mark 1:21 – 22   John 7:45-46

Mark 1:21-22 *"And they went into Capernaum; and straightway on the Sabbath day he entered into the synagogue, and taught. And they were astonished at his doctrine: for he taught them as one that had authority, and not as the scribes"*. The first words that Jesus spoke in the beginning of his ministry, astonished the people. In John 7:45-46 a warrant has been issued for Jesus. The Pharisees had sent the officers to arrest him and we pick up with "Then came the officers to the chief priests and Pharisees; and they said unto them, Why have ye not brought him? The officers answered, Never man spake like this man".

I am sure all of us realize that you can tell what kind of person an individual is by listening to them talk. A man always lets other folks know what kind of person he or she is by the things he is interested in and the way he talks. If a man is crude and vulgar, then you know where his mind is, you know where his heart is. If a man wants to talk about his job all the time, you know what motivates him. If he talks about money, you know what motivates him. You can always tell what kind of person or what motivates a person by his conversation. Jesus said the same thing when he said, "out of the abundance of the heart man speaketh".

Did you ever think about the power there is in words? Did you ever think about the times this world has been held by the words of individuals that were speaking? Remember when Hitler whipped Germany into a frenzy of hate by his words. Perhaps you remember Franklin D. Roosevelt when he aroused the spirit of America with his fireside chats. People have power in words and there is power in what people say. For instance, go back a few years ago when men like Moody, Fenny, and Sunday preached. Billy Sunday used to preach in those big tents with sawdust floors and would hold people spellbound by his words and when he finished preaching, he would leap over the pulpit into the front aisle and would for a long time and with great energy, urge men and women to enter the kingdom of God. Thousands were entered into the kingdom of God through the words of Sunday, Graham, and others. People have said there is power in those convincing words.

Did you ever imagine what it would be like to hear Jesus himself speak? Not just to read what Jesus said, but to be able to hear him speak. And the words of Jesus have thundered down through the ages of time to convict and to convince, and to condemn and convert. There is power in what Jesus said and is saying today. The Jews, in the days of Jesus, were used to going to church just like we do each week. They would go to the synagogue and they would take their seat and listen to a scribe as he taught them from Old Testament scriptures. On one occasion, Jesus went to the pulpit and he began to teach Old Testament scriptures. Those who were sitting in the congregation said, that Jesus did not teach us like the scribes did last Lord's Day. But that man, Jesus, spake as one having authority of the word. Of course, we know that he was the authority of the word. He was the word made flesh to dwell among us. The other occasion, in the scriptures, Jesus was to be arrested. The soldiers came back empty handed. The Pharisees said, "Why didn't you arrest that man like you were ordered to do?" The soldiers replied, "Never man spake like that man". Can you imagine the officers being bound by duty and law to do what they had been instructed to do? They were to arrest a man and bring him back. They certainly had no love in their heart, and they were certainly men that were given into any kind of fear. But Jesus' words were so powerful and overwhelming and astonishing that they did not arrest him. They went back and said to the people who sent them, you have never heard a man speak like that man. No man ever spoke like Jesus.

The first words that Jesus spoke, that we have record of, almost the first words are found in Luke 2:49. Joseph, Mary and all the people of Nazareth and all the other little towns around had all gone to Jerusalem to attend the Feast of the Passover. It was about a three day celebration, much like people used to do in our country, when church associations were held. People would go in wagons, buggies and stay at some little Free Will Baptist Church somewhere. The Jews travelled to the Passover, they were there for three days, and they were eating together, fellowshipping, going through the rituals of worship and being instructed and taught in the word of God. This had gone on for three days and they began to make their journey back home. After they had been gone from Jerusalem quite a while, I can imagine Joseph saying to Mary, "Have you seen Jesus lately?" "No, but I am sure he is with Jacob's family". So they began to search and they could not find Jesus anywhere. They suddenly realized that he was not with the company. Immediately they went, very sorrowfully in their heart, looking for Jesus all the way back to Jerusalem and then through the streets of Jerusalem. When they found this twelve year old boy, he was at the temple discussing the things of God with the teachers. When Mary and Joseph entered into the temple, they scolded Jesus, just as you would scold your 12 year old son or daughter. In verse 48, they asked him, "why hast thou thus dealt with us?" They had sought after him sorrowing. Jesus said to Joseph and Mary, "wist ye not that I must be about my Father's business?" Those were his first words.

Now that was the spirit that went with Jesus from the time he was 12 until the time he went to Calvary. He had to be about his Father's business. He said, I must work while it is day, for the night cometh when no man can work. Jesus continued to do the work of the Father, he continued to be about the Father's business from the time they lost him, through his ministry with the miracles, through his ministry with the parables, through his ministry of healing and raising the dead. All the way to Calvary, Jesus was about his Father's business until he could say from the cross, "It is finished". From the time he came from glory until he hung upon that tree, he was about his Father's business.

Today, the business of our Lord is still the biggest business in the world. It is the biggest business that men and women can be engaged in. You and I, as children of God, have the Father's business to attend to. It is not confined to the preachers, deacons, or Sunday school teachers. It is the major concern of every born again child of God to be about the Father's business. You hear a lot of talk today about the new evangelism. The new evangelism, but it is not at all redemptive, it is all social. There is nothing redemptive in the new evangelism. Preachers say today, churches need to be involved in the pressing human problems. We need to get involved in such things as world hunger, prison reform, the distribution of decision making powers. The big word is to get involved. Preachers are saying, let's get into the picket line and let's demonstrate and get involved in the pressing needs of the world. But not one word do you hear coming from the new evangelism about souls being lost and on their way to hell. Not one word do you hear about let's go out and take the message of the gospel of Jesus Christ to those who are lost and dying without hope. There is no word of salvation in there.

There is another word I hear among churches and that is the word, dialogue. They talk about new evangelism which is discussing prison reform with a bunch of kooks. I still agree with Maddox – the only way to have a better prison is to have a better class of prisoners. I think that is what we need to work on getting better prisoners. And while they are discussing that they are having dialogue. And what that means is let's do away with the word of God, let's close the Bible and lay it aside and let's talk in purely human terms about things that separate us. Let's talk about our differences, forget the word of God, forget what the Bible teaches and you and I sit down together and discuss humanistically our differences. Let's have dialogue. And while folks are having dialogue, the world is going to hell. No one is being saved by involvement, no one is being saved by dialogue, no one is being saved by the new evangelism and it is still our primary task to be about the Father's business. Not with eloquence on the part of the preacher, not with money, not with intelligence, not with our plans and our programs, but to simply preach the gospel of the Lord Jesus Christ in the power of the Holy Spirit.

Folks wonder why Free Will Baptist don't get involved with the National Council of Churches. You know all the churches have gone together to form one big governing body. Let me tell you something about the National Council of Churches, they met together not long ago for a conference. After their conference, sent out a report of those things which were covered at the conference. They discussed race relationships, they discussed getting all the churches together, they discussed artificial insemination, they talked about giving the homosexual his rightful place in society, they talked about abortion, and not one thing was talked about, during the conference, about doing the Father's business. Not one word about lost souls, evangelism, or revivals. They talked about birth control, war and peace, but nothing about the new birth. Which without, man has no hope. Jesus said, "I must be about my Father's business". That is what business you and I ought to be about also.

The second time Jesus spoke with great authority was when he said, "Suffer it to be so, now, for thus it becometh us to fulfill all righteousness". The occasion was John the Baptist preaching near the river Jordan and was baptizing the converts. John the Baptist was the only country preacher that did not have to go to town to draw a crowd. Great crowds of people came to hear him. Jesus went to hear John preach, and after John had preached, Jesus stepped down to the edge of the water and told John that he wanted him to baptize him. John said, "no, I ought to be baptized of you". But Jesus said, "Suffer it to be so now, for thus it becometh us to fulfil all righteousness". And Jesus went down into the river and there he was baptized by John. When he came up, dripping wet, a dove came down as a symbol of the Holy Ghost and lit on Jesus and the voice of heaven said, "This is my beloved Son, in whom I am well pleased". That ought to be the first desire of every convert, to follow the Lord in baptism. You may never preach a sermon, but in baptism you preach two sermons. In baptism you preach the death, burial, and resurrection of the Lord Jesus Christ which is the gospel that saves you. Not only do you preach a sermon about the death, burial and resurrection of our Lord, but you also preach a message of the coming again of our Lord Jesus Christ.

The third time Jesus spoke was in Mark 1:15 when He said, *"The time is fulfilled, and the kingdom of God is at hand: repent ye, and believe the gospel."* After Jesus was baptized, he went into Galilee and preached this message. He preached, "Repent for the kingdom of God is at hand". That was his message.

Ask yourself this question, how can I get through to God? Simply by coming to Jesus. Jesus said, "No man cometh to the Father, except by me". And he is waiting for all of us to repent and come to him in faith and accept him as our Savior. He lives for that purpose. Some folks have this idea that God is some kind of distant God. Some think he is an influence or some force, but you know God is nearer than hands or feet. God is nearer than the next breath you breathe. God is the God who is there. Those who want to find him, must seek for him with their whole heart. Men seek for God in all kinds of ways. Men seek to find God through some kind of ceremony, through some kind of ritual, through some kind of work. Men are always looking for ways to get through to God. But in the Old Testament, all men were told to repent to get to God. In the New Testament, John, Jesus, Paul, Peter, and others preached repentance. Repentance is not just being sorry for sin, not just turning away, though it is all those things. Repentance is a difficult doctrine that has to do with the whole change in the human heart.

I like the story about the little boy who went to the father and said, "I want to confess". The father said, "What do you want to confess?" He said, "I stole a load of hay last night". The father said, "How much did you steal?" The little boy said, "I am not sure, but I can get the rest tomorrow". Repentance is turning away from sin. Repentance is making up your mind that you will never again sin as long as you live. You will sin, but you make up your mind you are not. Repentance is not being sorry that you got caught. Repentance is not guilt for doing things that are wrong. Repentance is like a soldier, marching in order and the sergeant hollers, "halt". He stops dead in his tracks. The sergeant yells, "about face", the soldier turns around. The sergeant say, "forward march" and the soldier is going in the other direction. That is repentance – a man is going away from God, going to hell, the Holy Spirit says, "Halt". The Holy Spirit of God convicts us and stops us dead in our tracks, we turn 360 degrees and walk toward God away from hell. That is repentance. Jesus said, "Repent and believe in the gospel".

Then finally, these three words of Jesus spoke in John 1:38 *"What seek ye?"* Those disciples, who were following John, were there when John pointed to Jesus and said, "Behold the Lamb of God". Those disciples that had been following John began following Jesus Christ. And as they followed along after him, Jesus turned to them and said, "What seek ye?" They replied, "Master, where dwellest thou?" He told them where he was staying and they went with him and stayed with him in that home having him teach them the things of God. John the Baptist recognized that he had a great following. He had a lot of disciples. He knew he could not point to himself, so he pointed his listeners to Jesus Christ and said, "Behold the Lamb of God which taketh away the sins of the world". When the disciples turned to Jesus, he asked them, "What are you seeking?" Jesus said to them, "Come and see" and they went with him and they heard him and they followed him. You say that is not too striking an event in the word of God. One of those men followed after Jesus and said, "where doest thy dwell?" was a man named Andrew. After Andrew heard Jesus speak that day, he went and found his brother Peter and told him that they had found the Messiah. Andrew brought Peter to Jesus and that set off a chain of soul winning that climaxed on the Day of Pentecost, when Peter now was preaching and three thousand souls were saved.

What seek ye? What do you want out of life? What is that thing that motivates you? Have you stopped lately and just thought about your home, or your job? Have you asked yourself the question, where am I going? What am I doing? What am I accomplishing? Where do I want to go? Have you thought about that? What are you seeking in life? Do you just live for pleasure? The scripture talks about the woman who lived for pleasure. It says she is dead while she lives. Perhaps you seek after profit. Perhaps your one goal in life is to make money. Make all you can and can all you make. What do you seek after? Do you seek some kind of power? Those things that you are seeking after, are you really happy with? Can you say, I have found that which satisfies my heart? God so designed us to never be happy and satisfied until we are home with God. God made that a part of our soul that was made for God and God alone. You can cram all you want to into that spot but only God can fill it. What seek ye?

Jesus Christ is the answer to all our needs. You cannot find that which satisfies in science, profit, honor, pleasure, but only in Jesus Christ. If you seek peace of mind, Jesus Christ is waiting to fill that spot in your heart that is empty. That place in your heart needs to be filled and only God can fill. There is a song that talks about things people seek after: joy, peace, happiness, and then it says all of these things are all in the name of Jesus. So in the name of Jesus, I present Jesus, the need of your heart that which will make you whole, complete. I do not offer that which will give you a rose garden, something where there will not be trials or tribulations, but I offer that which can give you peace in tribulation. It will give you joy in the midst of sorrow and it will give you life in the midst of death. What see ye?

Chapter 20
Four Aspects of God's Glory
Psalms 51

It seems that God is getting his people ready for something. I don't know what it is. Maybe God is about to bring judgment down upon the church. Maybe God is about to bring a great revival. Maybe God is going to rapture the church and start the years of tribulation. I think God is getting his people ready for something. You and I, as God's people, are just in as bad a fix as the Methodist or anybody else. God needs to deal with us. God's spirit needs to come into this congregation and God's people need to respond to the Holy Spirit and to the teaching of God's word.

David in Psalms 51 had just listened to the man of God point his finger in his face and said, David, thou art the man. David you are the man that committed sin. You are the man that had everything a man could desire, because of lust in your heart, you had a man murdered and took his wife. And God is dealing with you David. God is not pleased. God is holding back his wrath, but God is going to judge you David. When the man of God left David, the Holy Spirit began to deal with David's life and heart.

In Psalms 51 there is not a better picture anywhere than the dispensation of the age of the Holy Spirit and the dispensation of grace. David is a man so heavy under the conviction of the Holy Spirit of God that he cries out more than one time. He feels the presence of God is so real and strong that he is trembling beneath the power of God. He cries out, *"Have mercy upon me, O God, according unto the multitude of thy tender mercies blot out my transgressions. Wash me thoroughly from mine iniquity, and cleanse me from my sin. For I acknowledge my transgressions; and my sin is ever before me. Against thee, and thee only, have I sinned, and done this evil in thy sight, that thou mightiest be justified when thou speakest, and be clear when thou judgest. Behold I was shapen in iniquity; and in sin did my mother conceive me. Behold, thou desirest truth in the inward parts and in the hidden part thou shalt make me to know wisdom. Purge me with hyssop, and I shall be clean: wash me, and I shall be whiter than snow. Make me to hear joy and gladness; that the bones which thou hast broken may rejoice. Hide thy face from my sins, and boot out all mine iniquities. Create in me a clean heart, O God; and renew a right spirit in me. Cast me not away from thy presence; and take not thy Holy Spirit from me. Restore unto me the joy of thy salvation; and uphold me with thy free spirit. Then will I teach transgressors thy ways; and sinners shall be converted unto thee. Deliver me from blood guiltiness, O God, thou God of my salvation: and my tongue shall sing aloud of thy righteousness. O Lord open thou my lips; and my mouth shall shew forth thy praise. For thou desirest not sacrifice; else would I give it: thou delightest not in burnt offering. The sacrifices of God are a broken spirit: a broken and a contrite heart, O God, thou wilt not despise. Do good in thy good pleasure unto Zion: build thou the walls of Jerusalem. Then shalt thou be pleased with the sacrifices of righteousness, with burnt offering and whole burnt offering: then shall they offer bullocks upon thine altar."*

David is a man in whom the spirit was moving. He was a man in whom the spirit was moving. He was a man whom the Holy Spirit of God was working, was alive and chastening him. The Bible says David was a man after God's own heart. God had anointed David personally as King over all of Israel. This Psalm, this testimony, is the making of the man David. What took place inside Psalm 51 was what made David a man.

I want us to look, first of all, that David has cried out in verse 1-6 for forgiveness of sin. I want you to notice the four kinds of sin. Verse 1 "Blot out my transgressions". What does it mean to transgress? It means to go beyond known limits. You know what God's standard is. You knew you could not go any further, but you went further anyway. That is a transgression of God's law. In verse 2 we find iniquity. What is iniquity? Iniquity is lawlessness and having a lawlessness spirit. That means you are not controlled by the Almighty God. You go your own way, you do your own thing. You make your own decisions. You have a lawless spirit and you listen not to the Almighty God. Also in verse 2, he mentions the word sin. To sin means to omit. To fail to do what you know you ought to do. The Bible says, "All have sinned and come short of the glory of God". In verse 4, he says against thee and thee only have I sinned. Sin against God is guile and deception. And he was guilty of all four. Since he was guilty of all four of these, he needed to be dealt with because he had done it all and he tried to hide it. He labored long and hard to cover up his sin with Bathsheba. He tried murder. He tried everything. He was guilty of all the commandments of God that said, 'thou shalt not'. And he tried to cover it all up and he needed to be dealt with.

In verse 5, in the school of the Spirit, God gave David a new revelation of sin. He let David see what sin really was. And this revelation to David, this thing that David saw, was so powerful to him that he cries out, "Behold, I was shapen in iniquity; and in sin my mother did conceive me." David begins to see, as the Spirit works on him, that sin was not what he had done, but he was a sinner because of what he was. He was a sinner, born in sin. He received a sinful nature and God opened up his eyes and let him see. And suddenly he sees sin like he never saw it before. Sin is what we are. There are some folks, today, who think they are alright because they have not committed murder or adultery, as David did. Sin is what we are. David saw sin under the search light of God. Not in his own wisdom or his own eyes, but he saw sin as God saw it. It almost floored David. He cries out, "Behold", three times.

Then in verse 6, he says, "Behold thou desirest truth". Where does God desirest truth? In the inward part. Where does God want or desire us to be clean? In the inside. We need cleansing on the inward part. And David says, Behold thou desirest truth in the inward part; and in the hidden part...". The hidden part is the part which no one can see. That part of you, your husband or wife cannot see and your children cannot see. That part that is you and you alone. That is where God wants cleansing. That is where God wants us to be truthful. What we are has to be true before what we do can be true. And that is where God works, on the inward part of the heart. God's people need a heart cleansing.

When God begins to open our hearts, when God begins to give us, as he did David, a revelation of sin and he goes down in our soul, He does not come unto us that he might condemn us, but that he might help us. That he might cleanse us. He goes down into that soul of ours to bring healing to the inward part. The light of God's word exposes sin for what it really is.

Jesus just stepped into the synagogue when he was in his ministry, he just walked into the church and the demons began to cry out in the presence of God. When men stood before Jesus Christ and before the Glory of God, they fell as dead men. Isaac, Ezekiel, John, no matter how holy they were or who they were, when they stood in God's presence they fell down as a dead man. You cannot sit under the teaching of God's word, and you cannot sit under the moving of the Holy Spirit and not see sin for what it really is. God opens your eyes and begins to show you what's in your heart. If you ever get a good revelation of what sin is, you too will cry out, as David did, "Behold, I see it Lord". I see sin where it really is. I see sin in my heart. You don't want me to reform, you don't want me to quit doing some things, you want to come into my heart and change me.

Behold if any man be in Christ, he is a new creature. He is not a reformed individual. He is not someone who has turned over a new leaf. He is a new creation. God creates a new heart in that man. I believe it is time for God to clean up the fold. I believe that is what God is trying to do to us, the household of God. God is trying to clean up the fold. I believe we ought to have that clean testimony that they had in the Old Testament when the temple of God became so polluted that God withdrew his presence from it. There was no singing in the house of God. There was no preaching, no reading of the Bible, no testimony, because the Spirit of God had departed from the temple. The Bible says, the priest and the ministers went into the house of God and there they took forth the corruption and the pollution from the house of God and the song of the Lord began again. Many of us today have our lips sealed because of sin. And the reason there is not that joyful singing of praises to God is for the same reason, our lips have been sealed by sin. We need to put it away. We need to clean up God's house. Clean up the heart of the Christian so praises of God can begin again. We've lost that. We've lost it.

I want you to see something that David saw and began to see. He began to weep and he began to cry because he saw sin in the inward part. He saw sin in his heart. Every one of you today or let me say, the most of you today, have your own little closet. You have in your heart and in your soul, your own private little closet that is under padlock and you yourself don't even open it. And we sing, "Come into my heart, Lord Jesus", and Jesus begins to come into your heart and we say, don't touch that part. That's my own secret little closet, God you can have all my heart, but God don't touch this. And Jesus begins to love you and he begins to make himself known to you and the Holy Spirit begins to speak to your heart and you come under the hand of God because God is going to someday reach to that private little closet of yours and he is going to snatch the padlock off of it and you are going to open the door of that dark cesspool of sin. Have you ever picked up a plank out in the yard that has been laying for a while? You pick it up and the bugs go running. They have been in darkness and they don't like the light and they scatter. One day God is going to get a hold of that closet in your heart and he is going to open the door and the rats and serpents are going to run. God knows where your little closet is. He knows what is in it. That is what God is after in God's people today – that private closet.

I believe that God took David and literally by the shirt tail, he dangled David over the pit of hell. I believe David could smell the smoke and feel the flame. God took him and literally shook him over the pit of hell and let him see what his sin was because David was a better man after the fall than he was before. I believe God will take you and I and he will dangle us over the pit of hell to make a man of God out of us, or a woman of God out of us.

There were three cries. He cries out, Behold, Behold. Why did he cry out like he did? In verse 1-6, he confessed his sin and he has been forgiven. Now why doesn't David stop there? Why, after confession of sin and having forgiveness of sin, why doesn't David just stop and rest. David sees something. David sees something that is more important to him than anything on the face of this earth and he cries out because he doesn't want to lose it. Now he has been forgiven and confessed his sin, now he cries out for God to remove the pollution that sin left there in his heart. There are two aspects of sin, you know. There is the guilt of sin and then there is that polluted nature of sin. David got a glimpse of something and cried out in verse 7, "Purge me with hyssop." Hyssop means bitterness. David is literally saying to God, God I don't care what you have to do. Do anything you have to do, but God take that pollution from me. He was forgiven, but he wanted something more. He says, "Wash me and I shall be whiter than snow". Now he is after something. Verse 8 says, "Make me hear joy and gladness..." Those are precious words. Notice David said, "Lord make me". Remember the prodigal son? What was it that made him a prodigal? He said to his father, father, "give me" and he became a prodigal. But not many days hence he came back to his father and said, "Father, make me" and he became a son.

Our testimony among God's people is Lord, give me. Lord, give me, pray for me, visit me, do for me. And we have prodigal Christians. But then they come back to God and say, God make me to hear and I want you to notice the next three words, "make me to hear joy and gladness and rejoicing". David saw something and he wanted it and he wanted it all. He wanted the anointing of God. He wanted to be saturated by the Holy Spirit of God. And he called upon the creator of the universe and said in verse 10, "Create in me a new heart". Take this old heart I have and create a new one, Lord. Now I want you to notice in the next two verses that which you and I have lost. The church of God has lost and David was in danger of losing and it caused him to cry out. You and I ought to be on our faces, as did David, lest we too lose what he was afraid he was going to lose. Notice the four aspects of God's glory here. He said, "Cast me not away from thou presence". God's presence. Secondly, don't take thy Holy Spirit from me. Restore the joy of thy salvation and then God give me a free spirit.

David is not afraid of losing his soul, is he? He is not afraid that God is going to cast him into hell. But he is afraid that the glory of God is going to depart from him. Most Christians think the only thing to Christianity is being saved. That is the height of success, when you get saved. Brother that is the minimum guarantee of God. You can have the minimum of God and still live. But David didn't want to live that way. He wanted the glory of God's presence. He wanted the anointing of God. He wanted the joy and the free spirit. That is what is driving this man. And the reason it is driving him so, is because he witnessed King Saul walking under the anointing, walking under the presence, the joy and the free spirit of God. He watched King Saul as God withdrew from him and David saw the difference. He saw Saul that had lost the anointing of God. David is saying here, don't let me do what Saul did. God do whatever you have to do, but don't let me injure the Holy Spirit and have it withdrawn from my life. I want the joy of God, the presence of God and the anointing of God.

That is what we have lost in our Christianity. That is what you and I, as Free Will Baptists, have lost in our relationship to God. The awareness of God's presence. The anointing of God's Holy Spirit, the joy of salvation and the free spirit that God gives to those who know his Son. We've lost that. You don't have to say, preacher, no we haven't, because I know we have lost it. All you have to do is come to church on any given Sunday morning or Sunday night and look for the joy. Look for the anointing. Look for the presence of God. It is not there, brethren, he is not there. We are saved, but that's all we are. We are just barely that. And we are in danger of losing what David saw Saul lose and he cried to God, God don't let me do anything and get to the place that causes you to do to me what you did to Saul. "Cast me not away from thy presence." Don't take your spirit from me. Give me the joy of salvation and God uphold me with a free spirit.

Notice he says, "Cast me not away from thy presence". There are two kinds of presence. There is that doctrine which Free Will Baptist believe – the omnipresence of God. God is everywhere present. Where two or three are gathered together in my name, there I am in the midst of them. We believe that God is everywhere at all times and circumstances. I can say to you today, Jesus is here. I would be speaking correctly. You can say, Amen that's good doctrine, brother. There is something better than that. There is something else called the manifest presence of

God. I can say God is here and you can say yes that's right, but you don't feel him, you don't see him, you don't hear him. You just know in your mind that he is here. But if I say Jesus is here and you feel him in your heart, you can saw Praise the Lord, I know he is here, I feel him in my heart. There is a difference in the omnipresence of God and that is what some folks have and only have. David didn't want that, he wanted the manifest presence of God. He wanted to hear God, he wanted to feel God, he wanted to sense him that he was there all the time.

Some people just live in the omnipresence of God, but Praise God there are those too, who live in the manifestation of God. God comes and you can feel him, hear him and touch him. Have you ever felt God? I know the Christian need never pray what David prayed, when he said don't take your Holy Spirit from me. I know Jesus said I will never leave thee or forsake you. But brother, God will withdraw from you and all you have left is the bare minimum. All you have left is dry bones that David cries out about. You may exist, but you are not living. You have walked away from God until that holy dove of God lifts off of your life and you walk in the omnipresence of God.

Have you ever wondered why, when Jesus was baptized, that the Holy Spirit came in the form of a dove? When you and I are baptized, the Bible says, the Holy Spirit comes to the believers as fire. When Jesus was baptized there was no guile in him. There was no sin in him and the Holy Spirit came as a lovely dove and rested upon him. But you and I have to be purged from sin. The Holy Spirit came to us as fire. David's cry is to let me not grieve the Holy Spirit. Don't let the Holy Spirit lift up off my life because I want the manifest presence of God and I cannot exist without it.

Then he says secondly, take not thy Holy Spirit from me. I think he was talking about the anointing. The most valuable thing in all the world is the anointing of God. People call it different things. Colored preachers used to call it the unction of God. He was talking about the anointing of God. He is talking about that which comes to you when you stand here behind this pulpit and you come sometimes with it and sometimes without it. And you tell people how valuable it is and you can get up to preach and you don't have it and you have to warm something up. The Nazarenes call it being sanctified. The Quakers call it overcoming love. The Assembly of God call it the baptism of the Holy Ghost. Whatever you call it, we ain't got it and we need it. That manifest anointing presence of God.

David said if I had the anointing of God, I would have three things: joy, power and rejoicing. And I would have the testimony to tell others. Joy, restore unto me the joy. I love that word. I love the word joy. It is something you look for on the face of a Christian. It is the mark of a mature Christian. The joy of the Holy Ghost is that unspeakable, flowing over, bubbling up, not fun, but joy. Have you ever been to a church and they have a welcoming committee and they stand at the back door and welcome you to their church and they are putting on? They sort of give you a cat grin from ear to ear. How are you? Good to see you. Welcome to the house of the Lord. I'm talking about joy that is written all over the place.

What's wrong? The problem is that you and I, as intelligent people, logical people, God loving, God fearing people wanting to serve God, you and I have squeezed all the joy out. Just the pure old simple joy, we have squeezed it out of our religion. I don't even know if that is a good word or not, but that's what we have done. We go out visiting people and sit here on Sunday morning with a long face. And if you were to witness to someone and say do you want to be a Christian?, they would say will it do for me what it did for you? Yes. Well thank you I don't want it.

David knew the joy. David had a marvelous way of worshipping God. He picked up the harp and when the manifestation of the Lord would come, he would start singing, pluck the harp and even dance before the Lord. No wonder he is repenting, who would want to miss all of that? He would play that thing, sing and jump all over the place and praise God. I don't want to lose that either. I don't want to lose the anointing of God. I don't want to lose the presence of God and the joy of God. And bless your heart, I refuse to let any man or any devil take away my joy.

Then he says, "Uphold me with thy free spirit". You can always tell a religious man, he is always hung up on something. When he sings, "Bless be the tie that binds", he is talking about a red tie. It just binds him up. Always afraid he is going to lose his salvation or afraid he is going to backslide. But the child of God has a free spirit. I'll talk more about the free spirit tonight.

Let me close by saying there are four aspects of God's glory. There is the manifestation of God's presence, the anointing of the Holy Spirit, the joy of salvation and there is God's free spirit. And David didn't want to lose them. He said, God don't let me do anything to grieve the Holy Spirit of God. He said, God, if you will do that my testimony will be so real that sinners will be converted unto thee. If all of us had what David was crying out for, our church couldn't hold those who are coming to know Christ as their personal

Savior. If all of us would get our hearts right with God, then sinners would be converted. If you would confess that sin that is in your life and be willing to do business with God, then sinners would be converted. Why? Because our testimony is empty. There is no joy in our testimony. Our lips are sealed. Why? In verse 15 he says, O Lord, open thou my lips; and my mouth shall shew forth thy praise." His mouth had been shut because of sin and the people of God today have mouths that are shut for the same reason. There is sin in their lives. There is no testimony. Our inward sin has shut out the joy. But David's testimony can be yours today. Child of God, if you will fall on your face before God, as David did, and say God there is sin in my life, I know that it is there, but I come to you to confess it today, before you withdraw from me that manifest presence of God. Come and say, restore in me the joy of salvation. That my lips might rejoice and be a happy Christian Are you happy in the Lord today? Do you have the joy of the Holy Spirit in your life? Are you the man of God you ought to be? Are you the woman of God you ought to be? Or has the Holy Spirit shown you that sin, that secret corner in your life that he wants to minister to today? Come to him today.

Chapter 21
Psalm 51
Message continued from Chapter 20

I want us to read a few verses in Psalms 51. This is the Psalm David wrote after the prophet of God, Nathan, had preached to him and brought the message of God to David, after David had committed adultery. David had tried to cover up his sin with murder. This is the Psalm that came out of David's heart as the spirit of God began to move upon him. David is very much convicted. The conviction was so strong on David's life that he said, I seem to just dry up on the inside and my bones are old. Day and night, the hand of God was heavy upon me, David says. This Psalm is a Psalm of repentance. It is the testimony of David as God worked upon him.

Psalm 51: 1-19 reads, *"Have mercy upon me, O God, according to thy lovingkindness: according unto the multitude of thy tender mercies blot out my transgressions. Wash me thoroughly from mine iniquity and cleanse me from my sin. For I acknowledge my transgressions: and my sin is ever before me. Against thee, thee only, have I sinned, and done this evil in thy sight: that thou mightest be justified when thou speakest, and be clear when thou judgest. Behold, I was shapen in iniquity and in sin did my mother conceive me. Behold, thou desirest truth in the inward parts: and in the hidden part thou shalt make me to know wisdom.*

Purge me with hyssop, and I shall be clean: wash me, and I shall be whiter than snow. Make me to hear joy and gladness; that the bones which thou hast broken may rejoice. Hide thy face from my sins, and blot out all mine iniquities. Create in me a clean heart, O God; and renew a right spirit within me. Cast me not away from thy presence; and take not thy holy Spirit from me. Restore unto me the joy of thy salvation; and uphold me with thy free spirit. Then will I teach transgressors thy ways; and sinners shall be converted unto thee. Deliver me from bloodguiltiness, O God, thou God of my salvation: and my tongue shall sing aloud of thy righteousness. O Lord, open thou my lips; and my mouth shall shew forth thy praise. For thou desirest not sacrifice; else would I give it: thou delightest not in burnt offering. The sacrifices of God are a broken spirit: a broken and a contrite heart, O God, thou wilt not despise. Do good in thy good pleasure unto Zion: build thou the walls of Jerusalem. Then shalt thou be pleased with the sacrifices of righteousness, with burnt offering and whole burnt offering: then shall they offer bullocks upon thine altar."

We learned this morning in verses 1-6 that there were four kinds of sin that David had committed. David had cried out to God for forgiveness. We believe verses 1-6 are a typical example of man with sin who comes to God to have his sin forgiven. Verses 7-10 is a cleansing from sin. The pollution that sin left behind, David cries out to be cleansed. Verses 11-12, we hear David's cry out to God that he might gain a free spirit. In verses 13-19, we see the results of that free spirit.

In verses 1-6, David confesses his sin and is forgiven. And we know that a man that is forgiven will go to heaven, don't we? So the question is why did David not stop there after repenting of his sin and after asking God for forgiveness? And after having the assurance that God had forgiven him, why did David not stop there? Why go on? David, for the first time in his life, saw sin as it really was. He had recognized that he had a sinful nature. He talks about God cleansing him on the inside. He recognizes he is a born sinner. And when the revelation of God same to him, the light of God's word exposed David's real self. It almost floored David when he saw how great his sin was. Behold, Behold, Behold – 3 times and in the Hebrew it is very strong. He is saying, I see it Lord. I see what you are after. I see sin as you see it. With the revelation of sin, comes a revelation of truth. David sees something and says to God, I know what it is you want. I know it is not just enough to be saved. It is not just enough to go to God and ask to be forgiven of your sin. David is saying, God, I see now that you need to take your truth and work it into my spirit. Now I want you to hold onto that. God wants to take his truth and he wants to take that truth and work it into your spirit. What does God want you to do?

Let's say that you are an alcoholic. You quit your drinking and refuse to drink again. What God wants to do is not take the bottle away from you, but God has to take that desire out of your heart. God just doesn't want to cause you to quit sin, he wants to take that urge out of your heart. He wants to work his truth in your spirit, so that you will not sin again. God doesn't just want to take you out of the bar, he wants to take the bar out of you. God wants to cleanse a man's heart and put his truth into our spirit.

Now if I bump into you, whatever is in your cup will spill out, won't it? Spiritually speaking, if I bump you, whatever is in that cup is going to spill out. Have you ever bought a new pair of shoes that were so pretty, but your corn hurt your foot so bad you couldn't stand it and you went to church and sat down and some clumsy teen-ager stepped on your foot. Now what happens in the next few seconds, is what I am talking about. When that happens, you immediately go for his throat and you say the shoes made me do it or this made me do it. In that moment, your human spirit manifested itself. What was really on the inside came out. That is what God wants to cleanse – what we are on the inside. David said, Lord I know what you want. It is not enough to confess my sins, but you want to do a work in my spirit. You want to restore me. David recognized that his human spirit had been made manifest. David had his human spirit under control until that woman took a bath on the top of the house. Then the human spirit manifested itself. David committed adultery. David committed murder. David committed guile and deception and every other sin in the book. Why? Because that which was in his heart from the beginning came out and manifested itself.

That is what God wants to change. God's truth has to be on the inward part. It is not enough to know forgiveness. It is not enough to know the Bible. We must have God's truth in our spirit. I know people talk a lot about memorizing scriptures. But you can memorize scripture and be as mean as a snake. The fact that you have memorized all kinds of scriptures has very little to do with your spirit unless the word, you have memorized, has done its work down in your heart. And God's truth has been worked in your spirit. Once that truth reaches your mind and begins to work its way into your spirit, something happens. God is Spirit. The Bible says, he that worships God must do so in spirit and in truth. What does God want to fellowship? God wants to fellowship your spirit because God is spirit. God wants to take his word and work it out in your heart so you will be, as David cried out, a new creation, a new heart.

David had received forgiveness. But he cried out for the right kind of spirit. Notice in verse 10, he mentions a right spirit. In verse 12, he talks about a free or willing spirit. And in verse 17, he talks about a broken spirit. David had received forgiveness, he had received cleansing from sin, but he wanted something more. He wanted to be restored. He wanted a restoration. He wanted a new heart, he wanted a renewed spirit. Why? So that it wouldn't come out again. You see, that's what happens to us when we get saved and we backslide so quickly. We got forgiven of our sin and cleansed, but we did not let God restore and we did not give God's word time or availability to get into our hearts. What happened? Our old spirit manifested itself again and we sinned again against God. David cried out, I not only want to be forgiven of my sins, but God I want to be a new man. I want a new spirit and a new heart, so that will not come out again. David did not want to commit adultery again. He did not want to commit murder again. And the only way he could be sure of that was for God to take it out of his heart. God had to take it out of David.

Whenever you got saved, God didn't run the devil out of your part of the country. When you got saved, God didn't close up all the bars. He didn't hide all the pornography. He didn't take away all those people who would lead you into temptation. God did not do that did he? I don't know how many times I have heard people say, well, I got saved and I was living for the Lord and I was a drunkard and one day I was walking down the street passed Joe's Bar, where I used to hang out, and there was something that just pulled me into that place and the first thing I knew I was drunk again.

That wasn't what happened was it? That bar was still in that man's heart. It was still there all the time. Now it had been manifested and it came out.

Nearly all of us think sometimes we are spiritual giants. We think we understand the Bible. I heard a fellow say the other day, there is one verse in the Bible I don't understand. And I thought, Glory to God, if I was that smart. There was only one verse he didn't understand. We all think sometimes we are standing strong and standing firm. What did Paul say? Take heed, lest you fall. We can go a long time and God can put us in the right circumstances at the right time, with the right people and something is going to happen. We will explode and that old human nature comes out. Why? Because it has been there all the time. I talked in the sermon this morning about all of us having a secret corner or closet in our hearts that even we do not go into. God loves us and brought himself to us because one day he is going to snatch that lock off of it and he will open up that closet in our heart. Whatever is in it is going to be exposed to the light of God's word. We think we are so strong, a lot of times that our emotions are controlled. Some folks are high tempered and they are always flying off the handle. That's not Christian, is it? You say, I've got that all under control, I haven't lost my temper in 3 or 4 months. God's taken it out of my heart and I've got it under control. Then your wife takes the car and runs over something and that which you thought was under control is made manifest again.

David realized that and realized that if God didn't do something in his heart, that the same feelings that caused him to commit adultery and murder, would come out again. He didn't want that to happen. So he said to God, forgive me, then purge me with hyssop, wash me, make me, cast me not away, restore unto me, create in me a new heart. He is saying just don't quit with forgiveness, but work me over God and take every bit of that out of my heart. You have heard people say well, people are always given into temptation because the eyes are the last thing to get saved. I heard a fellow tell me that one time and I don't buy it.

To see what David was clearly after, you have to understand I Samuel 15:26 and I Samuel 16:22. Saul has been anointed King of Israel. The spirit of God grew upon Saul and he walked under the manifest presence, the anointing of God. Then he sinned against God until the spirit of God withdrew from Saul and David saw him walking without the anointing of God and David said, God don't let that happen to me. In I Samuel 16:13 it says and Samuel anointed David's head and the spirit of God came upon David and he remembered how it felt to walk under the anointing of the spirit of God and David said, God I don't want to ever do anything that would cause the spirit of God to leave me. So he says to God, do a work in my heart. Take it out of my heart. The same thing can happen in our church services. You can come to church on Sunday morning and you can be thinking about your car, job, wife or food you are cooking. You come into church and everyone is singing, Amazing Grace how sweet the sound and you try to join in. You are just as dry as a bundle of sticks. Is God there? Sure he is there. He's there, but you don't feel him. God is not fellowshipping in your spirit. But then there are times when you come to church, sing Amazing Grace and God begins to manifest himself to you and you can say, Glory to God, he is here, I can feel him in my heart. That's the difference. And David saw that difference. He saw what it was to just say in his heart, God is here. That is good theology. Then David knew what it was to have the very power of God on his life and he said, God that is what I want.

If I sin and I repent to God and God forgives me, I need to be restored. Restore me, David says, to the joy of my salvation. He recognizes that he needs to be restored. Do you know what religion is? Religion is nothing more than Christianity with all the joy gone. As I said before, that's our problem. We have squeezed all the joy out of religion and Christianity. If you grieve the Holy Spirit of God, he will lift off your life just as he did Saul. You may be saved, but that's all you are. You have minimal knowledge that God is there. David's pray was don't just forgive me and leave me there. I want the anointing and I want to know that you are there. I want the power of God upon my life. I want it all and that's the normal Christian life.

You may say, preacher, I don't understand the difference in forgiveness and restoration. Those of you who are married, I can show you very quick. Let's say husband you do something wrong, and your wife gets mad at you. What happens when your wife gets mad at you? It gets awfully quite, doesn't it? She just don't say anything. And you finally recognize that you have done wrong. You go to your wife and say, honey I realize that I am wrong, I'm sorry will you forgive me? Now, some of you have never said that. Some of you wouldn't say it, if God hit you over the head with a concrete box. Some of the women could say amen to that. But you could say to your wife, honey, forgive me. Now she says, ok I'll forgive you. Now have you been restored or has your relationship been restored or is it still awfully quite. You ask your wife to forgive you and go to bed and say I'm sorry, will you forgive me? She says, I forgive you, good night. Now I know you know what I am talking about. It is not enough to be forgiven, the relationship has to also be restored.

God is saying to the church today, restore in the church, submission, deliverance, joy and the excitement the church once had and above all restore divine order in the church. Why? Because God is getting his people ready for something. In the very hours in which we are living, God is getting his people ready.

What is the effect of restoration? David says if you will restore me, I will teach transgressors. Do you know why a preacher knows about what he preaches? Because he has been through it. You know how I know about forgiveness? Because I have been forgiven of sin. David is literally saying, God if you will restore me, I will help the rest of God's kids. And that is the way I feel. God, if you will help me be a good husband, if you will help me to be a good father, I'll go try to help the rest of God's children. I will teach transgressors thy ways. From that restoration, sinners will be converted. Brother, if you have joy in your heart, if you have excitement in your heart, if you have been restored to fellowship with God, everyone is going to see it and they are going to want it. But brother, if they see you with a long face, and they see you losing your temper, and see you swearing, they don't want anything you've got. You have got to offer them something better.

Psalm 51:14 *"Deliver me from bloodquiltiness, O God"*. That is God take away the condemnation. Everyone could probably quote Romans 8:1 *"There is therefore no condemnation to them which are in Christ Jesus who walk not after the flesh, but after the Spirit"*. There is a great difference between quoting that verse and living in it. Living under no condemnation and knowing that my sin has been forgiven. Brother, every time David prayed, every time he thought to pray, he saw Uriah dead and Bathsheba expecting a child. That is what he saw when he prayed. And he said God I have got to get that out of my spirit and washed out of my heart and take it out of my mind, O God wash me thoroughly of my iniquity. Take away the pollution and nightmare of sin, cleanse it from my heart. If you are a Christian and you have sin in your life, every time you pray that sin becomes as big as the whole earth and stands between you and God. It gets bigger and bigger, the whole time you try to pray. The Holy Spirit keeps telling you there is something you need to get rid of. There is something you need to make right with God and it has to be forgiven and restored.

Then David said, "My tongue shall sing aloud". That is joy bubbling up in his heart. "Open thou my lips". What was wrong with David? His mouth was shut. His lips were sealed. He lost, first of all, the joy of his salvation and the next thing to happen was he had to shut his mouth. He couldn't talk about God. He couldn't tell sinners about the Lord because he himself was a sinner. He said, God if you will take all of that. That is what God does, isn't it? He washes us clean so that we can open our lips and speak for God.

In verse 19, David says "then shalt thou be pleased". God simply wants to be pleased with us. Jesus said, "I do always those things which please my father". Jesus was a father pleaser. We could reduce a lot of work to just simply bring pleasure to the heart of God. Doing what we know we ought to be doing.

You ever felt the pleasure of God? Isn't it marvelous to just feel the pleasure of God? I remember when I was a little boy and I would get into trouble and Dad would quit talking all of the sudden. I knew I was in for a licking and after I'd get a whipping I could tell it hurt him worse than it did me. But some time during the day, my father would walk up to me and put his hand on my head and tassel my hair up right good and I felt good. I knew that my father had forgiven me. It felt good. Have you ever felt the pleasure of God? You come into a situation and you make a sacrifice or something and do what you know is right and God says to you, you are a good kid. And you feel like saying, God say it again. Say it again, Lord. I love to heat that. I love to know that my father is pleased. A lot of people are going around trying to figure out what God wants them to do. I am glad I can say to God, God I'm glad I am here in Ashland City, trying to do your will and to please you Lord. That is the essence of Christianity.

Why does God go after our spirit? Because until God sets your spirit free, until God restores your spirit, until God takes the pollution from your spirit, you will never know restoration. You will only know the salvation of God. We have to have that, but brother, you can be saved and still be so bound up that you miss all God wanted for you in this life. God wants to make us free. That is our inheritance. But you need God breathing into your spirit to make you free. Let us as children of God say as David said, God I want to be forgiven, I want to know my sin in under the blood. It is important Lord that I be forgiven. And then, Lord I want to know that you are with me. I want to feel your presence. I want to have the anointing of God. I want the joy for service and joy for worship. God, I want a free spirit. So Lord, here is my heart, cleanse it not only of sin but of all the pollution and cleanse it so it will never come out again. I trust that is your prayer.

From The Shepherd To His Flock

Chapter 22
God's Plan for Your Life
Jeremiah 18

The purpose of this sermon is to celebrate what Christ has done for us. To celebrate his resurrection and to be challenged by his Word. I must preface my remarks by saying that everyone who is a member of the church not only has the privilege of criticizing, but most of them feel the duty to criticize. That's right – if you belong to something, you put your money and heart into it, you have the right to criticize. Occasionally, people say, "I don't like this or I don't like that. Who told you it could be done that way? or It was much better the other way."

This is what I think. I got to wondering. Every preacher ought to preach on injustice, don't you think? I think injustice ought to be exposed. I think minority viewpoints ought to be heard. So, the preacher has the right to say, "this is what I think". If I seem a little harsh in this sermon, I am only exercising my prerogative as a member of the church. I listen to what everybody else thinks, so as the preacher, I can say what I think. I may get scared before I get there and not do it, but in case I did, I wanted you to know.

When a preacher is preaching, and I can only speak for myself about this. But I get to preaching and say to myself, this is doing me some good. I don't know whether t is helping anyone else, but it is doing me some good. I hope that if I challenge you through this sermon or if I rebuke you, it is in the spirit of the Lord. It is not to chastise, but to correct and to give a word of understanding and a word to the wise.

Turn with me in the Old Testament to the book of Jeremiah, to a most familiar passage of scripture. Jeremiah 18 is one that you have heard, I'm sure, many times and there are all kinds of scripture lessons that you can get from Jeremiah, especially in this old familiar story. I'll be reading Jeremiah 18:1-11: *The word which came to Jeremiah from the Lord, saying, Arise, and go down to the potter's house, and there I will cause thee to hear my words. Then I went down to the potter's house, and, behold, he wrought a work on the wheels. And the vessel that he made of clay was marred in the hand of the potter: so he made it again another vessel, as seemed good to the potter to make it. Then the word of the Lord came to me, saying, O house of Israel, cannot I do with you as this potter? saith the Lord. Behold, as the clay is in the potter's hands so are ye in mine hand, O house of Israel. At what instant I shall speak concerning a nation, and concerning a kingdom, to pluck up, and to pull down, and to destroy it; If that nation, against whom I have pronounced, turn from their evil, I will repent of the evil that I thought to do unto them. And at what instant I shall speak concerning a nation, and concerning a kingdom, to build and to plant it; If it do evil in my sight, that it obey not my voice, then I will repent of the good, wherewith I said I would benefit them. Now therefore go to, speak to the men of Judah, and to the inhabitants of Jerusalem, saying, I frame evil against you, and devise a device against you: return ye now every one from his evil way, and make your ways and your doings good".*

The very best of men, sometimes, can become discouraged. That has always been a source of comfort for me to realize that the greatest of men, in God's service, have often been men who have been greatly discouraged. In this text, the prophet Jeremiah was called the weeping prophet. He was called the weeping prophet because as he looked out over the nation of Israel and saw their sin, his heart broke. As he preached to them and called them to repentance, it came forth from a heart that was broken and tears would come down his cheek. He would preach day after day, night after night, warning the people of Israel to turn from their wicked way or else God would deal with them in judgment. They went on in their sin. He pled with them to forsake it, but they went on living in sin. Sunday after Sunday, he pleads with his people to forsake the sin in their lives. He pleads with them to love one another. He pleads with them to be kind and gentle one to another. He pleads with them to be generous in their dealings with the church and with God. And Sunday after Sunday, he watched them go out and live in sin just as they had been doing.

God wanted to teach Jeremiah a lesson, so he sent him down to the potter's house. The potter who placed a lump of clay on a wheel and shaped it into a clay pot. The potter took this lump of clay and began to work it with skilled hands as the wheel turned. When he finished there would be this beautiful vessel. He must have said to Jeremiah, what do you think of this? Jeremiah probably said it was a beautiful piece of art. But the potter says no it has a flaw in it. The potter takes that pot, that's not yet cured, and he crushes it back into another ugly clump of clay. He begins to make a new vessel, one without blemish or flaw. The Lord said to Jeremiah, this is the lesson I want you to learn. Are not my creation, the men of the earth, like that lump of clay in my hands? Can I not just speak concerning a nation and a kingdom? Can I not see them turn from their sins and then change and repent of their sins? Can I not see them honoring me and repent and do good? Israel had been warned that God had a plan for them and they were going after other gods and marring this plan God had for them. God was saying to them, I can, with the sound of my voice, break you as that potter broke that first pot and I have the power to remold you and remake you again into a fit vessel. The application of the text was to the nation of Israel, but it has a personal application. Just as the potter had a plan for that lump of clay, God has a plan for every life seated in this congregation today. You can look at yourself and say, God has a plan for me. He has a plan for every one of you. Young children, middle aged, older people, God has a definite blueprint or plan for your life. That's the first lesson.

The second lesson is that we can, by failing, mar that plan. We can cause God to withhold the execution of his plan for our lives and we can mar what God wants to do, just as that first lump of clay was marred. Then God has the power, if we repent, to remake us into the vessel he wants us to be. There are a lot of points to make and I may have to finish in another sermon.

I want us to take this as a personal application. God has a plan for your life. You might say, preacher, tell me what God's plan is, then I can tell whether or not, God's plan is working or whether I have marred God's plan for my life. If we accept that God has a plan, then we ought to know what it is. Then we can tell if we are doing what God wants us to do.

The first plan for your life is that you recognize God as sovereign. That you recognize him as overall. The scripture says, he that comes to God, must first of all, believe that he is and that he is the rewarder of them who diligently seek him. So, first thing you do in your plan is to recognize God as God. Recognize him as Jehovah. Recognize him as the sovereign God. The God who controls our lives. We must, first say, God is. The fool hath said in his heart there is no God. But God's plan for us is to say, God is.

The second plan for your life from God is this. After you have recognized him as God, then you recognize and receive his son as your personal Savior. Now you can check along and see how you are doing in God's plan for your life. Do you recognize God as sovereign? Do you recognize him for who he is? Then, have you received his son as your personal Savior? Acts 4:12 says, *"Neither is there salvation in any other: for there is none other name under heaven given among men, whereby we must be saved."* No other name, no other name given under heaven than the name which has been given, which is Jesus Christ, the Son of God. Neither is there salvation in any other. Now this is where the world is divided. In fact, this may be where this congregation is divided this morning. There may have been some of you today who sought to be saved some other way. You know that he died, but still you are hoping against all hope that your goodness, your works, your morality, your faithfulness, your doings will make you acceptable to God. Neither is there any name given under heaven among men except the one name of Jesus Christ. People think, or they believe, they are saved by works. And if they compile or build up enough good works, God will say, my what a fine fellow he is, and give him eternal life. As we soon discover, you can work for the wrong reason. So, we recognize Christ as our personal Savior. The Bible teaches that salvation is in Christ. No man is saved until first, he repents of his sin; second, he confesses that sin unto God, forsakes that sin and third, receives Christ as his personal Savior.

There has gotten to be sort of a general thinking about salvation and it sort of runs like this. Everybody is doing the best they can. Everybody is working for the Lord, just in different ways. And everybody is on the road to heaven. Some of you may have that idea. In fact, I think some of you do have that idea. The idea that everybody is on the road just on different directions and we are all going to get there in the end. Brother, let me tell you something, you are not on the road to heaven until you have had an experience with the one who put you on the road and his name is Jesus Christ our Lord. Salvation is not in works. It is not in morals. It is in a person and that person is the Lord Jesus Christ, the divine Son of God. The one who died on Calvary, that whosoever believeth on him should not perish but have everlasting life. Ephesians 2:8-9 says, *"For by grace are ye saved through faith; and that not of yourselves: it is the gift of God: not of works, lest any man should boast."* Salvation is in a person.

Thirdly, it is God's plan (and remember my preface in the beginning) to live separated lives. I know some of you are saying, there he goes again, that Free Will Baptist is going to preach on separation. We have forgotten something, brethren. We have forgotten something as modern-day Christians. The something we have forgotten is this – when God saves an individual, he changes that individual. God does not save you in your sin, he saves us from our sin. Now you can put that in your little black book. You can put that in your pipe and smoke it, as somebody said. God does not expect us to live the same kind of life after we were saved as we did before we were saved. A lot of us have forgotten that. A lot of us have forgotten to remain separated from the world. Not for the purpose of being laughed at or being called fanatics, but there is a real born in God reason for separated living. And when I'm talking about separated living, I'm not just talking about staying out of the bars or away from the gambling table. I'm not only talking about physical separation, you do need to stay away from that, but I'm talking about a spiritual separation as well. I'm talking about where you used to be mean and contrary, you are now sweet and kind. Separated in your heart because there has been wrought a spiritual change in your life. You are not the same person; therefore, you don't live the same way. When you get saved, your wife ought to have a new husband. Your children ought to have a new father. You are different. God does not save an individual then let that individual continue to live like he has always lived. Why? There is no harm in a little drink, some might say. There is no harm in a friendly game of black jack or poker. Let me tell you something real. You know why God saved you? You know why Jesus Christ died on the cross for your sin? To save you from sin and then to put you here on earth as an example to win others from their sin.

Now let me tell you something else. If you continue to live, after you are saved, the way you did before, you continue to have your drinks and all the other things, all the people that you know, may think you are a sport. They may think you have the best personality of anybody they know. They may think you are the most generous man or woman they ever met and they may think you are the best friend they ever had, but they don't think peanuts about your Christianity. They don't think nothing of it. Not one thing of it. Even if it's alright, they don't think nothing of it. You know why? Because the world expects more of a Christian than Christians do. They say brother, if he is a Christian, I'm a saint. The world has a great big expectation of the Christian, doesn't it? Before you got saved and some of you have told me, you looked at everybody in this church and said they are not living right. A Christian ought to do so and so. And if I ever get saved, I'm going to be that kind of Christian. You had great expectations of a Christian. The world has great expectations too.

Now you may think you are a Christian and you may think you have some influence on your friends. But if you are living the way you did before you got saved, you don't have a bit of influence on them. They laugh under their breath when you talk about spiritual things. I have had people come to me, in an insulting way, towards Christians that I know. When you are a Christian, and the world sees someone serving the church or the Lord Jesus Christ, but they continue to do things which are, at best, questionable, then you can do nothing for Christ because you have lost your influence. Even if we could argue the point that there is nothing wrong with what you are doing in the beginning, the point remains, you have lost your influence. Their expectation of a Christian is greater than yours.

Fourthly, God has a plan for us to be loyal to his church. Why is the church here? Why is there a church here at the corner of Main Street and Elm Street? Did some man think it was a good idea? No, the church is here because it was born of God. The church is of divine origin. Christ purchased the church with his blood, not because man thought it was a good idea. Christ founded the church to make his name known to the whole world. The Borden Food Company, a company I worked for, had its headquarters in Columbus, Ohio, but it sold products all over the world. It has branches in every major city, to sell and make known their products. The Lord Jesus Christ's headquarters in in heaven, but he has branches all over the world. You and I are his missionaries working from every locality to make his name known to the whole world.

People say, "I'm a Christian, but I don't go to church and the reason I don't go to church is because I don't believe in the local church". "I am a member of the church universal". Brother, you ain't got nothing to do with the church universal - that's God's business. And besides, if you are a Christian and you don't believe in the local church, where did you find out about Jesus Christ? I'll tell you, you found about Jesus Christ through a local church. You didn't find about him through the church universal because some of them folks are dead and have been dead a long time. Well, we might could say some of the folks in the churches today are dead too, but that's another topic. But the local church has cradled the gospel of the Lord Jesus Christ for centuries. The local church has kept it pure and kept it circulated among the world. Every Christian ought to be a part of the church, ought to work for it, ought to tithe and ought to support it.

Who is the pastor of the church universal? If you are a member, who is your pastor? Where does it hold its services? Where are its missionaries? You ain't got nothing to do with the church universal. Excuse my language. Therefore, you can chunk that excuse and find you another one. The devil will give you one if you want one. He's got some good ones. The church appears in the New Testament, one hundred fourteen times and ninety-six times it refers to a local body of believers. I'll tell you the church is God's purpose and design in the world.

Fifthly, God's plan for your life is that you live like Jesus. Not that you live in the same kind of house that he might have lived in or wear the same kind of clothes that he wore, nor perform the miracles that he performed. But we can still have his spirit in us, in such a way, that will cause others to see Jesus in us. That is a trite saying. People say it so often, folks don't even pay any attention to it much anymore. Lord, help me to live so that others might see Jesus in my life. We pray it all the time.

When the disciples walked down the street, it was said of them, they have been with Jesus. Now how in the world could anyone know they had been with Jesus? It certainly wasn't their language, nor their clothing, but their spirits and their countenance. Their soul was showing and they knew that had been with Jesus. They lived differently. They lived different from the world. Most of us, I'm afraid, may come to the Lord Jesus Christ and say, Lord, I want to be saved, here are the keys to my heart, save me from my sin. The Lord says have you given me all the keys to your heart – all of them. Well, Lord, all but one. There is one area in my life I don't want to change. I can't give it up, but Lord, the rest of my life is yours. The Lord doesn't take over until we give him all our heart. If we haven't given him all our heart, we haven't given him any of our heart.

Is there something in your life unsurrendered? Is there some secret sin you are still holding on to? What about your temper, for example? Folks say that's just the way I am. Get mad and fly off the handle. Brother, Jesus saved you to save you from the way you are. To make you a different person. Until God saves you from your temper, you are not truly saved. Ouch. If I knew it was going to hurt that bad, I wouldn't have said it. Maybe you still have a mean disposition. Maybe you are still contrary, like Pa Poole. I don't know that, Mrs. Poole just says he is. Whatever it is, give it up. And when you give it up, you will be filled with peace and power. Individual responsibility is the worst problem in the world. That is the biggest problem businessmen have - to get employees to be individually responsible and do what they know ought to be done without being told. When it comes to the church, that is the worst – individual responsibility. I wish to God, I pray to God, that we could have such an organizational meeting in this church. That we could have people involved in visitation, bus ministry, education, etc. But this is the way it goes. Preacher, I believe we ought to have a sound Sunday School, one that proclaims the word of God and will not compromise the word of truth, but don't ask me to teach it. I believe preacher we ought to have the best choir that we possible could have, but don't ask me to practice. Don't ask me to sing in it, but you get one preacher. I believe we ought to have a visitation program and we need to be knocking on doors, but I'm too busy to go. Individual responsibility. I believe we ought to have wonderful activities for our young people, but don't ask me to work with them. Jesus said, I must work. I must do the works of my father for the night cometh when no man can work. The night is coming on us brother, and I wonder if there is any work left undone.

I'm going to tell you something, while I'm at it. This half-hearted, indifferent, cold, most of the time devotion to the church is working havoc in our church. Let me tell you how we generally do. I look in your face every Sunday morning, and I know who is faithful and I'm not making this a general condemnation. But a lot of folks, in this congregation, say preacher, don't count on me, if its so I can, I'll be there. I may come to Sunday School but don't care much for church. I may come to church but not Sunday School. And about prayer meeting, preacher, if I can I will come just don't count on me. Some of us in the church need to rearrange our lives. Your kids ought not have to ask you, are we going to church today? They ought to know that when Sunday morning comes around, they are going to be in church. Some of you need to rearrange your day of visitation because at 6:00 on Sunday night we have services in the house of God. Some of you need to rearrange your day of rest because we have prayer meeting at church on Wednesday night at 7 o'clock.

Oh, how I love Jesus, but I don't know if I can go to church or not. Now you have to be honest with me, that is the way we do, isn't it? If it is so I can, if it is convenient, I will, but don't count on it. I used to be the same way. When my wife and I started going to Goodsprings Free Will Baptist Church years ago, I said, honey, I don't want you to take President of the Woman's Auxiliary. Don't you take a Sunday School class, don't work with the teen-agers. Let's just sit back and enjoy going to church for a while. And then if we don't want to go, we don't have any obligations to make us go. And that will be beautiful and we will be free. It lasted about two weeks. Sue was President of the Woman's Auxiliary and working with the teen-agers. I was Sunday School Superintendent and lead director – committed and obligated again! Had to be there every time the doors were open. Some of us need to rearrange our lives. Some of us are layman in the church. Do you know what layman are? People that lay in bed passed the time when church is going on. That is what layman are.

Here is God's plan. God's plan is that you recognize him as God. That you accept his son as your personal savior and that you live a separated life. Sometimes preachers bring this trouble on themselves. In this one church where they played bingo, in order to bring sheckles into the coffers. This lady went to play Bingo one night and she lost her purse. The father announced over the loud speaker that a purse had been found and if anyone had lost a purse could come and identify it and they would get it back. The lady went to the father and said I have lost my purse. He said tell me some objects that was in your purse so you can claim it. She said there was a billfold with pictures of the grandkids. He said yes. He was looking at her real harsh. She said there was a makeup case with lipstick. He said yes, what else lady? She said well father there was a pack of cigarettes. And the father very sternly handed the purse and as she walked away, he said, "Do you every suppose the virgin May ever smoked a cigarette". She turned and said, "No, neither did the Lord ever play bingo". Some of us bring it on ourselves.

But the question is, have you received him as the God who is there? Have you received his son? Or have you marred the vessel? You know what God's plan is for your life. Maybe you are not saved and you have heard sermon after sermon and song after song, but the story of God's redeeming love is an old, old story to you. You have heard it over and over. You have heard it until your ears are dull. And you sit and listen to a sermon just like this one and never apply the truth to yourself. I know what Mrs. Pocle's gonna say, "Brother, you told the men today". She likes to encourage me. She says, "Preach on them men, they need it". And when I do, she says, "Brother, you told them this morning". But you never apply the truth to yourself. God help you to hear today, the words of the scripture. If you are not saved, these words, "he that believeth on the Son hath life. He that believeth not shall not see life, the wrath of God abideth on him". Perhaps you are a Christian and you have received him as your Savior, but you have to say, preacher, I haven't lived for him. I haven't given him my best. I'm just sort of playing at this thing, just trying to get by. I try to keep a little respectability in the community where I live, hoping to get to heaven by the skin of my teeth. That is really my commitment to Jesus Christ.

God is not pleased with that kind of dedication. You may not like the way the church is structured, but you can go to church somewhere. You can be in the House of God, where they are worshipping God, somewhere.

May the Holy Spirit take and convict where we need to be convicted and challenge where we need to be challenged. You know occasionally, we need a good stiff kick in the pants. I do, and my wife is very faithful. God doesn't crush us when he reveals truth to us. God does it that he might save us. Let's sing Just as I Am and listen to the words. Ask yourself, here I am just as I am and I wonder if the Lord is pleased with that. Standing before the Lord, just as I am without one plea, but just standing, is God pleased with my life? If you are here and not saved, as you sing, I pray the Holy Spirit would convict you of sin and that you would recognize God as God and his Son as your Savior. Come receive him as your Savior and begin your walk with God through the Lord Jesus Christ.

Chapter 23
Marring God's Plan
Jeremiah 18:1-11

I want to finish the sermon I started this morning on God's Plan for Your Life. For the sake of brevity, let me recap the basic theme I was trying to develop. In the Old Testament, God had a prophet named Jeremiah who was a man truly heart-broken over the sin of Israel. He had preached day and night rebuking Israel, calling them to repentance, asking them to turn from their evil ways, lest God bring some terrible thing upon them. They rejected Jeremiah's preaching and he became discouraged, as all preachers do. I am sure Jeremiah resigned his pastorate every week. I used to meet with a lot of ministers each week. Everyone was always discouraged and down in the dumps, except Bro. Don Lamb, he never was discouraged. Every Monday morning, they would resign, you know. I always picked the meeting up because I told them I resigned Sunday night right after the service was over. I resigned, slept on it, got over it and I was ready to go another week. But preachers do get discouraged when they preach and preach and preach and there is seemingly no response to their preaching. I have not had that much of a problem, basically, with my ministry because I don't look at my ministry as other preachers look at theirs. I believe that I am a pastor. I believe as a pastor, I am a shepherd for the flock. I believe, as the shepherd of the flock, my responsibility is to feed the flock of God. It is not evangelism. When folks get saved in our services, it is a wonderful thing. It is something we pray for, but it is an outgrowth of feeding the flock. So, I don't get upset one way or the other.

But Jeremiah was a man totally discouraged and was known as the weeping prophet, because he wept over this thing. God wanted to teach him a lesson. He wanted to use an object lesson so that he could burn this into Jeremiah's heart. So, God told Jeremiah to go to the potter's house and watch as he worked on the wheel for a while. After you watch him, God said, I'll have another word to say to you. Jeremiah went down to the potter's house and watched the potter as he picked up this lump of clay and began to wet it and get it pliable and workable. He watched as the potter put it upon the wheel and began to peddle. The potter began to shape the clay into some kind of pot. As Jeremiah watched, he saw the potter take the pot, he had just made, look at it and then crush it in his hands and make it back into a lump of clay again. There was a flaw in it, it was a marred vessel. Just then God spoke to Jeremiah and said, this is what I wanted you to see. I had a plan for the nation of Israel. I was going to make of them a vessel that I could use. But they, through sin, have marred my plan for their lives. Therefore, I have the power, as a creative God, to snatch from them their freedom. I have the power to make a nation great or a kingdom great or I have the power to withdraw my sustaining power from them. And he said watch the potter again. The potter began to place this lump of clay back on the wheel again and he fashioned another vessel. The object lesson was learned. Number one, God had a plan. Number two, that plan was marred. Number three, God can remake it and remold it and make it useful again.

This morning I talked about the first part of that and that is God has a plan for every one of us. You fit in somewhere in God's scheme of things. God has a plan for you to fulfill. You may never realize what it is and you may never fulfill his plan, but he has one for you.

We talked about what God's plan for your life was:
1. Recognize God as God,
2. Recognize his Son and receive him as your personal Savior,
3. That you live a separated life,
4. Live like the Lord Jesus Christ, and
5. Serve him faithfully. That is God's plan for your life.

Tonight, I want us to talk about how we mar God's plan for our lives. We often mar God's plan for our life. If you should see a drunkard staggering down the street falling in the gutter, or lying in his own vomit or you see a prostitute or other immoral degenerate, it is easy to see God had a plan, but they ruined it. But what is not so easy to see is they are not the only ones that mar God's plan for their lives. You and I do that too. You and I withhold God from completing his plan in our lives. Most people would say, I'm living a pretty good life. Maybe even now you are not conscious of failing or marring God's plan for your life.

We mar God's plan for our lives, first of all, through sin. Our mind goes back to the beginning and see Adam and Eve in the garden. We see they were perfect in their creation. There was no such thing as sin. The garden was a very beautiful place, there were no thorns or thistles. There was no crab grass or Johnson grass in the Garden of Eden. God's creation was perfect, both earth and man. But then we see Adam and Eve being deceived and falling into sin. We begin to see something happen to both the earth and to man. The earth begins to spring up thorns and thistles. We see now that man can't so easily live on earth. He has to make his living by the sweat of his brow. Bermuda grass gets in his tobacco crop and he has to spend all that time chopping it. Johnson grass gets in his corn. That was a part of creation falling. That was a part of the effect of sin upon this earth. They fell and creation fell. Then there was the prophecy that this universe would be remade. That it will be remolded like that lesson that Jeremiah was taught. This old world, in which we are living, will be remade someday. The prophecy says the desert shall bloom and blossom as a rose. God had a plan for this world. It fell, with Adam and Eve, through sin and that plan has been marred.

But God has the power to remake it. God had the power to remold Adam and Eve and make them again a useful vessel. But we sin and break God's plan for our lives. Do you know what sin is? Sometimes it is hard to describe sin, especially if you don't have too much education and not too thick between the ears. But this is what sin means to me. This is how I picture sin. I can remember all over this community, some of the most beautiful homes. I can remember the stately old homes that were painted and had beautiful gardens. Not what you call mansions, but just beautiful country homes. They were scattered all over Cheatham County. At night, when you went by, the house was lit up and there was perhaps laughter and singing inside the house. Perhaps someone you knew lived there and you can remember the good old times they had inside the walls of that old house. Now you drive down the roads of Cheatham County and there is an old dilapidated house, cobwebs where the light used to be. That, to me, is what sin does to us. We were, in Adam, perfect. But through sin we became like that old house. The owner long since died or moved away. For some reason, it has been deserted. Sin has the same effect on the human heart, as it did upon that house. We mar God's plan through sin.

Secondly, we mar God's plan through disobedience. Through just pure disobedience. Sometimes when our heart tells us what we want, it is awfully difficult not to disobey God. Sometimes we know what God's plan for our life is, but something we want desperately keeps us from doing that. Some pleasure, some material thing, something gets ahold of us and we must have that, at the exclusion of God's will for our lives. I remember the story that has been told many times of the young man who was studying to become a minister. He was studying in a Bible college. God had called him to preach and while he was there as a student, he met a young girl who was not a Christian. In fact, she was a very worldly young lady. He fell in love with this girl. He even asked her to marry him and she said she would if he would forget the idea and drop his plans to become a minister. I don't want to be the wife of a preacher, she said. So, he gave up what he knew to be God's will for the love of a woman. Not many years after that, this man was barely holding down a low paying job. His wife had died and his children were out in the world breaking his heart every day through sin. That's what sin can do. That is what our disobedience can do in our lives. God had a plan for that young man's life, but he marred it through disobedience.
In the Old Testament, I think of those men who knew what God's plan was but they marred it. I think of Saul, who was a handsome fellow. Very tall, strong and stood head and shoulders above the crowd, the Bible says. God made him king of Israel, a wonderful plan. But he, through disobedience, marred that and we see him coming to a

terrible end. Samson, another handsome fellow. God had a plan for Samson but Delilah had other plans for him. And Samson, through disobedience, sinned against God's known will for his life. We see him with his eyes being gouged out with a hot iron. We see him spending his last days as a beast of burden, pulling a mill. Then in his final moments, we see him being brought out into the arena to have some fun and they are insulting him. Finally, he gets the strength to die with his tormentors. God had a plan for his life, but he disobeyed God, he marred that plan for his life. But God was able to at least begin to remake him even in his death.

Mark was a man God loved and could use. But Mark marred God's plan for his life. We see something happen to Mark and we see him writing the second gospel. You see he was like that lump of clay. God had a plan, Mark marred it and so God had to remake him into a fit vessel. Peter was another example. Peter said, I love you Lord and I'll die for you. I'll let no one come near you. But then he denied the Lord. He marred God's plan for his life. The Lord looked upon him and Peter went out and wept the scripture says. Years later, we see Peter preaching on the Day of Pentecost. We see him, as if he were remembering the look that Jesus gave to him and poured out his heart and see 3,000 souls saved. God was able to remake him into a fit vessel.

When I think of Jesus and his disciples, these men who walked with him every day, who saw his miracles, who enjoyed the prestige of being in the company of Jesus Christ. Who is the treasurer of the group? Judas – capable and efficient. What happened to Judas? He marred God's plan for his life and we see him lying dead in the garden through suicide. Why? Because God's plan was marred in his life. He sold Jesus for 30 pieces of silver.

There is another point I would like to make. Before the potter remade the vessel, he had to break the old one. Most of us, who try to do anything for the Lord, are not worth a plug nickel until the Lord breaks us. Most of us must be broken before God can use us. Most of us have to at least experience brokenness. When you look through the hymn book and see that hymn, 'What a Friend We Have in Jesus', the story behind the author who wrote that was in love with a beautiful woman. They were about to be married and his bride died suddenly. Just a few hours before their wedding, the bride died. Through his brokenness, through his crushed soul, his crushed heart, he wrote," What a Friend We Have in Jesus", all our sins and grief to bear. He found that from being broken by the Lord, he found a friend in Jesus Christ.

Do you remember the hymn, 'O Love that will not let me go'? The man who wrote that was engaged to be married. Young, strong, healthy and looking forward to a great future. He began to have some problems with his eyes. He went to the doctor and the doctor examined him and told him he was going blind. He staggered out of that doctor's office, a broken man. He thought he had someone who would sympathize with him, someone who could help him bear the burden. He went home and told his bride-to-be that he was going blind and she said she would not marry a blind man. Further crushing his heart, he sat down and wrote, 'there is a love that is real'. Did you ever run into some fellow who is real cocky? And he knows all the answers. But he has never had the trials and tribulations that the older men have had. He has never been broken.

But if we would just be patient, the time will come when he will go through those experiences. There will come a time when he will be driven to his knees and he will be a better servant of God.

Bunyan's Pilgrim Progress came out of those hours of persecution and darkness in Bedford jail and a man who was broken. The greatest sermons, greatest songs, greatest books come from people who have been there. I read a moving story about the missionary Jetson, who returned on furlough from Burma. He was a man who had been broken in his health. When he arrived, he had to be carried to the platform. Ten thousand people met to hear him speak. He was so weak and his body so diseased. He was so weak he had to sit in a chair to speak and he could barely move his lips. The crowd could barely catch the words that he was saying. He began to talk and share his heart. As the crowd watched this broken man, the crowd began to weep. Twenty-one young men came forward during the invitation and volunteered to take his place in Burma. God broke him and then made him a blessing.

The greatest lesson I ever learned came through just an experience. When somebody talks about heaven, you really can't put it into words. But heaven is some kind of a catch all phrase that is out yonder somewhere very far away. Somewhere you think you will go when you die. But then you let that little child of yours slip out of your arms into death, to go home to be with the Lord. All of the sudden, heaven is so sweet. Heaven is such a special place because your loved one is there. You don't have to know some great speech. But because God has broken your heart, he can now make you a blessing to someone else who has a broken heart. So, after the vessel was broken, it was remade.

Let me ask you a question in closing. Are you giving your life totally to the things of the world? And perhaps Christ has some tiny place in your heart. Why wait till God chastises you? Why wait until God brings you to your knees? Why wait till then? Look in the Bible and see how God made men over again. Men like Peter and Mark. Perhaps you have sin. Perhaps you have slipped up somewhere. Perhaps you put everything else in your life before God. God is saying to you, in love, you marred the plan I had for your life, but I'm not going to cast you out. All is not lost. Just as I told Jeremiah to preach in that day, if you will return unto me saith the Lord, I will use you and remake you. Maybe we will not be a great worker for God, but God has a plan for us. his plan for you and me is that he can make us into the image of his son. And we mar that image he is trying to make of us through sin and disobedience. We need to be restored. We need a Savior. And aren't you glad he is the God of the second chance? Aren't you glad God doesn't throw you away the first time you fail? Aren't you glad he can remake you, remold you and make you a fit vessel?

At the last supper, Jesus said, "one of you is going to deny me". In turn, every one of the disciples said, "Lord is it I?" That is a good question for us to ask today. Lord, is it I? Is it me that is not living for you? Is it me Lord that has lost my first love for you? Is it I who has turned down that place of service? Lord, is it I who was too busy? Was it I who has grown cold in my prayer life? Is it I who has grown indifferent to the word of God? If there is anything in your life that is lacking, I hope all of us can realize it now, and be willing to become as a lump of clay in the potter's hand. I hope we can say, Lord, put me back on the wheel and remold me and remake me into the kind of vessel you want me to be.

Chapter 24
Waiting for Your Ship to Come In
I Kings 22:48-49

I would like to invite your attention to the book of I Kings chapter 22. I will be reading a couple of verses that we might set the theme for the message today. Beginning in verse 48, *"Jehoshaphat made ships of Tharshish to go to Ohir for gold: but they went not; for the ships were broken at Eziongeber. Then said Ahaziah the son of Ahab unto Jehoshaphat, let my servants go with thy servants in the ships. But Jehoshaphat would not."*

Notice in verse 48 that he made ships to receive gold. And then there is that horrible sentence that says, "They went not". They went not because they were broken on the rocks at this particular port. I would like to bring to your attention the theme that we are waiting for our ships to come in, in one way or another. Jehoshaphat, king of Judea, was not the kind of man that would sit idly by and dream of the day when his ship would come in. Jehoshaphat was a man who coveted gold. He coveted that which would make him rich and powerful. He did not just wish for the gold and just sit down and idly dream his hours away, but he made very carefully laid plans to get that gold which he had coveted. He built some ships. He didn't wait for someone else's ship to come in, he built his own ships. He built them according to the Tharshish ships which were very stout, strong and very swift. He sent those ships to receive the gold that he coveted but they went not. The gold was never shipped because the ships were broken on the rocks.

I got to thinking. The king of Judea, Jehoshaphat was not the first man, nor was he the last, to dream and have his dream smashed on the unyielding rocks. How many of you have started out with a carefully laid plan, with a dream in your life, and suddenly have that dream smashed before your very eyes. Have the plan you so carefully laid out, stripped from you and your dream died. Jehoshaphat was not the last man to be disappointed. Mankind literally thirsts today for that pot of gold that is at the end of the rainbow. Mankind has never been as greedy as he is today. Mankind has never been as bad at coveting what other people have as they have today. The problems that you and I face with inflation is caused by the sin of greed. Pure and simple, from Satan himself, the greed to have and to have more. The greed to have more for less investment. Greed is destroying us as a nation. All of us dream someday that our dream that just lies over the horizon is going to come true. There is a pot of gold at the end of the rainbow and one of these days, some way we'll get it.

I think the beaches are literally crowded with those people waiting for their ships to come in. Let me tell you about a few people who had dreams and their dreams were smashed. As we go through the Old Testament, there was a young man by the name of Absalom. He was the king's son. He was David's son. Absalom was not happy to be living in the king's house. He was not happy to be the king's son. He wanted to be king. He did not want to wait till his father died, he wanted to be on the throne now. He wanted his dream to come true now. So, Absalom began a very treacherous carefully laid scheme to throw his father off the throne, so he could be made king over all of Israel. Now he put together a coo. He was going to leave no detail undone. His ships were built very carefully and very strong and very warlike. Absalom had a dream and he wasn't willing to wait. He was going to make that dream come true himself. During those early years, he caused rumors to come around the kingdom and he began to eat away slowly his father's political power. He had some help on the inside of the government in making his plans. But his dreams were smashed. Instead of living to become king of Israel, we find him back in II Samuel riding on a mule, going to battle against his father. He was riding through the forest of Epharim and with his long hair running under the bough of the big oak tree, his head caught in the limbs of the tree and the mule ran out from under him. There he was suspended between heaven and earth, caught like an animal in a trap and the enemy saw this young man, who had dreams of becoming king, hanging helplessly in an oak tree. Ten of them used him for target practice, running their spears through his body as it hung suspended in that oak. He had his dream. He lost his ships and his dream was smashed. His dream was smashed on the rocks of selfishness. How quickly fortunes change. In the morning, he was sweeping to glory and by nightfall, he was a helpless target. He sent his ships for gold but they never came in.

Jesus knew of such a man in the New Testament. He was a farmer. In the book of Luke, chapter 12, he tells the story. There was a certain rich man whose land had delivered much. And this rich farmer had to be very smart to be a rich farmer. I farmed for a long time and any man that can get rich farming is a smart man. We can give that to his credit in the beginning. This man could not fill barns fast enough to hold his harvest. He was making so much profit and so much money, he didn't know what to do with all his assets and profits. I know what I would have done and what we could have done today. We could declare a shortage and put the price up twice as high. But he wanted all he could harvest, so he began to build bigger barns and he planned for a retirement. He planned for security and a better kind of life. He had his dream and he said to himself, I know what I'll do, I'll just build bigger barns and fill up those barns and then I know what I'll do. I'll eat, drink and be merry. He built his ships and he sent them for gold but they broke on the rocks. He never lived long enough to realize his dream. He set his heart on something, he planned for greater things, but he never lived long enough to see it. That night, scripture says, his soul was summoned into eternity. He died so quickly, he didn't even have time to make a will. We know that because the scripture says when he died, the question was asked who will these things belong to? We plan, we dream, we connive, we do all we know how to do to assure us of a future. Something happens to it and it's smashed in a moment's time.

There is another beautiful example of that in the Old Testament by a young man by the name of Haman, who was a political genius. He was a man who wanted to work his way up through the political ranks until he became the right-hand man of the king. He worked very carefully, even conniving and treacherous at times. He began to make his plans and work his way up in the political affairs of the kingdom until he would become one of the highest men in the kingdom. The only thing that stood in his way was the Jew. He began to have the Jews killed. There was one particular man that was giving him problems and his name was Mordecai. And Haman built a gallows, a place to hang people, and put it in the courtyard to hang Mordecai. He wanted to get him out of his way because he was on his way up. You know the story and how it ended. The scripture says the king said, "Hang Haman on the gallows he built for Mordecai. The same rope that Haman put up to hand someone else, he had to hang there himself. His dream was good, he thought. His plans were very carefully laid out. But he himself was hanged. The scripture says in the book of Esther that the king promoted Haman, advanced him and set him over the princesses. All the servants bowed and reverenced him. The ships were just about to come in, but they were wrecked.

Now why did I bring all of that up? Because there is something very important that you and I as Christians need to learn. There is a lesson we need to learn and relearn it. We need to get into the habit of making our plans around God. You know how you make your plans? Generally speaking, here is how you make your plans and all of us do it. We've got a dream in our minds and hearts and we know exactly what it will take to get it. We want to reach retirement with certain funds. We want to do certain things. The house must be paid off by a certain year. We must make X number of dollars per month to live the kind of life we are living. We put all out plans together and then we say, God we want you to put your rubber stamp of approval on my plans for my life. Is that not the way we live? Lord, I'll make the plans, I'll show you the plans and I want you to approve what I'm going to do in life.

James said it very well when he said, do not say that this year I will go into a certain city or next year I'll go into a certain city and there I will work and build and so forth. He said, say this, if it is the Lord's will, I will do this or do that.

One final illustration. There was another man who stood on the shore and waited for his ship to come in, but it never did. His name was Belshazzar. He was a man who was so sure of himself because of his mighty army and mighty fortress. On the night of his death, he gave a great feast and invited a thousand of his lords to come. He began to drink in front of his guests and he became drunk. In his drunken stupor, he began to blaspheme God. And the hand of God came and wrote upon the wall. He felt very safe, he had invited everyone except God. He was very certain of his plans. I'll tell you no man sobered up as quickly as Belshazzar when he saw the handwriting on the wall. God Almighty came and wrote his obituary on the wall of his dining room. He sobered up quickly. The scripture says, he died that night in front of the Persian army that invaded his kingdom. He died at the hands of the Chaldeans that night. I want to ask you today, are you making plans without God? Have you already got your life planned out pretty good? Have you left God out of your plans? Do you know exactly what you are going to do and how you are going to do it? Let me tell you something, God is sending this preacher to you this very moment to warn you about making plans without God. To warn you about making a life without God. To young people who are about to be married, expect to be married, or have just married, have you left God out of your plans? I want you to look back at those marriages that left God out and see how they ended. You are headed for trouble. You are headed for sorrow if you try and start a family and home without God in the center of it. You college students have every avenue of study opened before you. Your mind is being expanded daily by all the studying you have before you. Are you making your study and research without a thought of God? Listen to the wisest man who ever lived, who said, "to get wisdom for the sake of wisdom is ignorance". Wisdom for the sake of wisdom, for the sake of knowledge, Solomon said, is vexation of spirit. He said with all thy knowledge get understanding. Put God into your research. Put God into your planning. Put God into your life. Jehoshaphat suffered. He suffered because he joined himself to an unholy league. That is what caused the shipwreck of his dream. When he made plans, when he was thinking about his life, he invited those who did not believe in God to be a part of his fellowship, a part of his kingdom. He invited the unholy into his life. But he learned a valuable lesson. This unholy league, after the ships were wrecked, said let my servants go with your servants and he finally had sense enough to say no.

How many of us have built our ships and dreams and invited someone on board, who we thought was our friend, only to find our fellowship with them caused our dream to become smashed? There is only one way to get from here to there. To get from where you are now to your dream. To get from where you are now to your destiny. To get from where you are now to heaven. There is only one way. That is by faith in God's son, the Lord Jesus Christ. A marriage, a home, a career needs a pilot. We need someone who can carry us through life. Someone who can carry us through the dangerous rocks so our dream won't smash. We are not the captain of our souls. We are not smart enough to outsmart Satan. We are not strong enough to keep Satan out of our marriage and our homes. He wants to destroy that and sits and laughs at you and uses you as an example to the world that there is nothing to Christianity.

You need a pilot to guide your life. It doesn't pay to be ignorant, but neither does it pay to ignore God. Does God have a place in your plans? Have you considered God as a part of your life? Between you and your goal, there are a lot of hidden snares. But with God's help, you can stand like one man who did a long time ago and said, "I have finished my course, I have fought a good fight, I have kept the faith, henceforth there is laid up for me a crown of righteousness which the Lord the righteous judge shall give to me and not to me only but to all them who love his appearing". He was a man who had a dream. He planned his life and asked God to go with him step by step to show him where he made his plans wrong. To show him where to increase his plan. He walked with God and when he finished his life he could say, I finished it and I kept the faith and I received the crown.

Young people that is the kind of life you need to build. That is the kind of life you need to live. Count on God now. Walk with God now. Include him in your life and he will carry you around the treacherous shoals that would wreck your ship of dreams.

Chapter 25
The Second Coming
Matthew 24: 27-31

I would like to speak to you about a subject that needs to be preached on more. It is a topic that is almost lost in many churches and that is the second coming of the Lord Jesus Christ. Turn to Matthew 24. I would like to just pick out some verses of scripture, let's begin in verse 27. It is talking about the way in which the Lord will return. Matthew 24:27 – 31: *"For as the lightning cometh out of the east, and shineth even unto the west; so shall also the coming of the Son of man be. For wheresoever the carcase is, there will the eagles be gathered together. Immediately after the tribulation of those days shall the sun be darkened, and the moon shall not give her light, and the stars fall from heaven, and the powers of the heavens shall be shaken: And then shall appear the sign of the Son of man in heaven: and then shall all the tribes of the earth mourn, and they shall see the Son of man coming in the clouds of heaven with power and great glory. And he shall send his angels with a great sound of a trumpet, and they shall gather together his elect from the four winds, from one end of heaven to the other"*. It goes on to talk about some other signs and in verse 44 it reads: *"Therefore be ye also ready: for in such an hour as ye think not the Son of man cometh"*.

I think the teaching of the second coming of the Lord Jesus Christ is the most comforting scripture to be found in the word of God. It is and has been persecuted. It has been soul to those who have been bereaved. It has been the power of the church. Not only do we have a risen, living Savior, but we also have a soon coming King. We have the Lord of glory waiting to be revealed from heaven. That has been giving power to the church. That is the one thing that church people have rallied around, knowing that someday, in such an hour we think not, the Son of man cometh with power and great glory. I believe one of the reasons many churches have lost its power and perhaps churches in general all across the land of all denominations, because we have not been preaching and not been living and believing in the eminent return of the Lord Jesus Christ.

There are three things which the devil hates. The devil hates with all his power, first, the atoning blood sacrifice of the Lord Jesus Christ. The devil hates the royal red blood of the Lord. He hates that blood, which when we come to it we find cleansing from sin. He hates any preaching of the gospel which mentions the sacrifice of the Lord Jesus Christ or he knows in the blood of Christ sinners lose all their guilty stains. He hates the atonement and he does all he can to keep men away from the atoning work and power of the shed blood of Christ.

The second thing the devil hates, with all his might, is the intercessory Christ. He knows that Jesus Christ is standing, this very moment, before the throne of God and he is praying for you and he is praying for me. The very weakest of Christians have the Lord Jesus Christ in heaven praying for us this very moment. The devil knows that as long as a weak Christian realizes that Christ is there, as his lawyer, as his advocate, in the court of God, continually bringing us before God the Father, the devil is constantly accusing us before God. Jesus is there as our advocate taking our place and interceding for us. The devil knows that, as long as, he is there and we know he is there that his work is being defeated in the lives of Christians and he hates the intercessory office and ministry of the Lord Jesus Christ.

Not only does he hate the blood and hate the interceding of Christ, but he hates the doctrine of the coming again of Jesus Christ. The devil knows that as long as Christians believe in the second coming, it is a powerful incentive for us to live right. It is an incentive for us to be about the Lord's work. For in an hour, we think not, then cometh the Lord Jesus Christ. So, the devil hates the fact that we, as Christians, know and believe that Christ is coming again. For he knows, that when Christ comes, his work is over. He knows that he is being defeated when Christ comes. He knows when the Lord comes he will be cast into the lake of fire, so he hates all three of those things.

Despite all of that and all the devil has done to try to defeat us, the Lord is coming back. If we believe any of the scriptures, we must believe that Jesus is coming again. A lot of people say they believe the word of God, but they are not sure whether or not the Lord will really come the second time to this earth and that he will stand upon the earth visibly, bodily before the world. If you believe in heaven, you must believe in the second coming. The only reason you know about heaven is because it is in the word of God. Because the Bible tells you there is a heaven you believe it. The Bible tells you about the second coming therefore, we must believe it. Some people believe in hell. All you ever know about either one you get from the word of God. If you believe the word of God on one point, you must accept it in the other. The Lord is coming again.

We have, first of all, the promise of his coming. It runs very deep throughout the word of God. It is that promise. There is more said about the second coming than there is about his first coming. Three hundred eighteen times in the New Testament alone, it talks about Jesus Christ coming again. We have that promise from the Lord. There are three reasons why, I, as a minister, believe that the Lord Jesus Christ is coming back personally, visibly and bodily.

There are those who say when you die, that is the second coming of the Lord. There are those that say when you are saved it is the second coming of the Lord. No. One day the eastern sky will split and the Son of man will come at the sound of the trumpet. He will walk this earth again. I believe it because, first, it is according to the scripture. Jesus said so. Jesus said in Matthew 16:27: *"for the Son of man shall come in the glory of his father with his angels and then shall he reward every man according to his works"*. Mark's gospel records these words in Mark 13:26: *"And then shall they see the Son of man coming in the clouds with great power and glory"*. John said in chapter 14 verse 3, quoting the Lord Jesus Christ, *"And if I go and prepare a place for you, I will come again and receive you unto myself; that where I am, there ye may be also"*.

I have heard preachers say that it is a figurative passage of scripture. That we are really not going to be in heaven after we die. Well, if I'm going to be somebody after I die, I must have somewhere to be somebody. That someplace is heaven. it is the promise of the word of God. The Apostle Paul says in I Thessalonians 4:16 -17: *"For the Lord himself shall descend from heaven with a shout, with the voice of the archangel, and with the trump of God: and the dead in Christ shall rise first"*. Then we which are alive and remain *shall be caught up together with them in the clouds, to meet the Lord in the air: and so shall we ever be with the Lord"*. James said, *"Be patient, therefore, brethren unto the coming of the Lord"*. Jude said, *"Behold the Lord cometh with ten thousand of his saints to execute judgment upon all..."*. I believe Jesus is coming because the scriptures say so. It is in full accord with the word.

The scripture teaches us that when the Lord comes, those of your loved ones who have died in years past, who knew the Lord, will be the first ones resurrected. The scripture says, we shall not proceed them. In other words, we will not go before them, but they will be raised first. Then we who are living will not die but we will be translated and caught up with our loved ones who have been resurrected from the grave and there shall we be with the Lord. That is beautifully pictured for us on the Mount of Transfiguration. You remember Jesus came down from heaven with two men, Moses and Elijah. He carried with him Peter, James and John and went up to the mountain and they had fellowship together. Think about those people who were present on the Mount of Transfiguration. Moses died, didn't he? Moses died and was buried. Did Elijah die? No. Elijah didn't die, he was translated, caught up in the twinkling of an eye. He was changed and carried up to heaven. Peter, James and John are still alive. Moses was dead, Elijah translated and it shows us all three classes of people that will be here when the Lord comes. The dead will be resurrected. And we, if we are still alive, will be like Elijah. We shall be translated to not seeing death, go into heaven. Peter, James and John represent those who are living, at that time. I believe the second coming is according to scripture.

Secondly, I believe the second coming according to the angels, the testimony of the angels. Did you ever stop and think that any time God had a tremendous announcement to make on the earth, he sent angels to do it? The first time God sent an angel to make an announcement was at the birth of the Lord Jesus Christ. The angel came and said, *"Behold I bring you good tidings of great joy, for unto you is born this day in the city of David, a savior which is Christ the Lord"*. The angel made the announcement of the birth of Christ. When Jesus was crucified and buried in the grave and the women went on the first day of the week to embalm his body, an angel was there. An angel said to them, *"He is not here, for He is risen like He said"*. The first time the angel announced his birth, the second time the angel announced his resurrection and the third time the angel came, Jesus was standing on the Mount of Olives and they watched the Lord Jesus Christ as he went into heaven. An angel came and said, *"Ye men of Galilee why stand ye here gazing into the heavens. For this same Jesus that ye saw go up shall some again in like manner as ye saw Him go."* We believe the angel was correct when he said, he is born in Bethlehem. We believe the angel was correct when he said, he is not dead, he is risen. Therefore, we must believe the angel who said he is coming again. An angel made all three announcements.

The third reason I believe in the second coming is because of the Lord's Supper. Because the Lord has given to us a living memorial, a living example. He said as often as you eat this bread and drink this cup, ye do so to show the Lord's death till he comes. In the Lord's Supper, we look both ways. We look back to the cross and the death of the Lord Jesus Christ and we look forward to his coming again.

Now let's think for a moment about the purpose of his coming. Why is it necessary for Jesus to come back to earth? Why would he want to come back? Why does God feel it necessary for Jesus to come back to earth? In the first place, his purpose in coming again is to reveal his glory and his majesty. I Timothy 6:15 states, *"Which in his times he shall shew, who is the blessed and only Potentate, the King of kings, and Lord of lords"*. Jesus is coming back to reveal his majesty. The first time he came, he loved his enemies. You and I were his enemy when he came the first time. The Jew was his enemy. The Romans were his enemy. Everyone was an enemy to Christ. He came unto his own, but his own received him not. The second time he comes, his enemies shall love him. We who were estranged, whom God hath quickened and made alive shall love him. The first time he came, he was rejected. He was insulted and spit upon. The next time he comes, the Bible declares that every knee shall bow and every tongue shall confess that he is the Christ to the glory of the Father.

The third reason he is coming is to reward the saints. After the rapture, after the church has been caught up in the air, there is going to be a great marriage feast. The Lord, who is the bridegroom, will be joined together with the bride, who is the church. There is going to be a great wedding feast and all the saints of God in days past and those who were alive when he came, will be caught up together to take part in that great marriage feast of the Lamb. At that supper, the Lord Jesus Christ will set up his judgement seat and he shall judge. Not whether we are saved, not whether we are going to heaven, but he will judge us for the deeds which we have done in the body, whether they be good or not. At that great banquet, the Lord is going to pass out some rewards, some crowns. I have mentioned those five crowns many times. I want to give you the five rewards the Lord is going to give us.

The first crown is the Crown of Life. The Crown of Life is a special crown given to that Christian who died for Christ. Whoever died because of their faith in Christ will receive that crown. No one else will get it. The second crown will be the Crown of Glory. And some very special people are going to get that crown. That crown goes to the pastor of the folk. It goes to the shepherd, those whom God called to shepherd the flock. Then, there is the Crown of Rejoicing. A very special crown for a very special group of people. That crown will be given to every Christian who ever won a soul to the Lord Jesus Christ. If you have been responsible for a soul finding Christ as their Savior that is the crown you will receive. The fourth crown to be given out is the Crown of Righteousness. Remember Paul's words, the crown of righteous will be given to those who love his appearing. Those who looked forward to his second coming. Those who love his appearing Paul said, after he said, I have finished my course, I have fought the fight. Henceforth, there is laid up for me a crown of righteousness which the Lord, the righteous judge, shall give to me and not to me only, but to all those who love his appearing. The fifth crown will be the incorruptible crown. It will be given to those who have successfully withstood temptation. Those who fought the battle of the lust of the flesh and the temptations of life and have overcome them. Those who have separated themselves from the world and lived Godly lives shall receive the incorruptible crown.

The third reason he is coming is to reject the lost. Matthew 25:41 declares, *"Then shall He say also unto them on the left hand, Depart from me, ye cursed, into everlasting fire, prepared for the devil and his angels"*. In Revelation 21:8 he speaks of the same thing. He is coming first to reveal his glory, to reward his saints and to finally reject the lost.

Let's think briefly about the preparation. We have talked about the promise of his coming, the purpose of his coming, now let's think about the preparation for his coming. The first thing you ought to do is to make sure, beyond any shadow of a doubt that you are among those whom the Lord will receive. We ought to know, beyond any shadow of a doubt, that we have done what the Bible says we ought to do to be saved. That promise of the Lord receiving us was made to believers and to believers alone. The promise was not made to the world, it was made to those who believe in the Lord Jesus Christ. It is interesting to note, Judas was a part of the disciples of the Lord Jesus Christ. By the way, in the movie, Jesus of Nazareth, I want you to notice how many times the movie goes the opposite of what the Bible teaches especially this matter of Judas in betraying the Lord. That movie portrays Judas as a devoted follower who did what he did because Christ told him to. His revolution was getting out of hand and the Lord said if you'll betray me, I'll go to trial and this whole thing will come out. Jesus didn't know he was going to die, Judas was so upset after that he went and hanged himself. That is not what the Bible teaches, but that is what you will see in the movies.

The promise is made to believers. Jesus had them all there, Judas included and he said, some things to them and he dismissed Judas. Judas went on so he could lay the groundwork for the betrayal of Christ and it wasn't until Judas left that the Lord said, I go to prepare a place for you and if I go and prepare a place for you, I'll come again and receive you unto myself that where I am there you may be also. He said that after Judas left. He said that to those who believed. The promise was made to the believers. The preparation is to be ready and accept him as our personal Savior. To accept the scriptural plan of salvation as it is revealed to us in the word of God. You can be a part of the group accepted by the Father. Not only can you be a part of it, you ought to desire the coming of the day of the Lord. You ought to be earnestly, as the church in Revelation says, even so come quickly, Lord Jesus.

A Christian who does not want the Lord to come, has something wrong. A wife that does not want her husband to come home is a wife who is unfaithful to her husband. A church, who is the bride of Christ, who does not look forward to his coming back has been unfaithful to him. Therefore, we ought to desire the coming of the Lord Jesus Christ. We ought to do that which pleases him. The Lord said, *"Blessed is that servant who when He comes, finds so doing"*.

I am thankful he is coming again. I am thankful he is coming the same way he went. He is coming visibly. The Bible says no one knows the time, it is known only to the Father. So, the first thing we want to do is make sure we are saved. Make sure we are a part of that group that is waiting for the Lord to come. And the people said, even so come Lord Jesus.

Chapter 26
What Is Your Faith?
Matthew 6: 30-32

As we look over the past year, there is not much we can change. There are some things we wished had not happened, some things we wish we had done differently, but it is in our power to a large degree what the New Year shall bring. One of the things we need to be aware of is that Satan does not want us to be successful. He does not want us to be victorious. He does not want us to enjoy God's blessings and he will do all he can to hinder us from receiving the best that God has for us. One of the most effective tools of the devil to use on God's people, to whatever degree God allows him to use, is the emoticn of fear. Fear is one thing that hinders our growth perhaps more than any other thing that could happen in our lives. We are afraid of what our actions might prove to be. We are not sure about other people. We are all sometimes very fearful about the future.

When we use the word fear, we remember there are two ways in which the word fear is used. One is a dread or terror. One is a very painful emotion when we are afraid of punishment. The other fear is a submissiveness. It is a reverence that is produced in our hearts by the Holy Spirit. It does not dread God, but it dreads God's displeasure. We are afraid of God's displeasure. We want to please God. In that sense, fear is a good, godly emotion that God produces in us. We come to the point where we desire God's favor above all else. We reverence his holiness. We are grateful to him for his many benefits. We sincerely want to worship him and obey his will.

In Matthew 6:30-32 it says, *"Wherefore, if God so clothe the grass of the field, which today is, and tomorrow is cast into the oven, shall he not much more clothe you, O ye of little faith? Therefore take no thought, saying, What shall we eat? or, What shall we drink? or Wherewithal shall we be clothed? For after all these things do the Gentiles seek: for your heavenly Father knoweth that ye have need of all these things".* As we face different circumstances in life, one of the things we ought to ask ourselves is not what I am afraid of, but we need to ask ourselves what is my faith? There are people today, who are asking many questions about what they should do in the future. There are those who say, well, we want to have children, but we are entering in a world in which we are not sure if it is a good thing to have children in such an evil world. The question is not how bad the world is or any such thing as that. The question is what is your faith? Many times, we look forward to something and we wonder if it is going to work out. The question should not be will we have many enemies or will we face certain failures, but the question is what is our faith? What do we believe about a particular situation? The scripture says, be it to you according to your faith. Webster says that fear is a painful emotion marked by alarm or dread. Fear is as old as sin itself. It is one of the first things the sinful nature produced in man. It is one of the first emotions that we see that is so different from what God created. In the Garden of Eden, as far as we know, there was certainly no barrier between Adam and Eve and God. They fellowshipped together. They talked together and had wonderful fellowship together. That was the purpose of their creation. As far as we know, there was no fear or dread between the two. But as soon as Adam sins, we find him saying, I hid myself for I was afraid.

Fear is something that the devil produces. There are certain fears that babies have. There are certain fears that teen-agers have. There are fears that middle-aged and older people have. Some of that fear is good. Sometimes, fear of things will protect us. We ought to have some fear about some things. I never will forget when I was a Bible College. We had one class with Bro. Forlines. Bro. Forlines loved for people to be prompt to his class. There was one fellow who was late to class every day. You could see this boy as he came across campus. If he was ten minutes early or ten minutes late, he walked at the same gait. Bro. Forlines wouldn't let you come into his class late, you had to knock at the door. Then he decided whether to let you come in. So, this particular morning, Bro. Forlines was quite upset with this young fellow so when he opened the door to let him in, he kept him up front and sort of dressed him up and down real good. One of the things he said to him, and I've always remembered was, "Son, there is something wrong with a man who can't get in a hurry or can't get scared". Something is wrong with a man that can't have the sense to be afraid of something and something wrong with a man that can't get in a hurry.

Fear produces protection in our lives in many ways. But there is a kind of fear we need to avoid. We need to have a godly fear which we see evident in the Old Testament. We stand in awe at the Psalmists as they write and the Old Testament people write. We are amazed at their reverence for God. They simply stand in awe and reverential fear of

God. It permeates the Old Testament, this reverence for the holiness of God. Psalmist David said, God's blessings are for those who fear him. And the scripture says in the Psalms, I will teach you the fear of the Lord. In that sense, it is talking about worship. A worldly fear destroys. It destroys friendships, relationships, and futures. A godly fear produces strength. It produces confidence. It produces growth in the Christian life.

The key to overcoming fear is faith. Faith in God. How much do you know about God? You know God loves you. God so loved the world that he gave his only begotten Son. You know that God loves you more than any other person on this earth can love you. Greater love hath no man than this, that he lay down his life for a friend. God laid down the life of his Son, when we were not his friends, but his enemies. So, we know that God loves us. We know that God is not willing that any should perish but that all should come unto repentance. There is no doubt in our minds about how God feels about us. Not only does God love us, but God holds the future. It is God who is sovereign in the affairs of man. Not much happens by accident in our lives or in this world in which we live. God is sovereign. There are times when it seems God is silent but he is not. He knows what is going on and what is happening. Now if God is sovereign and God loves us and God holds the future, then if we fear the future, then we are not men and women of faith. If we have faith, we cannot live in fear.

There are many who say, I just can't help it, I'm just anxious about everything. I'm afraid of what's going to happen. There are folks who just worry all the time. My father was that kind of man and that is probably why he died at an early age. Worry and fear brought on high blood pressure.

High blood pressure brought on a stroke and it shortened his life by many years. He was the most worrying man I ever met. I think he would worry if he didn't worry. Every time we left the house or no matter what was going on, my father was always afraid of what was going to happen.

Turn to Revelation 21:8: *"But the fearful, and unbelieving, and the abominable, and murderers, and whoremongers, and sorcerers, and idolaters, and all liars, shall have their part in the lake which burneth with fire and brimstone: which is the second death".* Here John gives us a list of sins that will keep people out of heaven. It is important that we read that and that we understand it. Would you notice that the first sin listed in that verse is the fearful? To be anxious and to be afraid is sin. The reason it is sin is because it is not of faith. Whatsoever is not of faith is sin. We cannot have faith and fear at the same time. It's a matter of whether we are going to trust the Lord or whether we are going to fear the future.

David was a man hounded by Saul and lived his life in fear. David never knew, and in fact, he said on one occasion that there is but a step between me and death. He recognized there was a great jeopardy on his life. David found help for that fear. In Psalm 34 he says, *"I sought the Lord".* David brought his fear to God. God heard him and delivered him from all of his fears. David had a fear and he did what everyone ought to do with fear. He sought the Lord and the scripture says, God heard him and delivered him of all his fear. Then David added a little bit later, the angel of the Lord encamped round about them that fear him.

The promise of God's word is that if we will put the Lord first in our lives and revere him, worship him, he will deliver us from fear. There are many Old Testament references to God's deliverance from fear. Psalm 23, *"I will fear no evil"*. Psalm 27:1, *"Oh Lord is my light and my salvation; whom shall I fear? The Lord is strength of my life; of whom shall I be afraid?"* The psalmist said a God who loves me and is in control of the universe, of whom shall I be afraid? Psalm 34:9, *"O fear the Lord, ye his saints: for there is no want to them that fear him."* God says if a man will have a proper reverence and respect for God, he will lack for nothing. There is no want to them that fear the Lord. That is what David meant, wasn't it, when he said, I was young and now I'm old and I have never seen the righteous forsaken nor his seed begging bread. Psalm 56:3 says, *"What time I am afraid, I will trust* in thee". When I am overcome with fear, I will immediately put my trust in the Lord.

There are four great fears in all our lives, both the saved and the unsaved. Psychologists tell us that men and women basically have these fears all their life. One of the great needs of emotional stability is to deal with these fears. God's word answers every fear man has. First, the greatest fear man has is the fear of want. What if I lose my job? What if I must take a cut in pay? What if I get sick and cannot work? What if I have a pile of doctor's bills? What if my expenses go up? What's going to happen to me? The fear of want, by the way, is one of the fears God gave us to prod us into working. To be afraid of being in want. If there had been, in the days of the Old Testament, a Department of Health, Education and Welfare, we never would have had the beautiful story of the prodigal son. He never would have had to have gone back home. He never would have had to repent. He would have been taken care of by some government agency. God put a fear of getting hungry into our being to prod us to work. The Proverbs are filled with warnings about those who will not work coming to want. The question should be what is your faith?

The Bible says these fears are not legitimate fears. That we should not fear these things. Why? Because God is the great provider, as we see in Matthew 6. We will seek first the kingdom of God and his righteousness; and all these things shall be added unto us because he already knows what our needs are and he is the great provider. Therefore, any fear we have of coming to want are not legitimate fears. In fact, they are, if not sin, very close to sin. The anxiousness distrusts the Lord God Almighty.

Is Jesus sufficient for our needs? Can he supply our needs? Does he, in fact, clothe the grass of the field? Does he, in fact, take care of the sparrow in the air? Does he not much more look after us? Is he sufficient? Can we count on his love? Is he faithful to us? The issue is whether we will have fear or faith.

They tell us that the second great fear that man has is the fear of suffering. Not just pain in the body, but there is the fear of being pained in body and in spirit. The worst hurt that man can have is an emotional hurt. We can just about stand physical pain, but sometimes emotional pain is more than we can bare. We have a fear of loneliness. It is common to man, it is human nature to be afraid of being lonely. To be afraid of being sick. To be afraid of facing grief in our lives. We find that God cannot only help us in that area, but God does help us. He will not shield us from suffering. God will not protect us from suffering, but God will limit it and he will control it. If we have to go through those times, God will use it for our good. For all things work together for good to them that love the Lord who are called according to his purpose. How many times have you heard testimonies of people who have gone through great times of suffering and come out on the other side great men and women of faith. Because God allowed them to go through times of suffering. Someone asked the question, does God bring that upon us or does God allow or permit it? It doesn't matter. The question is how will you respond to those situations in which you find yourself in? What is your faith? The question is not is God being faithful? Or is God doing what he is supposed to do? The question is am I doing what God wants me to do? We come out on the other side, many times, with the opportunity to know his presence and his power.

God demonstrated that to the Apostle Paul when Paul sought the Lord with that thorn of the flesh three times. God said to Paul, I am not going to remove the thorn, but I will give you grace to bear it. My grace is sufficient for thee, Paul. And Paul said if that's the case, then I will glory in my infirmity. Instead of complaining about it, I will glory in it because your strength is made perfect in my weakness.

Then there is the fear of failure. The most common kind of fear, I guess, is the fear of failure. We want to do well in school, especially in college. We want to do well on our jobs. We want to achieve and be successful in social situations. Any competition we find ourselves in, we want to do well. That's our problem, we want to achieve in our own strength. We fear failure because we really do trust in ourselves and not in the Lord. We really want what we want and not what God wants. God is concerned with faithfulness. We are concerned with every kind of circumstance in life, but God is concerned, basically, with faithfulness. He is concerned with obedience and an uprightness of character. If we set our sights on doing God's will, the promise of the Bible is, he will help us succeed. And if God be for us, who can be against us.

In Hebrews 11, there is a whole listing of the heroes of faith. One thing you find in common about all those people is that they made it their business in their lives, not only to believe God but to do his will. The book of Joshua tells us that we need to trust God and be guided by his word. Then God promises us, I will never leave thee or forsake thee. We need not fear failure when God is with us.

Finally, a fear many have in different degrees is the fear of death. The scripture says that the last enemy that shall be destroyed is death. It is one of the fears that is going to stay with us up until the last. That is the last thing God is going to put under his feet. I Corinthians 15:26 describes the last enemy. It says that God will destroy it. But until then, it is very much an enemy to society. It is an enemy to us and our families. We fear death. The truth is the Lord Jesus Christ won victory over death and because Jesus was victorious we need not fear death to the degree that it shakes our faith. Jesus said, if I live, ye shall live also. Jesus came and one of the purposes was to destroy the fear of death. The scripture says before he came we were held in bondage to the fear of death. We were a slave to our fear of dying. We didn't know what happened after death. We worried about our loved ones. We were chained to fear. The scripture says Jesus came to set us free from our bondage to the fear of death. Jesus took part in the same that through death he might destroy him that had the power of death, the devil, and deliver them who through fear of death for all their lifetimes in bondage. God delivers us.

From The Shepherd To His Flock

We are living in a world that is filled with fear. God has an answer for all of our fears. But only as we believe him and only as we trust him completely can we be delivered. We have a choice. We can either live our life in fear or we can live our lives in faith. The Lord calls us to live by faith, trusting him for all the circumstances of our lives. We have not received the spirit of fear again unto bondage, but we have been given the spirit of a sound mind and love whereby we cry, Abba, Father.

Chapter 27
Have You Kept Your Promise?
Genesis 41:9

I want to speak to you on my favorite New Year's text, Genesis 41:9. This is the time to remember. This is the time to balance up the books of the old year and turn over a new page and begin to write a new year. It is time for us to make good our vows we made unto the Lord. Genesis 41:9 reads, *"Then spake the chief butler unto Pharaoh, saying, I do remember my faults this day:"*

The chief butler of Pharaoh had made a promise to Joseph when he was in prison some two years before this. He promised Joseph that if he were released from prison, he would remember Joseph to Pharaoh. He would speak a word on his behalf. Some two years have passed and suddenly the butler remembers the promise he made. He said, I do remember my faults this day.

My daddy used to say that a man's word was as good as his bond. There was a day when a man's word meant something. There was a time when a man would do a business transaction simply on his word. My father was a mule trader and I remember he had a fine team of mules. He sold them to a man here in Ashland City. I remember very distinctly he got $360.00 for that team of mules, which was a lot of money in those days. The man came and got the mules and left. My brother, Ralph, who was three years older than I and always had an eye for business, asked my father, "Didn't you get him to sign a note". Daddy said, "no, I didn't need to, his word is as good as his gold." I must have been very small at the time, but I have always remembered that saying.

Many of us from time to time make some wild promises. All of us, at some time or another, have promised God some things. The Bible says when we make a vow unto the Lord, God never forgets that we made that vow. We forget it or we try to hedge a little bit on that vow, but God never forgets the vow we made. This man in our text, finally remembers that he gave his word. A promise is a lot easier given than it is kept, isn't it? It is easy to promise things, but not too easy to keep them. The Bible says when thou vowest a vow unto God, defer not to pay it for God takes no pleasure in fools. The Bible tells us that when we promise God something, we must not dilly dally about doing that which we promise. Defer not to pay it, the Bible says because God looks at us as foolish when we vow a vow and do not keep it.

I want to ask you, by way of stirring up your mind, have you kept all the promises you made unto the Lord this past year? You remember when you said, "Lord, I will …?" I'll do this or that. Do you remember that? You remember you said, Lord, if you'll be with me, as Jacob said, this one time, I'll do so and so. Do you every wonder what would happen if the Lord were to make folks as sick as they say they are on Sunday morning and give that as an excuse for not coming to church? Just suppose God said well, if you are that sick, I'm just going to make you that sick. Did you ever wonder what would happen if God would make people as poor as they say they are when you ask them to help in the work of the Lord? Just suppose God would take away those children from those families that are being used as an excuse for not going to church? The most ridiculous thing I ever heard is, "I don't go to church because my children are small". Listen, there is no better place in all the world for a child than in church. So, what if he gets cantankerous? You did when you were a child. So, what if he tried to out preach the preacher. People are used to that. Folks are using their children as an excuse for not going to church. What if God took that excuse away? Suppose God would allow all of us as parents to consider the future and just see portrayed before our minds what our example and our influence has done to our children in the years to come. It's time our deeds line up with our talk. If a man vows a vow unto the Lord, or swear an oath to bind his soul, he shall not break his word. He shall do all according to that which he promised. What did you promise the Lord this year? Do you enter this New Year with broken promises?

You fathers, did you promise God sometime back in your life that you would take your family to church and Sunday School? Have you kept those promises? What kind of Daddy did you promise God you would be when he gave you that son or that daughter? Have you kept those promises that you made unto the Lord? We have a little service from time to time, which is called a child dedication service. There have been many parents who have dedicated their children unto the Lord. A part of that dedication is for those parents to make a vow, just as a marriage vow, before God and the witnesses. They say, "We promise we will bring our child and our children up in the nurture and admonition of the Lord. And we will use every occasion of the church to teach our children to be faithful unto the Lord. It is strange when people make promises like that and then they don't keep them. They forget about the promise they made. The scripture says, there shall be a place, where the Lord your God shall choose and there ye shall pay all your choice vows.

Since I have been in the ministry, many young people, from time to time, have come to this altar and they have dedicated their life to the Lord. They said in effect, Lord, I'll do whatever you want me to do. I'll go wherever you want me to go. I'll serve you all the days of my life. They made a promise unto the Lord. God has a place of service for each of us and that service which God demands of us will demand the very best of our dedication and our consecration. Have you kept that promise to God, young people? When you said, Lord, I'll give my life to you. I dedicate my life to you. You know one of these days, we will not only come to the end of a calendar year, but one of these days we will come to the end of our life. It will be a time of balancing the books. It will be a time of remembering. How many of us will face God in eternity with unkept promises?

Do you remember when that child of yours was sick and you prayed to the Lord and said, Lord, if you will heal him, I'm gonna straighten up my life and I'll live for you. I have had folks make that promise to me personally. If God would spare that child or heal that child or go with an adult when he was in surgery. I'll live for the Lord, I'll straighten up. Today, those promises are unkept. The Bible says, there is coming a time and place, and God will be the one to choose it, and you will pay your choice vows unto the Lord.

Do you remember when your home was threatened and you asked God to give you one more chance? Do you remember when that person that worked next to you died or that very special friend of yours was killed in an automobile accident? Do you remember what you promised God? Some time back when we had a tragic death in our church family, several young people made promises unto the Lord. They told me about those promises they made to the Lord. As far as I know, those promises are unkept.

Remember when you asked the Lord to make you successful and if he would go with you and bless you, you would give him a tithe? You remember, Jacob said that. He said, Lord if you will go with me and bring me back to this place and if you will help me Lord, I will surely give thee a tithe of all that thou hast blessed me with. Jacob was in a hard place. His whole future was threatened, so he made a vow to God. Have you ever made a promise like that? If you are holding back that which belongs to the Lord, today, let me urge you to surrender it. God has the most effective collection agency in all the world. Jonah was a man who was brought to his senses. He got in so deep, he couldn't get out. He said these words, "I will sacrifice unto thee with the voice of thanksgiving and I will pay that which I vowed unto thee." Jonah remembered he had made a promise to the Lord.

Perhaps the biggest unkept promise in this community and perhaps in this church is the promise those have made to give their hearts to the Lord. Perhaps there are some who said, Lord, this year, I am going to accept Christ as my personal Savior. You have come through this year and you have yet to keep that promise. God has been gracious, he has extended his grace to you. He has kept you alive and given you every opportunity. Will you keep that promise which you made to the Lord? The promise that you would give your heart to the Lord. How often have people said, I am going to accept Christ? I am going to join the church and live for the Lord. The old year is gone and the new one is beginning and you have never kept that promise. Perhaps you have not made peace with God. My friend, this might be God's fiscal year with you. This may be the year when God brings to a close your life here on earth. My spirit, God says, shall not always strive with man. Now is the accepted time, now is the day of salvation. Don't let God have to come down into your life and write over your life bankrupt. Will you, like this chief butler, say today I do remember. I do remember all the promises way back in my life that I have made unto the Lord. In times of sickness, in times of rejoicing and other times, I promised God something. And will you, like the butler, say I do remember?

Don't wait till eternity to remember. Don't take a chance on hearing God say to you what he said to the rich man. Remember in your lifetime you enjoyed the good things of life. Don't let it ever be said of you what was said of Israel, the harvest has passed, the summer is ended and we are not saved.

Jesus is waiting to make certain that cry will never escape your lips. Jesus keeps his promises. Christ gave his word. He said, "If a man come to me believing, I'll save him. He keeps his promise. Have you kept your promise?

Chapter 28
Jesus Never Fails
Hebrews 13:1-9

Today I want to share a subject with you that you already know. Something that you already have experienced in your own lives. Something that we need to remind ourselves of and that is the fact that Jesus never fails. Our text today is Hebrews 13:1-9: *"Let brotherly love continue, Be not forgetful to entertain strangers: for thereby some have entertained angels unawares. Remember them that are in bonds, as bound with them; and them which suffer adversity, as being yourselves also in the body. Marriage is honourable in all, and the bed undefiled: but whoremongers and adulterers God will judge. Let your conversation be without covetousness; and be content with such things as ye have: for he hath said, I will never leave thee, nor forsake thee. So that we may boldly say, The Lord is my helper, and I will not fear what man shall do unto me. Remember them which have the rule over you, who have spoken unto you the word of God: whose faith follow, considering the end of their conversation. Jesus Christ the same yesterday, and today, and forever. Be not carried about with divers and strange doctrines. For it is a good thing that he heart be established with grace; not with meats, which have not profited them that have been occupied therein."*

There is a verse of scripture that comes to us in the book of Joshua as Joshua was taking over for Moses. He needed some reassurance from the Lord. The Lord said unto him, *"there shall no man be able to stand before thee all the days of thy life. As I walk with Moses, so shall I be with thee. I will not fail thee, nor forsake thee"*. It is good to know that there is something that does not fail.

Everything I can think of, in this world, has failed. There is nothing in this world, I know of, that has not failed. We are today suffering from and being advised daily that so many banks have failed. The economy has failed. Political platforms have failed. If you don't believe that just remember, watch my lips, no new taxes. Five out of nine homes last year failed. More than one church has failed. But I want to tell you about someone who has never failed and we call his name Jesus. Jesus never fails.

I want to name to you some areas in which Jesus has not failed. They are by no means conclusive. First, let me remind you that Jesus never fails in His purpose. Jesus came for a decisive purpose. There was a purpose for God to have Jesus slain from the foundation of the world. There was a purpose for him becoming incarnate or being born and taking upon himself flesh. Jesus said in John 12: 27, *"Now is my soul troubled; and what shall I say? Father, save me from this hour: but for this cause came I unto this hour."* Jesus is facing the cross and says what shall I say. Why did he come? Luke 19:10 tells us the purpose of his coming. *"For the Son of man is come to seek and to save that which was lost."* His number one purpose, in coming, was to save the lost. And he has not failed in that purpose. As many as will come to him, he is able to save to the uttermost. Them that cometh unto him, seeing that he ever liveth, to make intercession for us. His number one purpose is to save the lost. He was faithful to the prophecy of the angel, when the angel said to Mary, thou shall call his name Jesus for he shall save his people from their sin. Paul said in I Timothy 1:15, *"Jesus came into the world to save sinners, of whom I am chief"*. So, Jesus came to save. That was his purpose. As many as would believe were saved and given eternal life. That purpose continues today. Jesus is still strong and able to save those who come unto him.

Not only did he come to save, but he came to bless the saved with abundance. Abundance of what? We can go through the scriptures. When God saved the sinner, God blessed the sinner. And says to those who are saved, I am come that they may have life and have it more abundantly. Speaking to the ones he came to save. Once they are saved, he said, I have come to give unto them abundant life. I am convinced that God wants to give his children the best that he has. Not only to save us, but to give us abundant life. Paul said in II Corinthians 9:8, *"And God is able to make all grace abound towards you; that ye, always having all sufficiency in all things, may abound to every good work"*. The Psalmist in Psalms 36:8 said, *"They shall be abundantly satisfied with the fatness of thy house; and thou shalt make them drink of the river of thy pleasures"*. Peter said in II Peter 1:11, *"For so an entrance shall be ministered unto you abundantly into everlasting kingdom of our Lord and Savior Jesus Christ"*. So, he came to save and to give those who were saved abundant life. We rejoice in the fact today that he has never failed in that purpose to save and to bless.

Jesus also came to bring a sword. Jesus said think not that I am come to the earth to bring peace. I come not to bring peace but to bring a sword. The first coming of the Lord Jesus Christ was not to bring peace. He said, I am come not to bring peace, but to bring a sword – for father shall rise up against son and son against father and mother against daughter and daughter against mother. I am come to bring a sword. A sword divides. Hebrews 4: 12, speaking of the sword, which is the word of God, he says, *"For the word of God is quick and powerful, and sharper than any two-edged sword, piercing even to the dividing asunder of soul and spirit"*. The word of God divides. The word of God is like a sword that cuts through society. It divides in many issues. It divides in issues of moral standards. There are some things that God requires of his people. God requires that his people live on a higher standard of ethics and living than the unbeliever. There are certain moral standards that every Christian ought to have and support and demand among God's people. The word of God divides in these moral issues. The word of God condemns adultery. The word of God condemns homosexuality. The word of God condemns abortion. The word of God is sharp and quick and it will cut asunder and divide. You let one member of a family decide he is going to live according to the word of God. I am going to live, in my life, the standards God set forth for me in his word. I am going to agree with God on moral issues. You let one member of the family do that and the son will go his way, the daughter will go her way, it divides. The word of God is quick and it is powerful. It says what it says. It demands certain standards, ethics and morals from his people. Because some people will not go along with what the word of God says, father against son, mother against daughter. Christ said, I am come not to bring peace, but am come to bring a sword. I came to save, I came to give abundant life and I come to bring a sword.

He also came, a part of his purpose, to be an intercessor. Romans 8:34 states, *"Who is he that condemneth? It is Christ that died, yea rather, that is risen again, who is even at the right hand of God, who also maketh intercession, for us."* He intercedes for us today. God looks at your sins, God looks at my sins and he wants to send judgement upon that sin, but Christs is interceding at his right hand. He is praying for you and me. Who is he that condemneth? It is Christ. Christ, who died and was risen. Christ, who died for sin. I have told you this story many times, but it made such an impression on me. A woman came to me when I was going to preach a man's funeral. She said, I understand that you are preaching so and so's funeral. I said, yes, I am. She said, well you know he is going to hell. I said, I didn't know God put you on that committee. If I had known, I would have been better to you. Who is he that condemns? It is Christ who died for sin. It is Christ who raised from the dead to vindicate and bring resurrection and bring triumph over sin and death and hell. No man has the right to condemn another. It is Christ that condemneth. But he also intercedes. When we sin, he intercedes for us. Jesus never fails in his purpose.

Jesus never fails his people. He says, be content with what things you have, because I will never leave you nor forsake you, so that you can boldly say, the Lord is my helper. God has never failed his people. Now his people have failed. His people have come short of his glory. Have you come short of his expectations and his demands and commandments upon our life. But he has never failed his people. The Psalmist said in Psalm 121:1-5 says, *"I will lift up mine eyes unto the hills, from whence cometh my help. My help cometh from the Lord, which made heaven and earth. He will not suffer thy foot to be moved: he that keepeth thee will not slumber. Behold, he that keepeth Israel shall neither slumber nor sleep. The Lord is thy keeper: the Lord is thy shade upon thy right hand."* He never failed his people. He has never failed them in provisions. Deuteronomy 2:7

states, *"For the Lord thy God hath blessed thee in all the works of thy hand: he knoweth thy walking through this great wilderness: these forty years the Lord thy God hath been with thee, thou hast lacked nothing."* In Psalm 37:19 and 25, *"They shall not be ashamed in the evil time: and in the days of famine they shall be satisfied. I have been young, and now am old; yet have I not seen the righteous forsaken, nor his seed begging bread."* Jesus never fails his people in provisions and in their protection. Isaiah 54:17 *"No weapon that is formed against thee shall prosper; and every tongue that shall rise against thee in judgment thou shalt condemn. This is the heritage of the servants of the Lord, and their righteousness is of me, saith the Lord."* and Deuteronomy 11:25 states, *"There shall no man be able to stand before you: for the Lord, your God shall lay the fear of you and the dread of you upon all the land that ye shall tread upon, as he hath said unto you."*

Jesus never fails in his promise. There are three things he has promised. He promised us he is coming again. He promised us he will answer our prayers. And he promised us he will lift us up. In John 14:1-3 we read these words, *"Let not your heart be troubled: ye believe in God, believeth also in me. In my Father's house are many mansions: if it were not so, I would have told you. I go to prepare a place for you. And if I go and prepare a place for you, I will come again, and receive you unto myself; that where I am, there ye may be also."* He promised to come back. You have that promise today in your heart and in your spirit. Jesus said he is right now preparing a place for you, if you belong to him, he is coming to get you.

He has promised to answer prayer. It shall come to pass, He said, that before they ask, I will answer and while they are yet speaking, I will hear. It is good to know that you can pray and God will hear you. And aren't you glad that even if we don't' know how to pray, he will pray for you? Aren't you glad before you ever get through telling him the burden of your heart, he is already answering your prayer.

He also promised to lift us up. Look at John 6:39, 40 and 44. *"And this is the Father's will which hath sent me, that of all which he hath given me I should lose nothing, but should raise it up again at the last day. And this is the will of him that sent me, that everyone which seeth the Son, and believeth on Him, may have everlasting life: and I will raise him up at the last day. No man can come to me, except the Father which hath sent me draw him: and I will raise him up at the last day."* Jesus has never failed you in your protection. Jesus has never failed you in your provision. And Jesus has never failed you in his promise. Which leads me to say, If the Lord said it, you can stand on it. Amen. I went to a sales meeting one time and I gave a report. My boss questioned me on whether my report was true or not. He said," is that true"? I said, "Brother, if I tell you an ant can pull a bale of hay, you can hook him up". If Jesus says it is so, it's so. You can depend on Jesus' promise.

Jesus never fails in his principle. What is a principle? A principle is a basic truth. A principle is something that is fixed or a predetermined policy. Jesus said my doctrine is not mine, but my doctrine is of the one who sent me. God has never recalled his doctrine. God has one way for every man to be saved. He has never changed it. He has never remodeled or reshaped it. God never fails in his doctrine. The scripture says, whosoever calls upon the name of the Lord shall be saved. If you believe in your heart that Jesus said God raised him from the dead, that belief in your heart is counted unto righteousness. And whosoever calls upon the Lord shall be saved. Let me tell you something about his plan of salvation. It is something the church must preach repeatedly. I don't care how well you are acquainted with the doctrine of salvation, the church must keep preaching it. We can't ever stop preaching the doctrine of salvation. Salvation is the message that every church must preach over and over again. It must be the very center of our mission. Faith cometh by haring and hearing comes from the word of God. We are saved by grace through faith. God never changes. He never fails in his doctrine.

Jesus never failed in his doctrine of separation. Here is where Christians split hairs and fellowship and go one way or another. But God has commanded his people to be separate from the world. He said come out from among them and be ye separate. There is the doctrine of separation. There are some things you cannot have fellowship in. There are some things you cannot participate in and be pleasing unto God. II Corinthians 6:17 states, *"Wherefore come out from among them, and be ye separate, saith the Lord, and touch not the unclean thing; and I will receive you"*. Not the preacher, not the parents, but the Lord said it. "and touch not the unclean thing, and I will receive thee." Separation. What are some things we need to separate from? First, we need to separate ourselves from being yoked with unbelievers. We have already seen the mess that gets you into. Being yoked with unbelievers in marriage, in visits, in association, God never fails on this matter of principle or doctrine, now you will fail in that. But he still requires you to be separate in matters of the Christian life. If you have a friend that is leading you away from God into the world, drop that friend. If you have a friend who is leading you into a situation where Christ is not welcome, brother, drop that friend. There are some things that will never change: God's word and God's doctrine. There are some things that were right for our forefathers and they are right for us. Some things never change. Sin never changes. There are some things that were right for the apostles, and there are things that are right for us. We may change, but God has never changed in his doctrine of salvation and the doctrine of separation.

Thirdly, He has never failed in his performance. Jesus Christ, the same yesterday, today, and forever. One of the things you learn when you study the doctrine of the scriptures is that God is immutable. Immutable means he doesn't change. Aren't you glad that God doesn't have good days and bad? Amen. My wife knows when I am having a good day or not. Aren't you glad God doesn't wake up in the morning in a bad mood? God doesn't have good days and bad, he is immutable. He changes not – the same yesterday, today, and forever. We talk about the godhead, Colossians 2:9 says, *"For in him dwelleth all the fulness of the Godhead bodily"*. He is still God. He is still a part of the Godhead and he will be forever. He is the same in his position. He is high and lifted up. Today, we lift him up. We exalt his name and every knee shall bow and every tongue confess that he is Christ to the glory of God, the Father. He is the same. He is always the eternal son. Hebrews 1:8 reads, *"But unto the Son he saith, thy throne, O God, is forever and ever"*.

Now let me say this in closing. Because he has never failed me, I must not fail thee. Because he has never failed you, you must never fail him. We all know of folks who failed the Lord. I have failed the Lord. I suppose all of us have failed the Lord at one time or another. I think about Peter who failed the Lord. Especially making such a statement that he would die before he would deny the Lord. And the Lord looked at Peter and said, "Before this night is over, you will deny me three times". Peter denied the Lord. Some of us have failed the Lord in our service to the Lord. Some of us are guilty of sin of omission: things we have left undone. Things that we should have done, but haven't. Some of us have failed the Lord in service. The scripture says do not forsake the assembling of yourselves together in so much as that day is approaching. None of us can say, we are not guilty. Where were you last Sunday morning? Sunday night? Where were you Wednesday night? I say that with all the love in me. If you are a child of God, why don't you want to be with God's people? If you are a part of the family of God, why don't you want to be in the house? I don't understand how a blood bought, blood washed Christian can stay away from God's people week after week and never miss it. I long to be here on Sunday morning. I long to be here on Sunday night and Wednesday night. But some of us have failed the Lord. Some of us have failed the Lord in our homes. Some of us have failed the Lord in our work. Your fellow workers don't even know you are a Christian, because you have never told them. You work with them all day and none of them know you are a Christian. Perhaps there are some here who have failed him in that you have rejected the knock on your heart's door. He said, behold I stand at the door and knock and if any man will open I will come in and I will sup with him and he with me. Some of you have rejected that knock and you have failed the Lord.

Whatever the failure is today, why don't we just take care of it? If we have failed the Lord in rejecting his son, then why don't we just receive him today? If we have failed him in service, why don't we commit ourselves today and do better? We are going to support the Lord, support the house of God, we are going to support the kingdom. Have you failed him? Jesus said, Come unto me all ye who are weak and weary and I will give you rest. Jesus said, I am the door. If any man come to the father must come by me. He said, I am the good shepherd. I give my life for the sheep. I am the way, the truth, and the life and behold I stand at the door and knock at your heart today. Why not make today the day we get things right with the Lord?

From The Shepherd To His Flock

Chapter 29
A Great Sermon by a Great Christian
Acts 13

We have explained before and we will explain it again that which makes any written word or spoken word great is that it contains universal truth, that is, it fits all ages and all times. It is true in the Stone Age and it is true in the Computer Age. We are going to look at a great sermon by the greatest Christian who ever lived. I feel that we are within the realm of truth when we say Paul was probably the greatest Christian who ever lived. Where influence is concerned, Paul was among the greatest.

Today's sermon is going to pick up in Acts 13 beginning with verse 14. Just a verse or two of introduction and then we are going to read the first recorded sermon of the Apostle Paul. Acts 13: 14-16, *"But when they departed from Perga, they came to Antioch in Pisidia, and went into the synagogue on the sabbath day, and sat down. And after the reading of the law and the prophets the rulers of the synagogue sent unto them saying, Ye men and brethren, if ye have any word of exhortation for the people, say on. Then Paul stood up, and beckoning with his hand and said, Men of Israel, and ye that fear God, give audience."* He begins his sermon in verse 17-44, "The *God of this people of Israel chose our fathers, and exalted the people when they dwelt as strangers in the land of Egypt, and with an high arm brought he them out of it. And about the time of forty years suffered he their manners in the wilderness. And when he had destroyed seven nations in the land of Canaan, he divided their land to them by lot. And after that he gave unto them judges about the space of four hundred and fifty years, until Samuel the prophet. And afterward they desired a king: and God gave unto them Saul the son of Cis, a man of the tribe of Benjamin, by the space of forty years. And when he had removed him, he raised up unto them David to be their king; to whom also he gave testimony, and said, I have found David the son of Jesse, a man after mine own heart, which shall fulfil all my will. Of this man's seed hath God according to his promise raised unto Israel a Savior, Jesus: When John had first preached before his coming the baptism of repentance to all the people of Israel. And as John fulfilled his course, he said, Whom think ye that I am? I am not he. But, behold, there cometh one after me, whose shoes of his feet I am not worthy to loose. Men and brethren, children of the stock of Abraham, and whosoever among you feareth God, to you is the word of this salvation sent. For they that dwell at Jerusalem, and their rulers, because they knew him not, nor yet the voices of the prophets which are read every sabbath day, they have fulfilled them in condemning him. And though they found no cause of death in him, yet desired they Pilate that he should be slain.*

And when they had fulfilled all that was written of him, they took him down from the tree, and laid him in a sepulchre. But God raised him from the dead: And he was seen many days of them which came up with him from Galilee to Jerusalem, who are his witnesses unto the people. And we declare unto you glad tidings, how that the promise which was made unto the fathers, God hath fulfilled the same unto us their children, in that he hath raised up Jesus again; as it is also written in the second psalm, Thou art my Son, this day have I begotten thee. And as concerning that he raised him up from the dead, now no more to return to corruption, he said on this wise, I will give you the sure mercies of David. Wherefore he saith also in another psalm, thou shalt not suffer thine Holy One to see corruption. For David, after he had served his own generation by the will of God, fell on sleep, and was laid unto his fathers, and saw corruption: But he, whom God raised again, saw no corruption. Be it known unto you therefore, men and brethren, that through this man is preached unto you the forgiveness of sins: And by him all that believe are justified from all things, from which ye could not be justified by the law of Moses. Beware therefore, lest that come upon you, which is spoken of in the prophets; Behold, ye despisers, and wonder, and perish: for I work a work in your days, a work which ye shall in no wise believe, though a man declare it unto you. And when the Jews were gone out of the synagogue, the Gentiles besought that these words might be preached to them the next sabbath.

Now when the congregation was broken up, many of the Jews and religious proselytes followed Paul and Barnabas: who, speaking to them, persuaded them to continue in the grace of God.

And the next sabbath day came almost the whole city together to hear the word of God." That is the sermon Paul preached.

We are going to look at some of the great universal truths that are contained in this sermon. The Apostle Paul, the man who preached this sermon, is a man we all know very well. You know that when Paul wrote to the people of Philippi, in the book of Philippians, that Paul introduced and described himself to them as being an outstanding Hebrew. He said to them in Philippians 3:5-6, *"circumcised the eighth day, of the stock of Israel, of the tribe of Benjamin, a Hebrew of the Hebrews; as touching the law, a Pharisee; concerning zeal, persecuting the church; touching the righteousness which is in the law, blameless."* The Apostle Paul, when he wrote to that little Roman colony, Philippi, there were not enough men to even have a synagogue. All they had was a place a few women and children met together to pray. They were the poorest of people. The Apostle Paul writes to them and tells them who he is and it almost seems as if Paul is very arrogant when he says who he is. It seems he is trying to be arrogant and lord over them. And yet he is not at all being arrogant. Paul is saying to them, I was a Hebrew of the Hebrews. I was an outstanding Hebrew, but all of these things I have said unto you that were mine because I was a Hebrew were useless to me when I tried to find Jesus as my Savior. He is not saying to them look what a marvelous experience I have had and one you will never have. He is simply pointing out to these folks that all the advantages that were his, were useless to him in gaining Christ. In fact, he said, those things which were gained to me, I count but loss that I might win Christ. Paul said, as far as being a Jew, I had great credentials, but when it came to receiving forgiveness of sins, all those credentials of mine were useless. These credentials, on the part of Paul, were not useless to Jesus though. They were useless in helping him become a child of God. They were not useless to Jesus after he was saved.

The Apostle Paul, because he was a Pharisee, a Hebrew of the Hebrew, he was a man that was disciplined. A man that could stand up under the worst of circumstances. He was a man who could endure hardships, a man because of his discipline, could overcome great obstacles. Those things that were useless to Paul in order to be saved, became great benefits after he was saved. Jesus used all this discipline, his personality, and his rigor of not giving up. Jesus added some grace to all that Paul had and all that Paul was. He used Paul as an instrument. Now Paul became, no doubt, one of the most influential Christians who has ever lived. The gospel was to be destined to be preached into all the world. God was sovereign, he could carry the message into all the world, but God used Paul as that instrument.

Here in Acts 13, we have, as far as we know, the first recorded sermon. He is a distinguished Hebrew and apostle and you will see he was a distinguished preacher of the word of God. Let's notice some universal truths in his message. First, Paul points out to the nation of Israel, the truth that God is an active participant in history and that he is seeking to have a relationship with men and women. He is trying to teach Israel that God walks through history. He is assuring them that God is not in his own little world and the world is in its world. He is trying to straighten out the fact that God did not wind this world up like an alarm clock and let it run out on its own. He is convincing them that God has been active in history. The fact that God has intervened time and time again in history. The Apostle Paul was, of course, a master preacher. He lived in a time when denominationalism was as pronounced as it will ever be. There were the Jews and the Gentiles, about were as opposite as you could get. But notice the truth that Paul preaches to these two groups, which both had in common. The scripture says, standing up Paul motioned with his hands and said, ye men of Israel and you Gentiles are ye that far from God. Now listen to me, Paul is not confused about the scope of the gospel, the Jews were. The Jews thought the gospel was for the Jew only. Paul knew the scope of the gospel was to every man. And he was not confused about the depth of God's love. It was not for the Jew, or the nation of Israel. It was to the Jew first and also to the Greeks. He said the God of Israel chose your fathers. Now that sounds awfully Jewish at first, but it is universal. He is saying God took an active part in history. God reached down from heaven and he chose this nation of Israel, not because of who they were, not because of their power, intellect or wealth, but in his sovereignty, he decided to make them his people. He would love them with an everlasting love. God is active in history, he chose our fathers. We did not choose him but God chose us. He chooses, he blesses, he desires to have a relationship with man. He said God chose Israel. His acts with Israel were not weak, they were not pitiful, but they were with authority and power. His power was displayed when he brought them out of Egypt. His patience was demonstrated when he suffered their matters in the wilderness. His faithfulness was demonstrated when he brought them into the Land of Canaan. The reason God is active in history is because he is seeking a people to have a relationship with.

Secondly, Paul reminds them that Christ is God's Messiah chosen to fulfill the Old Testament prophecies and bring about a reconciliation and a right relationship with man. Paul is a master here. Before he can confront these people with the greatest fact in history, he is going to tell them about Jesus Christ being born. The greatest fact in all of history. He is going to tell them about the word becoming flesh and dwelling among them. He is going to tell about the incarnation when God came into this world in the person of the Lord Jesus Christ. But he can't tell them that first. Before he can tell them that he has to tell them God has been active all these years. God chose the nation of Israel. And God chose, that through Israel, would come the Messiah. Now there is a reason he has to do that. If you just think about God's relationship with Israel, you can figure out why the Jew feels the way he feels about God's relationship to Israel. You see, take everything that God did for Israel. First, he chose Israel. He brought them out of Egypt, out of slavery. He, with many miracles, brought them through the Red Sea and the wilderness. Where he fed them, and suffered with patience their conduct and their manners. He took them into the Promise Land having defeated their enemies. Now that could be the whole story. That could be the end. All that God had done for Israel, Israel could have been envisioned as the end in itself. That is how God has been related to us. But Paul is reminding them that all God has done in Israel's history was but a foundation. He is going to build on all these facts, the super structure of salvation through the Lord Jesus Christ.

Then he enters the third truth. That this Christ is God's Messiah who has come to fulfill the Old Testament prophecies and Old Testament law. He comes to fulfill all of that, not to destroy it. This foundation of the law of the prophets of God's dealing with Israel is very important. Paul had to lay that foundation and had to show them how God had worked in their history. On that foundation, he is going to build a super structure. He is going to build a building. I know some of us have, even in churches, where a church may start out to build and not have quite enough money, so they build a basement. They worship in the basement until they can afford to build a structure upstairs. Some people have started out to build a home and they decide to pay for things as they go, so they build a basement and live in the basement until money becomes available to build on that basement a house. But sooner or later you move upstairs. All that Paul is reminding these folks of is their basement, the foundation. He said, you Jews have been in the basement for all these years. Now it is time for you to move upstairs. It is time for you to go into the house of God and worship the Lord Jesus Christ. Jesus did not come to destroy the law and the prophets, but he came to fulfill. Now you must move upstairs and worship God. Paul is a master here in making that truth a reality. You see the Jews had been living in the basement. They had memorized all the words of the prophets. But Paul said, God has sent his only Son so it is time for you to move. Now moving out of the basement is not going to destroy the basement.

Paul is saying to them, now that he has come, you need to respond by beginning to worship upstairs. Worship on a higher plane. Why? Paul gave them the greatest reason that has ever been given to man. Why they should worship this Christ, in these words, "God raised him from the dead". That is the truth on which all of salvation hinges. Paul did not say, "If Christ is now raised, our faith is in vain, our preaching is foolishness, and we are still in our sin. But Paul said, God raised him from the dead. If Christ did not come forth from the grave, you and I are going to die and our spirit is gonna just disappear somewhere. Paul said, If Christ be raised, we shall be raised with him. The scripture says, it does not yet appear what we shall be, but when he comes we shall be like him. That was the testimony of the Lord Jesus Christ himself. He said, I am the resurrection and the life. So, we know God acts in history. Every act he has been involved in has been an act that he has initiated. Each historical moment, each isolated incident, all were done that he might perform the ultimate climax, which was the gift of his son and with him the gift of salvation for all men. Thirdly, Paul says men and women have the power to choose whether this Jesus will be a great man in history or whether he will be a personal Savior. All of God's acts culminate in Jesus. Why? Paul gives the answer when he said, Therefore, my brothers, I want you to know it is through Jesus that the forgiveness of sin is proclaimed to you. Through him everyone who believes is justified from everything from which you could not be justified by the law of Moses. What fellowship does God have with evil? What fellowship does righteousness have with unrighteousness? The answer is none. The Bible says, there is none righteous no not one. We are not righteous, but God wants to have fellowship with us. So how does he do it? Well, somehow, he has to make us righteous. And the Hebrews tried that with the law for more than a thousand years and they couldn't do it. We are sinners, God wants to fellowship with us, but he cannot look upon evil. We must be made right in God's sight. Isaiah said, even our righteousness is as filthy rags.

Finally, Paul said, God sent forth his son to become our righteousness. And in that miracle moment, salvation became more than a probability, it became a possibility. But is isn't automatic. Someone said preaching the universal salvation every man is saved because Christ died for all sin. All we need to do is tell them about it. Salvation is not universal in that it is automatic. It is through faith in the Lord Jesus Christ, Paul says, who loved us and gave himself for us.

Paul's first sermon is very powerful, isn't it? Filled with universal truths. Truth that is as relevant for us as it was two thousand years ago. The question is, have we chosen him? Has forgiveness become a reality through faith for us? Has righteousness been imparted? Do we have fellowship with God? And do we realize, today, our sonship to the Lord Jesus Christ?

Chapter 30
The Love and Justice of God

I would like to quote several passages of scripture. I want to quote scripture that has to do with the love of God and the justice of God as love and the justice of God comes together in the salvation of souls. I want to show you that both love and justice are clearly shown in the Lord Jesus Christ making himself a sacrifice for sin.

John 3:16 – "For God so loved the world, that he gave his only begotten Son, that whosoever believeth in him should not perish, but have everlasting life."

Romans 3:26 – "To declare, I say, at this time his righteousness: that he might be just, and the justifier of him which believeth in Jesus."

Isaiah 53:5-6 – "But he was wounded for our transgressions, he was bruised for our iniquities: the chastisement of our peace was upon him; and with his stripes we are healed. All we like sheep have gone astray; we have turned everyone to his own way; and the Lord hath laid on him the iniquity of us all."

I Corinthians 15:3 – "For I delivered unto you first of all that which I also received, how that Christ died for our sins according to the scriptures;"

I Peter 2:24 – "Who his own self bare our sins in his own body on the tree, that we, being dead to sins, should live unto righteousness: by whose stripes ye were healed."

I Peter 3:18 – "For Christ also hath once suffered for sins, the just for the unjust, that he might bring us to God, being put to death in the flesh, but quickened by the Spirit:"

Matthew 20:28 – "Even as the Son of man came not to be ministered unto, but to minister, and to give his life a ransom for many."

I Timothy 2:5-6 – "For there is one God, and one mediator between God and men, the man Christ Jesus; who gave himself a ransom for all, to be testified in due time."

Galatians 3:13 – "Christ hath redeemed us from the curse of the law, being made a curse for us: for it is written, Cursed is every one that hangeth on a tree:"

Titus 2:13 – "Looking for that blessed hope, and the glorious appearing of the great God and our Saviour Jesus Christ; who gave himself for us, that he might redeem us from all iniquity, and purify unto himself a peculiar people, zealous of good works."

Hebrews 10:10 – "By the which will we are sanctified through the offering of the body of Jesus Christ once for all."
Hebrews 9:12 – "Neither by the blood of goats and calves, but by his own blood he entered in once into the holy place, having obtained eternal redemption for us."

Revelation 5:9 – "And they sung a new song, saying, Thou art worthy to take the book, and to open the seals thereof:

for thou wast slain, and hast redeemed us to God by thy blood out of every kindred, and tongue, and people, and nation;"

I John 4:10 – "Herein is love, not that we loved God, but that he loved us, and sent his Son to be the propitiation for our sins."

Galatians 2:20 – "I am crucified with Christ: nevertheless, I live; yet not I, but Christ liveth in me: and the life which I now live in the flesh I live by the faith of the Son of God, who loved me, and gave himself for me."

The love of God and the justice of God are both shown in the dying of the Lord Jesus Christ for our sin. Now if you would take the time today to consider the love of God on the one hand and the justice of God on the other hand, then the logical conclusion of discovering both truths would teach us that the only way to be saved is through substitution. The only possible way of being saved, the only possible way of salvation, when you consider both attributes of God, is in substitution. Someone dying for us. God's justice on the one hand, made it necessary for Christ to die for our sins. In John 3:14, the scripture says, *"For as Moses lifted up the serpent in the wilderness, even so must the Son of man be lifted up"*. Why is it so, in God's justice, that the Son of man should be lifted up? Romans 3:26 answers it. *"To declare, I say, at this time his righteousness: that he might be just, and the justifier of him which believeth in Jesus."* God's justice made it necessary for Christ to die. And God's love made it possible for him to die for our sins. God so loved the world that he gave his only begotten Son, that whosoever believeth in him should not perish but have everlasting life. Brother, what you and I ought to desire to know today; the one priority in our hearts today as men and women of God and even those who are not in God, but are seeking after the way of salvation – the only thing that we ought to desire to know is simply God's way. What does God say? What does God demand? We like to rationalize and we like to argue about what God said and what did he really say when he said this or that. We simply ought to want to know what God wants from me. Or what is God's way of salvation?

The scriptures I quoted makes it clear that the sinners only hope lies in Jesus Christ dying. And not so much just that he died but the sinner's only hope lies in the fact that Jesus died in my place. That is our only hope. He died in your place and he died in my place. The reason he died in our place was that he might set us free from the justice – the penalty- of your sin. You see, God is just. God said, "the soul that sinneth it must die". Therefore, God could not turn his back upon justice and let man go free. Man, on the other hand, could not save himself, so God's love and justice joined hands and provided a substitution for man, and Jesus died in our place. Not only did he die in our place, but he died to pay the full penalty for all iniquity. He paid it all. When Jesus hung on the cross and said, "It is finished", he meant the full weight and penalty of sin had been paid by his own precious blood for all iniquity.

It is rather amazing how many people like to raise objections to Jesus dying on the cross for the sin of the world. Isn't it amazing how even today, the teachers in theological seminaries have joined hands with the most blatant infidels to cry out against Jesus dying on the cross saying it is morally wrong for an innocent man to suffer for one who is guilty. And Jesus died, the just for the unjust.

Jesus died, the innocent for the guilty. And liberal theologians have joined with infidels. it reminds me of Luke 23, verse 11 and 12 where Pilate and Herold were enemies with one another and the scripture says they joined hands together in the order to set Jesus at naught. The hands of liberals have joined hands with their enemy to set Jesus at naught. And they use the argument that it is unthinkable that the guilty should have their sins paid for by someone who is innocent.

Let me say to you, today, not only was the innocent dying for the guilty, a part of God's plan, but it fits into the highest and noblest of mankind in the human race. Let's suppose I was going down the street tonight and I heard some groaning in the ditch. I take a light and I go to the source of the groaning and I find two men, who in a drunken street brawl, have almost killed one another and they are laying there, their faces gashed and bleeding to death. I pick them up, I see to it they are carried to the hospital and that they don't die. Isn't that the innocent paying for the guilty? To say that it is morally wrong, would say that we are condemned to pass by day after day seeing the festering wounds of the blood shot eyes and the sin of the human race and have to walk by it. We would say it would be morally wrong to walk by the other side. Do you remember the parable of the Good Samaritan?

First, let me say, it is not morally wrong for the innocent to pay for the guilty because God did it. If God did it, it cannot be morally wrong. Let's suppose you have a son. And your son becomes a drunkard. Your son wastes his substance in riotous living and comes with his health ruined and wrecked and his life shot. You, as his father, go to him and bring him to your home and you nourish him and take care of him because of a father's love. Is that not the innocent paying for the guilty? Could you not say, if you use their argument, well, he is the sinner, let him pay his own debt for his sin. No, it would condemn you as a father, to pass by day after day seeing your son die a horrible death and not being able to do anything about it. I am not afraid to face the question of whether it is morally wrong for the innocent to die for the guilty. It is the highest and noblest of the human race that the innocent pay for the guilty. You and I are paying tax dollars for the guilty, brother. It is costing us an arm and a leg to feed and house and care for medically those who are guilty of sin. Don't you know you are feeding families of men, who will not work? Who don't want to work and wouldn't work if they had the opportunity. You are paying for that. Don't you know you are buying food for people who are too lazy to work? Is that not the innocent paying for the guilty? Either one thing or another, God did it and God is wrong or it is right because God did it. Now if those who objected said that Jesus Christ was forced to lay down his life for the sinner, they might have an argument. But I want you to listen to the words of Jesus Christ: "I lay down my life of myself. I have the power to lay it down and I have the power to take it up again." No man taketh my life from me, Jesus said, I had the power to look at the human race and say no and I had the power to look at the human race and say, yes. I'll die in their place. No man took my life from me. Some people like to say that Jesus' death on the cross was something that got out of hand. That it was a surprise to God. That it was a natural conclusion to a revolutionary who tried to change the way the world was thinking. It was no mistake that Jesus died. Jesus laid down his own life. He had the power to take it up, but he laid it down. He took upon himself the form of man and was obedient even unto the death on the cross.

Some say this is the great exception. This was the one exception to the question of the innocent dying for the guilty. No, it wasn't any exception. Neither was it some kind of makeshift redemption as the blood of goats and bulls. It was a one-time real full redemptive ransom that God's Son paid for the human race. Just as a captain of a ship can give himself to the enemy to free his own men, just as the diamond can be used to redeem the debt of many dollars and just as one man can pay the debt of another and just as one man can pay the courtroom fine for another, even so Jesus gave himself a ransom to pay for the penalty of sin.

It was not just the nails being driven through the quivering flesh of Jesus Christ nor was it the physical pain that he endured, but it was the Lord laid upon him the iniquity of us all. He was made sin for us. He was suffering in the sinner's place. The just for the unjust. II Corinthians 5:21 reads, *"For he hath made him to be sin for us, who knew no sin; that we might be made the righteousness of God in him."* Instead of trying to avoid or change or rationalize the plain meaning of the word of God, should we not bow in reverence to such love? Should we not bow our bodies and hearts before such a manifestation of the love of God? Jesus died in my place. Should we not rather realize it was for you and for me that he died and through his suffering and no other way we can escape the just penalty of our sin and have eternal life with God?

Isn't it funny how we change our thinking from physical to spiritual things? Did you ever notice how illogical people are when it comes to spiritual things? You now the man, who says of spiritual things, I believe in predestination. I believe that if I am predestined to be saved, I'll be saved whether I want to or not. Did you ever get that man who thinks that way to transfer that kind of thinking to his natural life? For example, in the morning when it comes time to go to work, don't get up, don't shave, don't put on your clothes, if God intended for you to get to work, you will get there whether you want to or not. It is the same reasoning.

We pick up the newspaper and there is a story on the front page about a fireman in some city, who had a family of his own, goes into this burning building and there is a little girl. He picks up the little girl and as he runs out of the building, he inhales too much smoke and he dies saving this child from the burning building. The whole world weeps for that man. And then they coldly, scorn and reject the Son of God and the salvation of Jesus Christ for substituting himself in the sinner's place. The pride of the human heart. Brother, don't you sit in the seat of the scornful. Don't sit in the seat of the scornful, but rather sit with those who will say in that day, worthy is the Lamb who was slain and purchased unto God by his blood, the redemption of men from every tribe and every tongue and every nation.

What does the Bible mean when it says, Christ died for our sins? What does it mean when it says he gave himself for our sins? What does it mean when it says he bore our sins in his own body upon the tree? It means clearly, that he died in order that God might be just and the justifier of them that have faith in Jesus Christ. How can God be just and how can he justify the sinner? That is a good question. You cannot answer that question apart from the fact that Jesus Christ died on the cross of Calvary.

There are three things God could have done. God could have been a God of justice without no love at all. Can you imagine what this world would have been like had God just been a God of justice? Demanding an eye for an eye and a tooth for a tooth. It would have been hell on earth. He could have been just a just God, one that everyone feared, with no love at all. He could have been mercy and love and no justice. If that had been true there would have been no moral law. And we would have had hell trying to get rid of hell. So, there was one possible way that love and justice of God could come together in the form of his Son, the Lord Jesus Christ, and pay the penalty of sin for the human race. God had to be just and the justifier of them that have faith in Jesus Christ. The greatest crime ever committed is to reject so great a salvation. We shudder when we read in the paper about the crimes being committed. The crimes today are so above our thinking and understanding, but far greater and far blacker is the crime of rejecting the love of God as it was manifest in Jesus Christ on the cross of Calvary. Oh, what a crime, to realize that God did the only thing he could do to purchase your life and mine. And that the only way possible for us to have eternal life with him, was that God's Son die in our place. He sent him and through his love, he loved us enough to die for us. While we were yet sinners, Christ died for us. I can do nothing but bow in the presence of such love and say to my father, worthy is the Lamb to receive honor and praise and glory and power.

The only reason folks reject this kind of love is what I call intellectual pride. They are too smart. Or religious pride or more frequently, love for the world and secret sin in their own lives. I have had the occasion recently to visit several people who have just quit coming to church. Wondering and realizing that someone may have said something that offended them. Wondering if perhaps, I said something that offended them. And without exception, you can talk to those who no longer come to church, their first response is I don't like this or I don't like that about your church. You leave disheartened and discouraged and you cry to God. You tried to get folks to be friendly. You tried to get folks to speak to them. Then, you find out that there is sin in their life and they are guilty of gross immorality. That they have committed the grossest sin before God. Brother, that's why they don't come to church because there is sin in their lives. And when they come to church, the word of God exposes that sin and makes them uncomfortable. In order to cover up not being there, they use some excuse, like, someone hurt my feelings. Now when I visit someone who has quit coming to church, my first impulse is to say to them when I shake their hand, what sin is in your life? I don't do it, but that is my first impulse. That is why folks don't accept Christ. They don't want to give up that sin in their life.

God had given you sufficient proof God has made his word plain so all can understand the way of salvation. It is an awful step to reject God's way of salvation. It is a step never to be retraced. To reject God and go out into the dark unending future beyond this grave with no hope in God unredeemed from iniquity with no hope, when God has plainly warned us, without the shedding of blood there is no remission. It is an awful eternal crisis when you see God's only provision for you. The only provision so complete, so final, so perfect, so sure and then you face the warning, that God said, I call heaven and earth to witness against you this day. I have set before you life and death, blessing and cursing, therefore choose life.

I, as a minister of the word of God, can say to you that I call heaven and earth to witness against you today. For I have set before you life and death. I have set before you blessing and cursing and my invitation to you is therefore choose life. Therefore, choose God's way and accept Christ as your personal Savior.

I talked to one lady who was quite intellectual who said, quite frankly, I could be saved if I really felt that I had something to repent of. I cannot see myself as a sinner. I cannot bring myself to repent, to confess because I don't feel that I am a sinner. Folks like that have got a problem, you know it. Folks like that are too smart and their intellectual pride is keeping them from heaven and will send them to a devil's hell, where all of their intelligence can be used in screaming day and night with the gnashing of teeth and wailing. They will remember with that intelligence every opportunity they had to receive Christ and let it go by. One said, I cannot see what the relationship of Jesus Christ dying on the cross has to me. It has all to do with you. It was a sacrifice for you. If I were sitting on a pier somewhere and someone came and jumped in the river to show their love for me and drown, it would not make any sense to me. Maybe I needed love. But the fact that he did that without any relationship to my needs, it wouldn't have any meaning to me. But if I were to fall into the river and someone came and jumped in after me and made my fate their fate and saved my life, I would have to declare, greater love hath no man than this, that a man lay down his life for a friend.

Jesus didn't just die as a historical event. Jesus died to identify with you, your need, your sin. Don't reject so great a salvation. God's love made the sacrifice possible. God's justice made it necessary. I'm going to ask you to ask yourself this question, have I taken God's way or am I sitting in the seat of the scornful? Have my sins been washed away by the blood of the Lamb? That's the only way. Because God loved us doesn't mean that he could turn his back on his own holiness and justice. And when love and justice come in conflict with one another, it is always love that must take the backseat. But in this instance, God's love and justice came together in perfect harmony to save your soul and mine. Have you made God's way, your way? If you have never accepted God's provision for your sin and your soul, I invite you to receive Christ as your personal Savior. If you are a Christian and have grown cold in your heart and indifferent, I invite you to rededicate your heart and life to Jesus Christ.

Chapter 31
Four Sides of the Gospel
I Corinthians 15:1-4

Let's begin in I Corinthians 15 verse 1: *"Moreover, brethren, I declare unto you the gospel"*. Let me stop right there and say this. If I get busy and don't tell my wife, but if I should die suddenly, if there is any money left in my estate to put up a monument or tombstone, I would like you to remind my wife, that I want this to be my epitaph, "I declare unto you the gospel." I know of no greater blessing, I know of no greater work on earth, than to declare the gospel for the Lord Jesus Christ. I would like for that monument to say that I declared the gospel of the Lord Jesus Christ. Now, let's continue in verse 1-4, *"which I preached unto you, which also you have received, and wherein ye stand; by which also ye are saved, if ye keep in memory what I preached unto you, unless ye have believed in vain. For I delivered unto you first to all that which I also received, how that Christ died for our sins according to the scriptures; and that he was buried, and that he rose again the third day according to the scriptures:"*

Some of you may have heard in the past few weeks about this particular religious organization, I don't know anything about it except its name. I think it originates in California. It goes under the heading of the Four- Square Gospel and it is preaching on radio and television and sending out literature. If it lives up to its name then it is fundamental because it is preaching the four-square gospel. The four-square gospel simply means there are four important Christian doctrines involved in the gospel of the Lord Jesus Christ. These people are preaching those four particular doctrines which make up the gospel.

There are many sides to the gospel of the Lord Jesus Christ. There are many avenues. One of the richest things I know about God is that God is love. And I know that a preacher could preach a lifetime and never exhaust the scriptures that deal with the love of God. But brethren, if that is all a preacher preaches then he has not preached the gospel. He has not preached it all. From time to time, in preaching the gospel of the Lord Jesus Christ, I might have offended some and I know that I have. I have had many people get mad at me because I preached on a particular subject and it was sin and I said that God would hold us in account for that. Brethren, anything less than the four sides of the gospel of the Lord Jesus Christ is not a gospel at all. A watered-down gospel is not gospel. If you preach of the love of God and never preach on the others, you are deceiving and leading astray those who listen to you. I made up my mind, a long time ago, having entered into the ministry later in life, that if I could not preach the gospel of the Lord Jesus Christ as it is revealed to me through the word of God, I would be better off fishing and you would be too. I would not deceive you if I just didn't preach. And you would not be deceived if you didn't have to listen to just part of the gospel. There are more sides to the gospel than just one. There are four.

It is a wonderful thing to tell folks Jesus saves. It is a wonderful thing to tell folks that God so loved the world that he gave his only begotten Son that whosoever believeth in him should not perish but have everlasting life.

But if I just preached that Jesus saves and did not preach that man needed to be saved I would not be declaring the whole gospel. If I did not preach that we are all born sinners and that all of us are under the penalty and wrath of God for sin and were on our way to hell and that Jesus came to save us from that hell and we be saved by expressing our faith in the Lord Jesus Christ by receiving him as our personal Savior, then I have offended you really and truly by not telling you the truth.

I want us to look at the four sides of the gospel. The first side of the gospel, very simply, is that Jesus lived. Jesus of Nazareth was a real person. He was a historical person, just as any other man whose record has been recorded. There was a Jesus of Nazareth. He walked the dusty roads of Galilee. And I know that this Jesus lived. I never heard him preach. I never laid eyes on him. I never saw him perform miracles. I know he was buried in baptism in the river Jordan. I know he lived to about thirty three and a half years of age. I know he was crucified on a cross. How do I know he lived? Because the most authoritative book of all the world, God's inspired Bible, told me that Jesus lived. I believe George Washington lived, don't you? How many of you saw George Washington? Anyone hear him speak? Did you ever see him? Did you see him when he crossed the Delaware? But you believe he lived because the history books tell you he did. I believe that Jesus lived because the most authoritative history book of all the world, tells me that Jesus lived. I know he did all those things I mentioned. I know that George Washington, for example, was born in Virginia. I know he was a general in the Army. I know he fought in two wars. I know he became the first president of the United States. I know Jesus laid his hands on those that could not walk and they leaped and went to their house praising God. I know that because the word of God told me that he did.

He lived, first, in heaven. I know Jesus lived even before the world began. I know that before there was any form to this earth, Jesus existed. I had a fellow get angry with me because I said that. This man had been a Christian for fifty years, at least he had been a member of the church for fifty years. He said, how in the world can you expect me to believe that a man can live before he is born? Because the word of God said so. Jesus existed before the world began. He and the Holy Spirit were with God when there was no form to this earth. They are both identified in the creation chapters. The spirit of God moved upon that chaos and turned it into beauty. Jesus was there when God said, let us make man in our image.

Not only did he live in heaven, but he lived on earth. He came to us in the form of a tiny baby, born to a virgin in the city of Bethlehem. The days came that Mary should be delivered, there was no room for them in the inn. They found shelter in a stable and when she brought forth her first-born son, she wrapped him in swaddling clothes and laid him in the manger. The word of God told me that. He lived on earth. I don't know how God did that. I don't know how the Holy Ghost came upon Mary and how she conceived and how she brought forth a son, but I know it did. And that is one of those things that is not any of my business.

Jesus lived not only in heaven and not only in earth, but the reason Jesus lived and the reason he didn't come into the world full grown was that Jesus lived to show us what God was like. The Old Testament prophets had said repent and turn to God. Their question was what is God like? What kind of being is God? Who is God that I should turn to him? Jesus came in the fullness of time to show us what God was like. When people saw Jesus, they saw the father. He said himself, "he that hath seen me hath see the father". When they saw him in his miracles, they saw the power of God. When they saw him take that little child and put him in his lap, they saw the compassion and love of God. He lived to show us what God was like. Do you want to know what God is like? Just look at Jesus. If you wanted to paint a picture of God, paint one according to what you think Jesus would look like.

A little boy sat down at an easel one day and began to paint. His mother asked him what was he doing. He said, I'm painting a picture of God. The mother said, son, no one knows what God looks like. The little boy said, they will when I get through.

Jesus came to tell us what God was like. He came that you and I might know God. Jesus said the Father and I are one, he that hath seen me, hath seen the Father. Yes, Jesus lived. Jesus is our example and teacher. He came to teach us how to live. Really you don't need a psychologist or psychiatrist to tell you how to live, that is why Jesus came. If we could put the principles which God gave to us through his Son Jesus, we would know how to live. We would know how to get the very best out of life. I'll tell you something, I believe with all my heart, there are a lot of folks in heaven that know Jesus lived. There are also a lot of folks in hell that know Jesus lived.

The second side of the gospel is Jesus died. This Jesus I just talked to you about walking the roads of Galilee, he died.

God said he would die, years before he died. He was wounded for our transgressions, bruised for our iniquity and the chastisement of our peace was upon him and with his stripes we are healed- Isaiah 53:5. He was cut off from the land of the living – Isaiah 53:8. That his death was surrounded by the rich and the wicked. God said he would die. I know that he did die. I know this Jesus, who lived, was betrayed by a disciple's kiss in the Garden of Gethsemane. The soldiers took him to two priests first and then finally to Pilate, the governor and there he was condemned to death. I know he tried to carry his own cross to Calvary, but he fell beneath the load and a man picked up the cross and carried it for him. When he got to the top of the mountain, there they stripped him of his remnant, put him to an open shame, spit in his face, drove spikes through his hands and feet, lifted him on a cross and pierced his side with a spear and he died. I know that he died. A lot of other men died in the same manner as Jesus died. What I want to know is why did he die? Why did he die such a shameful death? Why was he numbered with the wicked? Why was this young man, who never did anything wrong, crucified? He died to save us from our sin. He did not die because he was a revolutionary. He did not die because he was willing to die for a cause. He died of his own free will that he might save us from our sin. When God saw we were doomed to hell, that we were literally stumbling over one another into the pits of hell, he said I will send my Son, my only begotten Son, that if they believe on him, they would not perish. That is why he died. He died that you and I might be free from sin. He died that we might have our sins washed away. He died to fulfill the holiness and the justice of God and that those who believe on him might be saved. Yes, Jesus is our teacher and he is our example. Other people can teach us, other people can be our example, but only Jesus can be your Savior. Do you want to go to heaven when you die? There is just one way to go. No man cometh unto the Father but by me, Jesus said.

Do your sins bother you? Do your sins trouble you? What do you do when your sins trouble you? Do you hide them? Do you sweep them under something or put them in the back of your mind? What happens when a Christian sins? And we all do brethren, all of us sin. Do we lose our religion? Do we quit coming to church? What do we do with our sin? Bring them to the cross. That is why Jesus died. That was the reason he hung on the cross, that we might hear the gospel of the Lord Jesus Christ and bring our sins to the cross and have them lifted. Then when we were saved, when sin came to us, we could carry that sin back to the cross of Jesus Christ. If we confess our sins, he is faithful and just to forgive us our sins and to cleanse us from all unrighteousness. There is only one way and that is by the way of the cross.

A little girl was lost in England. She had strayed a distance from her home and she couldn't find her way back. There was this great cross in the square in one of the cities. It was sort of a landmark. She was lost and couldn't tell the policeman her name nor where she lived. He was trying to get all the information from her he could so he could find her home. She finally said, Mister, if you can carry me to the cross I can get home from there. Brother, that is true of all of us. If we can get to the cross, we can get home from there. But that is the first stop we must make. Jesus lived and Jesus died. Why did he die? That we might have salvation, forgiveness of sin. That we might be redeemed.
The third side of the gospel is Jesus rose from the grave. At three o'clock in the afternoon, Jesus bowed his lovely head

and died. Can you imagine what a scene that was? To see the Son of God hanging upon a cross and finally see him bow his head in submission and say it is finished. There was a lot of laughter and jeering around the foot of the cross, but I believe there was weeping in heaven when the angels saw the Son of God, the lovely unspotted Son of God, dying in shame and without a friend. They must have wept. It must have broken the heart of God as he had to turn his own back on his Son and darkness covered the whole earth. Jesus had two secret disciples. We know one of them because he was rich. His name was Joseph of Arimathea. The other was name Nicodemus. We know him because he came to Jesus under the cover of darkness to seek the way of eternal life. These two men, the rich and the ruler, came to Pilate and asked for the body of Jesus Christ. Given permission, they took that body down from the cross and very lovingly and gently, they placed it in the tomb. Fulfilling the scripture of Isaiah. He would die among the wicked. He died between two thieves. He would make his grave with the rich. He was buried in Joseph's own tomb in the garden, fulfilling scripture. They buried him and went their way brokenhearted. All the hopes and dreams they had for this Jesus were gone now because he was dead. Their whole dream was now crushed because their leader was dead and they would all have to go back fishing. Jesus had said, I'll rise again, but they didn't hear him. It went way over their head. As the women came to the tomb on a Sunday morning to embalm the body of Jesus, the angel said, why are you seeking the living among the dead. He is risen as he said. And he has gone before you into Galilee. He rose from the grave. That morning that tired, wounded, cold body of Jesus Christ began to become warm. It began to move and Jesus, the Son of God, with the power of God in his life took those grave clothes from his body, he folded a napkin and laid it aside and walked back into life. And because he lives you shall live also. Amen! They should have known. I could say to Peter and John and the rest of them, Oh ye of little faith. Don't you know the king of life was also the king of death? Don't you know the grave could not contain the Son of God? Jesus is coming again is the fourth side of the gospel. He ascended into heaven after his resurrection after some forty days. As he went into heaven, the angel, the man in white, said to the disciples who were gazing at him, why stand you here gazing into the heavens, this same Jesus which you saw go will come again in like manner. He is coming again. And his coming will complete my salvation and your salvation which began at the time you received him as your personal Savior. Then your salvation will be complete. Paul said, I would not have you to be ignorant brethren concerning these things. I will have you know that Jesus is coming and the events surrounding his coming, I don't want you to be ignorant of, so I'm going to tell you, by the inspiration of the Holy Spirit what's going to take place. If you are a pre-millennist, Jesus will come. He will come for two groups of people. He will come first for those saints of God who have died in ages past and he will resurrect them from the grave. And those Christians who are alive, at that moment, will also be transformed and changed and together those two groups of people will go into heaven with Jesus Christ. While they are gone, the great tribulation will hit this earth, like the world has never seen. There will be suffering, sorrow and despair for a period of a few short years and then Jesus is coming back bringing with him those he called up in the beginning. We will reign with him for a thousand years. During that time, Satan will be punished, Satan will be chained and out of darkness and the eternal ages will begin. Jesus is coming again. The truth of it leaps out at us from every page. His coming could happen at any minute. There is nothing in the word of God that must happen before Jesus comes. It has been fulfilled. Don't delay the Lord's coming by getting so involved in prophecy that you have a chart and say this has to happen or that has to happen. Don't be the character in that parable which the servant delayed his Lord's coming. You remember that parable? That is what folks are doing when they look at prophecy and say such and such must happen. Nothing has to happen. It has all been fulfilled. Jesus could split the eastern sky this moment.

I'll leave you with a question. If it were to happen this moment, would you be ready? If you are not saved, you wouldn't be ready. If you are not serving the Lord, you are not ready. If you Christians and this Christian, if we are not giving God our best, we are not ready for him to come. And if we have not received Christ, we certainly are not ready. He could come at any moment.

What a glorious time that is going to be for the Christian! To be able to see our Lord face to face. To be able to have all the questions answered to our satisfaction. To have a pure perfect mind and body. To never know what it is to cry again, or be discouraged, or heartbroken. To never be sick again and never again be interrupted by death.
Those are the four sides of the gospel: he lived, he died, he rose and he is coming again. Are you ready?

Chapter 32
Perfecting the Saints
Hebrews 11:33 – 40

Hebrews 11 is the history of the faithful, those who have gone on before us, especially those heroes of the faith. I want us to begin reading in verse 33. The apostle here is referring to or pointing to the Hebrew Christian, those people who had lived in the past. The Hebrew Christian, at this time, was enduring persecution. They were having a great deal of difficulty and the apostle is pointing out to them that their forefathers endured and had made it to heaven. If their forefathers could do it, they could do it also. After giving us men and women by name, he says in verse 33 – 40: *"Who though faith subdued kingdoms, wrought righteousness obtained promise, stopped the mouths of lions, Quenched the violence of fire, escaped the edge of the sword, out of weakness were made strong, waxed valiant in fight, turned to flight the armies of the aliens. Women received their dead raised again: and others were tortured, not accepting deliverance; that they might obtain a better resurrection: and others had trial of cruel mockings and scourgings, yea, moreover of bonds and imprisonment: they were stoned, they were sawn asunder, were tempted, were slain with the sword: they wandered about in sheepskins and goatskins; being destitute, afflicted, tormented; of whom the world was not worthy: they wandered in deserts, and in mountains, and in dens and caves of the earth. And these all, having obtained a good report through faith, received not the promise. God having provided some better thing for us, that they without us should not be made perfect."*

There are times, brethren, when we feel some things we cannot say. There are times when I feel very deeply about some things that I cannot find, in my mind, the ability to put into words. You, perhaps, have at times, been so grateful someone has done so much for you that a mere thank you seems inadequate. You felt something much deeper, something more elaborate to say but the words would not come. I feel some things today that are too deep to put into words. I can't find the words to express what I want to say. I have a particular feeling about verse 40 of chapter 11. I do not understand it and I'm sure I am going to take it out of context. I am sure theologians can tear me apart about what I am about to say. But I feel something in my heart about verse 40. Verse 40 says, *"God having provided some better thing for us, that they (those who have gone before us) without us should not be made perfect."*

There is, today, a special kinship between us and every individual who has been a believer before us. It is true about this church. All of us here today, we have a special kinship with the founder of this church, with the members who have been members for forty or fifty years. We are all one and in one family. That is what the apostle is telling the Hebrew Christian. He is speaking of the glorious achievements of the heroes of faith. He is bringing up the dead of the past, the mighty men and women of faith. He is passing them before the eyes of the present-day Christian and he is presenting them as men and women of faith who had done all these things. He names them and then the apostle turns to his readers and tells them they are better off. He says you are in a much better position and you are much more richly blessed that your fathers were. You possess the reality of that which they longed for. You are enjoying those things for which they labored and died. Therefore, you are much better off. You have some better thing. He is not talking about heaven because they will share heaven with us. The better thing he is talking about here is a better privilege, sanctification, a better salvation in fact. Good Friday, Easter Sunday, and Pentecost raised the level of our salvation far above that which they experienced. They have now entered into it in heaven. But we have a better privilege, a better position in life simply because of what they did.

Then he says not only are you better off than they are and more richly blessed than they are, but he adds something that speaks to me. He says those who have gone before are being perfected by you. There is a sense in which those who have already lived and worked here in this church and have died, there is a sense in which they are now being make perfect. They are now being satisfied. And there is a sense that we are bringing them satisfaction. We are fulfilling them. Don't you know that when Bro. Hudgens established the church, that he had dreams of what would be here in years to come. We are a part of his dream. His dream is not being realized. He died not receiving the promise, but today, we are fulfilling his dreams.

When I think of those people who taught Sunday School in years gone by, Mrs. Mary Patton and others. I think they are not really made perfect until their students become men and women of God and they in turn become teachers. There is a sense in which we are presently perfecting and bringing satisfaction to those who went before us. And that is what I read in this particular verse. He is saying, God having given us something better that without us they should not be made perfect. That is a truth that I understand better than I can explain it. I'm like the Pentecostal who was talking about the baptism of the Holy Ghost. He got a little confused and finally he said its better felt than telt. That's the way I feel about this verse. It is better to feel it than to explain it.

But I want us to notice in this verse that it is a glorious truth that it binds together the entire household of God. There is a special kinship today between you and Abraham, between you and Moses. There is a special relationship between you and those who were members of the church sixty years ago. We are all one family. And the reason that is true is because with God there is no past. God is not the God of the dead. God is the God of the living. We are all alive unto him. We are all one in him. We are all one family through Jesus Christ. In that sense, no individual saint of God can really be perfected until all the saints of God are perfected.

There is a sense in which individual members of this church cannot rise to that level of perfection until we all come to the statutes of that man or woman in the Lord Jesus Christ. We can try to grow in the Lord. We can try to build to our faith. But until every member builds to his faith and every member begins to grow; none of us can truly be perfected in Christ. There is a sense in which those who have gone before us and those who have lived and dreamed and have since passed away, I believe they are being perfected or satisfied as they view what is going on. The apostle said we are encompassed by a great cloud of witnesses. There are those watching us today as eager spectators, interested in what is going on because it was a part of their dream. It was something they lived for, prayed for and planned for. The church cannot really be perfected and complete until it becomes truly the bride of the Lord Jesus Christ. The kingdom cannot truly be perfected until it be established in all the earth, and until the church extends itself as it incorporates those in the body of Christ. I love the thought behind what the writer says when he says we are encompassed about a great cloud of witnesses. One age sowed, another age harvest. But the sower and the harvester are the same, they are one. The sower of the seed cannot be perfected until the harvester perfects the one who sowed. One begins to build, another finishes the building. One lays the foundation, another erects the edifice. But the layer of the foundation is not perfected until the building be built. The builder perfects the one who laid the foundation.

There is a sense in which we are, today, perfecting those who have gone before us. One begins a work, another accomplishes, but we are all one in the family of God. I think of those today who are being perfected. Those men and women of years and years ago who labored and fought for liberty. Those who fought for freedom. Those who spilt their blood on foreign fields so that you and I might be free. That was their dream. That was what they made the supreme sacrifice for. The way we use that freedom perfects those who gave their lives for it. We ought to be careful how we handle freedom and liberty. Especially, those who fought for the liberty of mind, the liberty of thinking and expressing oneself. Today, as we live as children of liberty, we are fulfilling and perfecting those who fought for it and had to die for it that we might have it.

I think of the missionaries that went forth to preach the gospel and those who gave their lives that the gospel might be preached. They died not having carried the word of God to everyone they wanted to so we carry the gospel on for them. By carrying the gospel on, we perfect and bring satisfaction to them. Without us, they should not be made perfect, the writer says. They left the work. The fighters for freedom and liberty and those who fought for the evangelization of the world, they died having not realized the promise.

There is a sense, I believe, in my heart, in which the Lord Jesus Christ has not been perfected. That is, he has not truly realized to the full extent the satisfaction of why he died. The scripture says when he saw the travail of his soul, he was satisfied. But Jesus will not be satisfied until all men are drawn to him. Jesus will not be satisfied until every man, woman, boy and girl has heard the gospel of the Lord Jesus Christ. There is a sense that our Lord will not be satisfied until the other sheep become a part of his fold. As long as there is a sheep today, out in the cold, there is a sense in which Christ is not satisfied. He will never be satisfied until the kingdoms of this world become the kingdoms of Christ, until the church be extended to all the world. So today, as we celebrate the 60th anniversary of this church, we are in fact perfecting not only the prophets and martyrs, but our forefathers, our mothers and fathers, brothers and sisters in the Lord. But we are also perfecting and bringing satisfaction to our Lord, who died that all men might be saved. May God give us the grace to add to the joy of the saints today. May God give us the grace to add to the joy of our Lord, in laboring for lost souls. Let us give ourselves to satisfying the Lord, to work that we might hasten that day when the Lord will truly be satisfied, when every knee shall bow and every tongue confess that he is the Christ, to the glory of God the Father. We owe a great debt today to a lot of people. Paul said, I am in debt and then he began to list the people to whom he was indebted. To all of men, Paul says, I'm indebted.

We are in debt today. I read the early minutes of the church and in the first budget of the church they allowed twelve dollars one year for electricity. You know that by them paying that twelve dollars for lights, you and I can pay what we pay for the same thing today. But if they had not begun a work, there would be those that would never have been saved. There are many today who will be in heaven because of the ministry of this church and because of those who laid the foundation. But we today are building the edifice, we are perfecting, bringing satisfaction, fulfilling those who went before us. Let's commit ourselves to finish the task they have given us and that is continuing to build and enlarge and extend the ministry of the Lord Jesus Christ at this place.

Chapter 33
The Voice of Jesus
John 7:37-46

"In the last day, that great day of the feast, Jesus stood and cried, saying, If any man thirst, let him come unto me, and drink. He that believeth on me, as the scripture hath said, out of his belly shall flow rivers of living water. (But his spake he of the Spirit, which they that believe on him should receive: for the Holy Ghost was not yet given; because that Jesus was not yet glorified.) Many of the people therefore, when they heard this saying, said, of a truth this is the Prophet. Others said, this is the Christ. But some said, Shall Christ come out of Galilee? Hath not the scripture said, that Christ cometh of the seed of David, and out of the town of Bethlehem, where David was? So, there was a division among the people because of him. And some of them would have taken him; but no man laid hands on him. Then came the officers to the chief priests and Pharisees; and they said unto them, why have ye not brought him? The officers answered, Never man spake like this man."

Wouldn't you have liked to hear Jesus speak? Wouldn't you have liked to have been present on the day of the Sermon on the Mount; and hear Jesus deliver the beatitudes? There must have been something very rich, something very full, and something very vibrant about the voice of Jesus. I would have loved to have been there when Jesus said to the children, Come to me. And when he said, become as little children we shall see the kingdom of God. There was something magnificent about the voice of Jesus. But more important than what or how a man speaks and how a man's voice is received, more important than all that is what a man says.

The Pharisees wanted Jesus arrested. They sent the officers to do just that. When they returned to the Pharisees they had not laid hands upon Jesus. The Pharisees asked the officers why haven't you done what you were asked to do to this Jesus? Why did you not arrest him as we asked you to do? The officers said to the Pharisees, when we heard him speak, never a man spake like this man Jesus. He said some of the most wonderful things. He said some of the most profound things and something happened in us and we realized here was a man that spoke not as other prophets had spoken, but here was a man who spoke with authority. Here was a man who spoke, with a kind of spirit that caused us to come back to you and say, never man spake like this man.

Jesus said some wonderful things and I said that was more important than the way he spoke. The message that he spoke. In those days, most of his preaching was by using very simple things. But there are some things he said then and he would say to you today. If he were here in this pulpit, here are some things Jesus would say to you today. He said on one occasion, I tell ye nay, but except ye repent ye shall all likewise perish. He made that statement in answer to really a trick to catch him. But Jesus said except ye repent ye shall all likewise perish. Do you know Jesus knows something about man that man is not willing to admit? Jesus knows that we like to hide. And Jesus knows what the whole human race has never been able to admit. And Jesus knows this, Jesus knows that man is a sinner. Man won't admit that. They will admit they made a mistake. They will admit they were wrong. They will admit to almost anything except to say those three words, "I have sinned". But Jesus knows what we are not willing to admit. He knows we are sinners and because we are sinners, we are lost. He knows that because man is lost they are separated from God. He knows that because they are separated from God, they will never inherit eternal life through Jesus Christ. He knows that and because he knows that, he would say today, except a man repent, they shall all likewise perish. To repent means, and I could talk a lot about what the word repentance means, but the best definition I ever heard was, like being in the army. The sergeant is giving the command to march. And you are marching north and while you are marching he says, halt and you stop. He says about face and you turn completely around. He says march. You are marching in one direction, you come to a stop, you turn completely around and now you are marching in the other direction. That's repentance. That is turning around and going in the other direction. One day you were going toward the devil and hell, the Holy Spirit of God hollered to you, halt! and you stopped. You turned about and now you are walking toward God and heaven. That's repentance. I could try to explain repentance, but it is impossible to explain without using the word faith. Faith and repentance are twin graces. They are so closely related you cannot describe one without the other. Man must have faith to repent. If a man repents, he will exercise faith. Paul said it like this, repentance toward God and faith in the Lord Jesus Christ. Why repentance toward God? Because it is God's law that we have broken. It is God's wrath that we have incurred. How do we repent toward God? By exercising faith in his Son, the Lord Jesus Christ. If we want to get back to God, we must repent toward God. To get back into fellowship there is only one way and that is by repentance. The explosion they had in Waverly, Tennessee reminded me of this illustration. There was a fire that occurred in a sanitarium years ago. The place was engulfed in flames and the fireman thought they had everyone out of the building. They discovered there were four patients that had been blocked on the fourth floor. They had gone room to room to escape the heat and finally they got to the last window. They were standing there in the window. It was impossible for the fireman to go into the building, so they set up a net outside the window. They began to beg these patients to jump. Three of them trusted and believed and jumped out the window to safety. But one looked out and saw the net and he didn't believe it would save him. He became panicked and feared jumping, he ran back into the burning building and they found his charred body. All because he did not have the faith to believe in the net. He didn't have enough faith to trust it to save his life. There was only one way for him to get out and he didn't have enough faith or trust to go that way. The Bible says those who are outside of the Lord Jesus Christ are in danger of eternal flames. There is only one escape. But there is an escape. The only escape is that we trust that way of escape. We trust God's provision for our predicament. That provision is the Lord Jesus Christ.

Another statement that Jesus made then and he makes today is, thy shalt love the Lord they God with all they heart and with all they strength and with all thy soul and with all thy might. I am going to ask you a question. Who do you love? I ask Jennifer that all the time when she comes and stays with us. I say, Jennifer who do you love? She says daddy first. I don't know why kids do that. Mommy carries them and gets up with them in the middle of the night. Then the first word a child says is Daddy. But Jennifer says Daddy first, then momma and then Terry, which pleases me to no end. But I ask you the question, who do you love? I'm sure that most of you thought who do I love? When I asked that question and you thought of who you loved, did you put God in that list? Jesus said, thou shalt love the Lord thy God with all thy soul, mind and strength. People say, I love the Lord. I Love God. But most of us put God somewhere down the line and we put others ahead of God. God said seek ye first the kingdom of God. Put your mind in the kingdom of God first and God will give you the things that you need. You might say, Bro. Terry that is why we are here today because we love God. Why else would you get up and go to church? Jesus said, if you love me you will keep my commandments. And I say to you this morning, that if you love God, you will follow God. And I say to you today, if you love God, you will join the church and you will serve him through the church. You will join the fellowship somewhere and I don't mean put your name on a piece of paper. You will get in God's church and you will serve him. If you love God, you will love lost souls. Not only will you love the lost, but you will seek to win them. If you love God, you will love the Bible and you will live by it. If you love God, you will love others, for whom he died. It is easy to say, I love God. The fact of the matter is, if you love God you will live a godly life. If you love God you will serve him. If you love God you will follow him. Let me tell you something, if you husbands lived in your relationship to your wife like you do in your relationship to God, you would be in a separation long before now. She would kick up out and she should. We say we love God, yet we do not follow him, or read his word. We say we love God, yet we do not win souls and do not attend church. Jesus said, if you love me you will love me with all your mind, soul and strength. Jesus said, what shall it profit a man if he gain the whole world and lose his own soul. What profit a man if he becomes so given over to material things and of making money? What good would it do him if he becomes owner of the whole earth? That he has a title deed to the whole earth and then die and lose his soul, what shall he profit? He would profit nothing. Nothing. I remember not too long ago a very prominent man died. It was rumored by many in town that he had money. I suppose he did, I never saw him spend any. Somebody asked the question, when they went by the casket, how much did he leave? Brother, he left it all. That's how much he left. He left every penny of it. The only thing that mattered then was what he had done for Jesus Christ. Death has a way of making us all equal. Death reduces us to a state of helplessness, to a state of hopelessness because nothing we shall do after death matters. Only what we have done for Jesus matters when we come to the end of our way. It doesn't matter how high you raised yourself in society. It doesn't make any difference whether you live in a cabin or a mansion, or whether you had a master's degree or no education at all. The only thing that matters is what have you done for Jesus Christ. And Jesus said, what shall it profit a man if he gain the world and then come to die without Jesus. Somebody said that when Queen Elizabeth died she had ten thousand dresses in her wardrobe and on her deathbed she said, millions for an inch of time. In other words, she said, I'd give my kingdom to live a minute or two longer. Jesus said, men ought to always to pray and faint not. Another thing about death is that its approach causes people to pray. Men who never bow a knee to God and men who never bow their hearts to God, kneel to pray when death approaches. Men ought not wait until they die to pray. Jesus said a man ought always to pray. That is, pray every day. Let me ask you a simple question. Why should we pray every day? We got into a discussion about asking the blessing in college. We were trying to be legalistic. When do you ask the blessing? Someone said, every time you have food. Well, if I a soft drink, that's food isn't it, should I pray? Somebody came up with a solution. If it costs ninety-eight cents or below, you don't pray. If it costs ninety-eight cents or more, then you ought to pray. I guess that is alright. But why should we pray every day? Doesn't God bless you every day? Why shouldn't we thank him every day? More importantly and more sobering, don't we sin every day? Shouldn't we pray for God to forgive us? Jesus said men are always to pray and to faint not. The greatest men of history have been men of prayer. Men who have let their spiritual lives put down roots into the source of strength, the Lord Jesus Christ. Jesus said, go ye therefore into all the world and teach all nations, baptizing them in the name of the Father, the Son and the Holy Ghost teaching them to observe all things which I have commanded you. Lo, I am with you always even to the end of the world.

There are three great words in the gospel. One of them is Come. Jesus says if you are lost and in a state of sin, come unto me for salvation. The next word is Tarry. When you come to me for salvation, tarry until you be endued with power from on high, until the Holy Spirit of God strengthens you for the task which is before you. Then the third great word is Go. Come to God for your own personal salvation, tarry until ye be endued with power from on high and then go and teach all nations. Go and make disciples of all nations, and I will go with you. One of the things Jesus said which is the most beautiful is, in my father's house are many mansions, if it were not so I would have told you. I go to prepare a place for you and if I go and prepare a place for you, I will come again and receive you unto myself, that where I am there ye may be also. Jesus said that and I am glad he said it.

I want to tell you the truth. If it were not for the joy that I get from my family, this life wouldn't be worth living. If it weren't for the joy of my family and that includes my brothers and sisters in Christ, to say in my own words, there isn't nothing worth living for. I am glad that this world in which I live is not all there is to it. There is something better coming. If I didn't think there was something better, I would have ended my life long ago. I can assure you of that. I am sure you don't feel that way, but I do personally. I wouldn't put up with this world if I didn't think there was a hereafter. If it were not for the pleasure I get from my family, I would have hung it up long ago. Jesus said, in my father's house are many mansions and I go to prepare a place for you and when I get it prepared, I'm coming back and receive you unto myself and there you shall live with me.

When I buried my son, and I walked away from that cemetery, I couldn't tell you who sent flowers. I couldn't tell you what the preacher said or what songs were sung. But in my heart, there was that still strong voice that said, let not your heart be troubled, ye believe in God, believe also in me. I go to prepare a place for you so forth and so on. If God hadn't said that to me that day, life would have become too unbearable to live. I wouldn't give you a nickel if it were not for the fact that I enjoy people, the love of people, life wouldn't be worth living.

Jesus is coming and thank God when he comes there will be no long hours of work. When Jesus comes there will be no troubles. When Jesus comes there will be no tears or broken hearts. When Jesus comes there will be no sickness, no death, no misunderstandings, no hurt feelings. When Jesus comes there won't be high heat bills, doctor's bills, rent, and all the other bills. Thank God when he comes there is something better. When Jesus comes there is no dark valley to walk through. To be honest with you, I have always been afraid to die. Ever since I was a little boy, I have had a fear of death. Folks say when you get saved, you don't mind dying. I don't want to die. In fact, since I got saved is the only time I have wanted to live. I don't want to die, but I'm not scared to die, because Jesus went to the grave and left it, he left a light behind and it is not dark anymore. There is sorrow to the Christian in death, but there is no terror. When Jesus left the grave, he left it lit, he opened it and we walk through it.

Back in history, we see a group of Christians who came to Nero's coliseum and you can hear the crowd anticipating the turning loose of the lions to tear them limb from limb. We see these Christians kneel and pray and history tells us exactly what happened. I can hear Nero, as he watches them pray and sees the glory of God on their faces, he says, they see something we don't see. Yes, they do. They saw something Nero didn't see. They saw another world. They saw beyond the tears, beyond the suffering and death. They saw Jesus, and another world. Yes, Jesus said in my Father's house are many mansions.

You have heard today some of the things Jesus would say if he were here today. If you are here today and you don't know the Lord as your personal Savior, he would say to you, repent or perish. If you are here and you have let some of the world come between you and your relationship to God, you can hear him say to you, come unto me all ye that labor and I will give you rest. If you are here today and are a born again Christian and you are living a godly life, you can hear him say to you, go ye into all the world and carry the gospel. Whatever you need, whether it be for salvation, rededication or commitment, come to him today and hear the voice of Jesus.

Chapter 34
I Know
II Timothy 1:12, Romans 8:28, II Corinthians 5:1

Let me give you some introduction to this message. A few years ago, Miss Pinky Christian, gave me a book that belonged to her father. Since then she took it back, but she gave it to me one time. In that book was a sermon preached in the year 342. Some of the sermons were 1500 years old. There was one sermon in there that was preached in London about the time the bicycle was invented. This whole sermon was dealing with the sin of bicycling. People were bicycling on Sunday and not going to church. I sort of laughed at this preacher saying that the craze of bicycling would ruin humanity because man was never designed or created to travel at that rate of speed. The preacher said if we continue in this speed craze of cycling, we are going to develop into a generation of high strung and nervous people. Then, the automobile came along and many medical doctors in that day said that the speed would not be good for mankind. Since then, we have the airplane. We sort of laugh at those preachers but they are right about one thing, we developed a high strung and nervous generation, didn't we? I don't know if it started with the bicycle or not. We are indeed living in a very rapid pace today. I boarded a plane in Atlanta Saturday afternoon and took off from the terminal and I thought I was on my way to Nashville and I sat on the end of the runway for thirty minutes. By my watch, every fifteen seconds a plane landed and one took off. I tried to imagine in my mind all the airports of the world and multiply that. They say at the largest airport in the world, a plane would land and take off every three seconds. You can't even comprehend the race and rapid age in which we are living. We don't think anything about the speed every day, but we have developed a high strung and nervous generation. If there is any one thing that would mark the age in which we are living, it would be anxiety. That is the one characteristic of our generation, worry and anxiety. The medical people say that some ninety percent of the beds in hospitals are filled with people who have anxiety problems or emotional problems. Their physical ailments are caused by emotional problems. We are living in a time of unrest. What makes that all even worse, we are living in a generation of religious unrest. The fundamentals are going beyond known bounds and the others are escaping from fundamental religion to find what they want in "isms" and in cults. Hoping to find that magic something that will satisfy the heart of man and to do that they have turned aside from the religion of God, the religion of Jehovah, and from the religion that is based on the word of God and have gone after these cults seeking to satisfy their heart. In their anxiety and unrest, they are searching. That religion that is based on something other than the word of God cannot satisfy the human heart, so that only multiplies the anxiety and unrest. Only Jesus, of course, has the answer to the heart and the problem.

Christianity based upon God and the word of God gives you something to hold on to. If the whole world goes crazy, you who are born again have at least something to stabilize your lives and something to hold on to. The child of God can say, if they have truly been saved and truly been born again, I know and I may not be able to explain the Bible, I may not understand a great many scriptures, but one thing I know, I know the author of Christianity. So, it gives us something to hold on to. The apostle Paul said at least three times, I know. Those three times he was answering a need of the heart of the Christians. One time when Paul says, I know is in II Timothy 1:12, *"For the which cause I also suffer these things: nevertheless, I am not ashamed: for I know whom I have believed and I am persuaded that he is able to keep that which I have committed unto him against that day."* I don't know about you but in the age in which I'm living, I pass by a man who says, I guess or I think. I go directly to a man who says, I know. If I wanted to know something about airplanes, I wouldn't go to someone who has never seen one. Speaking about airplanes, I remember suckering tobacco one day with Mr. Zollie Nicholson and a big plane came floating over and I said, Mr. Zollie, how would you like to be up there with that fellow? And he never did look up, he just said, I would hate to be up there without him. That's all he knew about airplanes. You would ask someone who designed, who drew the plans, or someone who flew the airplane to find the answers. If you get sick you don't want to go to a quack. You go to a doctor who can find out what's wrong with you and can give you something to help you. It is amazing to me, how in this age, people listen to those who have no credibility, especially in the realm of religion. For example, this Harry Flint, who is a convicted peddler of pornography, by his own definition says he is trying to publish in his pornography or pornographic magazine, since now he is a Christian, he still wants to be the king of porno and secondly, he wants to be some kind of voice about hypocrisy among Christians. Now I can tell you for a fact, if he wants to talk about hypocrisy and use himself as an example then you can look to him as an expert because he is one. But if he is going to do it from a Christian standpoint, brother, there is no bigger hypocrite than he is. But he will be a voice, I can guarantee you. Folks will listen to him.

I have been preaching or have been ordained now twelve years. I have preached for fifteen years and folks don't take me seriously. I have studied I don't know how many hundred hours and folks still don't take me serious, but a movie star or someone of position can get saved or say he is saved, and tomorrow he is an expert and folks flock to his door to hear what he has to say. If you want to know something about religion, you need to go to an expert. If you want to know something about Christianity, you go to someone who knows. The apostle Paul was the greatest Christian who ever lived. There is no doubt about that. He is everybody's hero, whether you are Catholic, Church of Christ, or Free Will Baptist. He is the greatest. He was beaten, he was shipwrecked, he was imprisoned, he went through it all and the apostle Paul can say with certainty, I know. When Paul say, I know, I can stop and listen to him because he is an expert in that field. He had an experience with Jesus Christ. He met Jesus Christ face to face. He talked and walked with him. When Paul says, I know, it is good enough for me. This verse is often misquoted to read this way, most people quote it, "for I know in whom I have believed". That is incorrect. It does not say "in whom I have believed". It says, "I know whom I have believed and whom stands for Christ. He said I know Christ and I believe Christ. I have met him in an experience and I know him, therefore, I trust him. If you are born again and saved you can say, I know Christ. Not, I know about Christ, but I know Christ. Not only do I know him but I am persuaded, since I believed on him, that he is able to keep that which I have committed unto him, which is my soul. And he is able to hold it and keep it unto that day. Until the day, of course, when Jesus comes again. A saved man knows a person. He knows the one who forgave him and walks with him and blesses him every day of his life. He may not understand the Bible in its entirety, but he can say, I know Christ. I know whom I have believed.

Mel Trotter was a very colorful preacher. It has been said of Mel Trotter that he said, don't know if it is true or not, but it was told many years ago. Mel Trotter was an alcoholic. He was so bad when his baby died and was laying in the casket, he went and took the shoes off that baby and sold them for whiskey to get drunk. Then left the whiskey store and on his way to the river, to commit suicide, he heard someone singing, Jesus Saves. He went into a little mission and gave his heart to the Lord. He became one of the greatest preachers that ever lived. Someone asked Mel one time, how do you know you are saved? He said, brother, I was there when it happened. I know because I was there. I know because of what he did to my heart. I know because I had an experience with Jesus Christ. And Paul says, I know whom I have believed. Free Will Baptist are sometimes afraid to preach on the last half of that verse when it says, I am persuaded that he is able to keep that which I have committed, because it sounds like eternal security. I think it is to tell you the truth.

Paul says since I met the Lord and since I have given my heart to him, I am persuaded there is not enough devils in hell, to rob me of my salvation. I am persuaded that he can keep me. Many Christians today are living troubled lives because of sin. They give their heart to the Lord, and then they commit some sin or allow the world to become so real to them they begin to lose the joy of their salvation. If sin ever troubles you, look back to the time when you committed your life to the Lord. And if you had an experience with him, you can say with certainty, I know he saved me. I don't have any doubt he saved me. Since he saved me, I am persuaded that he is able to keep what I committed to him. Paul says, I know. So, in the matter of salvation, we can listen to the expert when he says, I know whom I have believed and am persuaded that he is able to keep that which I have committed unto him against that day.

Turn with me to Romans 8:28 where Paul uses this assurance again. Paul says, *"And we know that all things work together for good to them that love God, to them who are the called according to his purpose."* Now if you ever quote that verse of scripture, quote it all. Don't stop at "we know all things work together for good". Go on and finish it. It works together for good to them that love God and to them who are called according to his purpose. Here is another occasion where the apostle Paul is speaking from his own experience. Now we are not listening to some graduate of the theological seminary sitting behind a walnut desk. We are talking about the bloody, battered, beaten, persecuted, imprisoned, shipwrecked apostle Paul. Out of his own experience he can say, I know that all things which have happened to me and to all things that happen to any Christian, work together for good to them that love God, to them who are called according to his purpose. I am sure that Paul, when he was floating in the middle of the sea, on a plank, didn't look up and say praise God, this is wonderful. I've got a library full of books and all of us got a good dose not long ago of praise God in everything from Lt. Caruthers book, Prison to Praise and Power to Praise. These books say there is great power in just praising God. One instance was where a child was born to a family that was retarded. His advice to them was to praise God for it. Well, I'm not going to questions his ethics or anything about him, but I believe the Bible says there is a time to weep with people, as well as, a time to rejoice with people. When someone is suffering, we don't go to them and say, well, just praise God brother. No, you put your arm around them and you weep with them. You let the tears fall down your cheek. But all the time, if you are saved, you know that whether or not this thing is good, there is, if this person is a Christian, there is something and someone working behind all this to somehow put it all together and work it for some good. So, if I go out here and have a wreck in my automobile, I don't jump out and say, praise God, that's a good wreck. I had a wreck not long ago and I didn't get out praising God, I got out holding my neck in case someone was looking. I held it for three or four days. When I was by myself it felt pretty good, but when I was in a crowd it stiffened up. Well, I've settled the case and it feels good tonight. Just kidding.

Paul could say after a while, this worked out for good. In other words, the shipwreck allowed me to preach the gospel to another group of people. It allowed me to preach with confidence to my comrades and companions on that ship. It allowed, in the midst of all that devastation, to show the power of God for saving all our lives. On another occasion, he said it has all worked out for the furtherance of the gospel. He wanted to go in one place, God caused some problems and caused him to go into another place and it all worked out for the good of sending the gospel to another place. I believe it was Joseph who said, when his brothers sold him into slavery, he said, you meant it for harm, but God meant it for good. You meant to get rid of me and you had nothing in your mind but evil, so all the time you were doing it, God meant it for something good. He went to Egypt and became ruler and delivered his own brothers.

Paul could say I know that all things work together for good to them that love God. I am convinced that nothing is too hard for us to go through. If it means bringing Glory to God, if it means bringing blessing to others, or if it means bringing salvation to souls. Nothing is too hard to endure. If God can use that for good or for any other reason. That's a hard scripture. There have been times when I said, Lord, I need help on that one too.

Then in II Corinthians 5:1 is the third time the apostle Paul says, we know. *"For we know that if our earthly house of this tabernacle were dissolved, we have a building of God, a house not made with hand, eternal in the heavens."* Paul, a man of experience, a man who is our expert is saying, we know, we don't guess or think, but we know that the minute this old body in which we are living dies, we know there is a better one waiting for us. There is a body which God himself has made and it is an eternal body that will never die. Now that is a wonderful verse of scripture. Every day we live, out bodies are decaying. Some of us are decaying faster than others. But every day, we live, we get a little weaker. I don't know whether you are the age or not, but there comes a time when you know that your steps are getting a little bit shorter. That your eyes are getting a little bit dimmer. Your ears are getting just a little bit weaker. You realize that all this means is you are making your way to the grave. Your earthly house is decaying. It is slowly but surely deteriorating. Our apostle Paul, the expert says, we know that the moment that happens, we have a new body, which

God has made for us. It is an eternal one not something made with hands, but eternal in the heavens.

Paul never guessed about life. He never guessed about death. He never questioned it. He said on one occasion, I know in my own mind and own heart that it would be better for me to die. It would be better, personally, for me to depart and be with Christ. Nevertheless, Paul says it is needful for you that I remain. He willingly stayed behind and willingly remained here and went on with the work God called him to do. He knew he was going to die. Not only did Paul know he was going to die, but he perhaps knew he would be killed. I guess a fellow that had come as close to being killed as many times as he had probably had a good idea that sooner or later someone was going to get him. He went on with the work. And he knew the moment his head rolled from his body, his soul would soar to be with God. We know that the moment we die, we have a building of God, a house not made with hands, eternal in the heavens. I would like to explain death tonight, to these little ones. I'm sure none of us like to think about it and most of us are frightened by it. There was a little girl one time, who knew she was going to die. Because she knew it, she was afraid. And this man began to talk to her about it. She said, I am afraid to leave this earth and go out into the state of death. He said, honey, would you be afraid if you were sitting here and dozed off to sleep watching television? Would you be afraid if I picked you up in my arms and carried you to the bedroom and tucked you into bed? Would you be afraid when you woke up? No, I wouldn't be afraid, she said. He said that is what death is like. Someone, a lot stronger than I am, Jesus is his name, who is a lot closer to you than I am and heaven is closer to you than the next room. When you die, this Jesus comes and picks you up in his arms and carries you to the next room and lays you down. Paul said when this body falls away that moment, God has for us a new body, better than the one we have. It is just waiting in the other room.

God took Moses up on a mountain one time and said to Moses, you can't go into the promise land. And I am sure Moses must have shed some tears. I am sure the tears must have come down that old warrior's face when he was told he couldn't go into the promise land. God said, Moses, I've got something better for you. I've got something much better than staying here and going into the land of promise. He said, you are going home to be with me. And Moses died and he has been with God ever since.

We know that if this body be dissolved we have a building of God eternal in the heavens. I think man has built into him a longing for that home. I believe the God who made us has put a sort of homing instinct in us just like he put into the pigeon or to the salmon. You turn a homing pigeon loose, he will make his way to the sky, circle a few times and fly home. Instinctively, because God put it there. I believe God put in us that homing instinct so we would long for home. Some day when this body is gone and life is over and the day of trouble is gone, then God will open the door and we will forever be with him. We can say with Paul, I know that I am saved. I know that since he saved me, he is carrying for me. God takes care of the past, present and future.

God took care of the past when he forgave us of our sins. God takes care of the present by caring for us. And God takes care of the future by having prepared for us a new body and a new home to live in. And that's enough.

There were three girls standing beside a store window one Christmas. They were explaining to the fourth girl all the toys and beautiful decorations that were in that store window because the fourth little girl was blind. The three were trying to explain to her the color of the bicycle, the color of the doll's hair, the size of the tree and the ornaments on the tree. They were explaining as best they could to show the little girl what the store looked like. A man was standing by and overheard them talking. He finally said, children, it is impossible for you to describe to her what that looks like. It is an impossibility. But what if that man could have given sight to the blind and what if that man could have taken them into the store and bought them all the beautiful things that they saw. That would have been like Jesus. That's a picture of what he is going to do for us one day. Someday, the earthly scales will fall from our eyes and we will not only see of the beauty of heaven, but we will inherit all the treasures of heaven.

Paul said three times, I know. He said, I know whom I have believed. He said, I know that all things work together for good to them that love God, to them who are the called according to his purpose. And then he said, we know that when this tabernacle be dissolved, we have a building eternal in the heavens.

Don't you want that? If you are here without Jesus Christ, don't you want that? Doesn't your heart and soul long for that? Don't you want him to forgive you? Don't you want him to transform you and give you peace and hope? And Christians, don't you love him? Then come and serve him better.

www.ingramcontent.com/pod-product-compliance
Lightning Source LLC
LaVergne TN
LVHW051108080426
835510LV00018B/1959